POPE PIUS XII LIBRARY, ST. JOSEPH COL.

3 2528 11322 5819

D1710918

Behavioral Mechanisms
and Psychopathology

Behavioral Mechanisms and Psychopathology

Advancing the Explanation of Its Nature, Cause, and Treatment

Edited by

Kurt Salzinger and Mark R. Serper

American Psychological Association

Washington, DC

Copyright © 2009 by the American Psychological Association. All rights reserved. Except as permitted under the United States Copyright Act of 1976, no part of this publication may be reproduced or distributed in any form or by any means, including, but not limited to, the process of scanning and digitization, or stored in a database or retrieval system, without the prior written permission of the publisher.

Published by
American Psychological Association
750 First Street, NE
Washington, DC 20002
www.apa.org

To order
APA Order Department
P.O. Box 92984
Washington, DC 20090-2984
Tel: (800) 374-2721; Direct: (202) 336-5510
Fax: (202) 336-5502; TDD/TTY: (202) 336-6123
Online: www.apa.org/books/
E-mail: order@apa.org

In the U.K., Europe, Africa, and the Middle East, copies may be ordered from
American Psychological Association
3 Henrietta Street
Covent Garden, London
WC2E 8LU England

Typeset in by Goudy by Circle Graphics Inc., Columbia, MD

Printer: Maple-Vail, Binghamton, NY
Cover Designer: Minker Design, Bethesda, MD
Technical/Production Editor: Kathryn Funk

The opinions and statements published are the responsibility of the authors, and such opinions and statements do not necessarily represent the policies of the American Psychological Association.

Library of Congress Cataloging-in-Publication Data

Behavioral mechanisms and psychopathology : advancing the explanation of its nature, cause, and treatment / edited by Kurt Salzinger and Mark R. Serper.
    p. cm.
 Includes bibliographical references and index.
 ISBN-13: 978-1-4338-0452-6
 ISBN-10: 1-4338-0452-2
 1. Psychology, Pathological. I. Salzinger, Kurt. II. Serper, Mark R.

 RC435.B44 2009
 616.89—dc22

                2008044294

British Library Cataloguing-in-Publication Data

A CIP record is available from the British Library.

Printed in the United States of America
First Edition

CONTENTS

CONTRIBUTORS

Lyn Y. Abramson, PhD, Department of Psychology, University of
    Wisconsin—Madison
Lauren B. Alloy, PhD, Temple University, Philadelphia, PA
Deanna M. Barch, PhD, Washington University, St. Louis, MO
Clara M. Bradizza, PhD, Research Institute on Addictions, State University
    of New York, Buffalo
Todd S. Braver, PhD, Washington University, St. Louis, MO
Lori Eisner, MS, University of Miami, Coral Gables, FL
Daniel Fulford, MS, University of Miami, Coral Gables, FL
David Grant, MA, Temple University, Philadelphia, PA
C. Peter Herman, PhD, University of Toronto, Toronto, Ontario, Canada
Assen Jablensky, MD, DMSc, University of Western Australia, Perth
Sheri L. Johnson, PhD, University of California, Berkeley
Richard Liu, MA, Temple University, Philadelphia, PA
Katherine L. Muller, PsyD, Albert Einstein College of Medicine,
    New York, NY
Janet Polivy, PhD, University of Toronto, Toronto, Ontario, Canada
Simon A. Rego, PsyD, Albert Einstein College of Medicine, New York, NY
Kurt Salzinger, PhD, Hofstra University, Hempstead, NY
William C. Sanderson, PhD, Hofstra University, Hempstead, NY
Mark R. Serper, PhD, Hofstra University, Hempstead, NY
Paul R. Stasiewicz, PhD, Research Institute on Addictions, State University
    of New York, Buffalo

Behavioral Mechanisms
and Psychopathology

INTRODUCTION: JUST WHAT ARE BEHAVIORAL MECHANISMS?

KURT SALZINGER AND MARK R. SERPER

Since the 1980s, many scholarly articles have extolled the "biological revolution" in the field of psychiatry. The coming and going of the "Decade of the Brain" has also ushered in the current *Zeitgeist* in the field—that mental disorders are basically mediated by biological mechanisms and, as such, require biological treatment. This notion is epitomized in Nancy Andreasen's book, *Brave New Brain: Conquering Mental Illness in the Era of the Genome* (2001), which seeks to discover "a brave new world in which mental illnesses, now painfully common, become infrequent and easily treated" (p. xi) through biological techniques and therapies. In short, the dominant theme in psychiatric research over the past quarter century has been that biological mechanisms govern the expression, course, and treatment of mental illnesses.

To be sure, the predominance of biology in the treatment of behavioral disorders governs the medical paradigms, with their embrace of diagnostic criteria as detailed in the *Diagnostic and Statistical Manual of Mental Disorders* (e.g., 4th ed., text revision; American Psychiatric Association, 2000). Such a diagnostic focus is governed, in turn, by a sophisticated and evolving symptomatology that frames the treatment of mental illness as the mitigation of the presenting symptom (the aberrant behavior). In the medical realm, going to the source—the cause—of the problem has a firm foundation in biology: Chest discomfort is a typical sign of ischemic heart disease, and the cardiovascular specialist prescribes a regimen of diet, exercise, and drugs (and possibly some quasi-surgical intervention) to reduce blood pressure, unclog arteries, and mitigate other physical symptoms. But does such a regimen go to the actual source of the problem? A treatment is offered up, but can we say the patient is cured if he or she goes back into a workaday world filled with the kind of stress that sustains hypertension? A cardiovascular psychologist would look at the patient's work and home environment as the ultimate (or at least another) source of coronary disease because the patient's interaction with his or her environment might well negate the biological intervention, as when the patient continues to expose him- or herself to stress.

Mental health diagnosticians, however, face a greater challenge when exploring the presenting symptom of aberrant behavior, particularly in tracing such behavior to its source, and especially when such aberrant behavior involves no obvious biological site. In short, reliance on biological causes alone may be necessary to explain some aberrant behavior, but it is in any case not sufficient. The identification of the offending behavior alone is not sufficient either. We need to identify the variables that control it. For this purpose, we need to examine the behavioral mechanisms underlying the various behavioral disorders. Broadly defined, a *behavioral mechanism* refers to

> a real-time principle of operation that describes the actual behavior of a living organism. . . . Thus, a behavioral mechanism is a comprehensive statement of the relations among inputs, outputs, and internal states of the organism at hand, where each state is defined by a set of equivalent histories. . . . The causes are the inputs together with the internal states. The states and resulting mechanisms are not necessarily physiological, although they may ultimately make some connection with brain physiology. Similarly, they are not cognitive, in that they do not appeal to elements of mental life, like representations and expectancies. . . . Explanation consists of theoretical specification of the underlying behavioral mechanisms, using the inputs and internal states as the calculus. (Moore, 2003, pp. 33–34)

In other words, behavioral mechanisms allow the clinician and the researcher to consider the entirety of behavior—the establishing operation, the discriminative stimuli, the reinforcement history, the "internal state," and the consequences of the behavior—in the examination and treatment of psychopathology. Behavioral mechanisms go beyond the diagnostician's necessary examination of the aberrant behavior; they specify its context.

Specifically, Figure 1 shows how the variables interact. Thus, a person who is hungry is under the influence of an establishing operation (deprivation of food for some time), making the presence of food (the discriminative stimulus) more salient, thus resulting in the behavior of eating and leading to

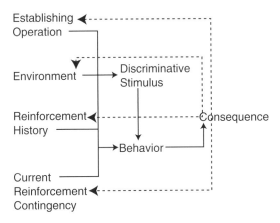

Figure 1. The behavioral mechanism. From "The Behavioral Mechanism to Explain Abnormal Behavior," by K. Salzinger, 1980, *Annals of the New York Academy of Sciences, 340,* p. 68. Copyright 1980 by Blackwell-Wiley. Adapted with permission.

the ingestion of food (now the reinforcer). Of course, the reinforcement history is critical here in that the person has in the past been sated when ingesting food (provided in the environment), and the current reinforcement contingency is such that when the subject of our discussion reaches for food (current reinforcement contingency) it actually becomes available—that is, there is no glass or other impediment barring access to the food (the consequence). Now, a person who eats when there is no "normal" establishing operation in effect (no hunger), and only the presence of food in the environment occasions eating, may cause us to talk about the power of this excessively powerful discriminative stimulus occasioning the behavior we have come to call *binge eating.*

Here is another example: We have discussed in other forums the notion of immediacy as an example of how a behavioral mechanism explains the abnormal behavior of patients with schizophrenia. Various reviews of the literature have shown that patients with schizophrenia have a tendency to respond to stimuli immediate in their environment (Salzinger, 1980, 1984; Salzinger & Serper, 2004). The critical question then becomes, "How does this response tendency produce schizophrenic behavior?" The suggested behavioral mechanism for that was basically an elaborated reinforcement contingency (see Figure 1; see also Salzinger, 1984), which raises such questions as the following: What if most reinforcers affecting behavior were the immediate consequences? What if most of the antecedent stimuli, the discriminative stimuli in the presence of which reinforcement is likely to follow behavior, were also predominantly immediate? How could this mechanism and others stemming from these relationships account for such schizophrenic symptoms as hallucinations or paranoid thinking?

One possibility, of course, could be that responding only to some stimuli in one's environment would lead to misinterpretation of one's surroundings. Thus, hearing a car horn but not responding to the fact that the horn is not attached to a car but sitting separately on a table might produce a car hallucination or at least make the afflicted hearer jump out of the way. Hearing an actor say "I'm going to kill you" might well make the patient think that he or she is in actual danger instead of responding to the other stimuli of a stage, audience of many people, and so on, all making clear that the threat is not directed at the patient—or, for that matter, that the threat is not even real. Responding to only some stimuli in one's environment might well make it difficult, if not impossible, to solve problems or to respond sensibly in a conversation; it would also mean that much behavior is conditioned by stimuli predominantly in the patient's immediate environment. One could then argue that this would relate to other symptoms of schizophrenia.

Whether to enhance theoretical understanding or improve clinical efficacy, emotional and behavioral problems must be understood in terms of the controlling variables (the behavioral mechanisms). Examination of the behavioral mechanisms that mediate psychological disturbances is crucial for a complete understanding of the origin, maintenance, treatment, course, and symptomatology of any mental disorder. We asked the authors of the chapters in this volume to examine in turn the behavioral mechanisms that mediate (explain?) cause and effect for a variety of behavioral disorders and discuss the treatments that result from understanding these mechanisms. Each contributor or group of contributors to this volume responded to our charge to examine the behavioral mechanism underlying a particular form of psychopathology in terms of its own reinforcement history. That charge was given to these contributors on the basis of the fact that they were the experts and that they thus would be able to provide the readers—students, scholars, and clinicians alike—with the most interesting and useful information.

We asked Assen Jablensky (chap. 1) to provide us with an exploratory bridge between biological and behavioral mechanisms, which he did using schizophrenia to demonstrate the nature of endophenotypes in the clarification of the nature of various forms of psychopathology. In his masterful chapter, he not only provides the bridge between behavior and biology (for an explication of various forms of these relationships, see Salzinger, 1992) but also submits a solution to the problem of the less-than-perfect relationship between genetics and disease processes. The endophenotypes that he lists include both biological and behavioral measures, suggesting a rapprochement between behavior and biology. Instead of relying on psychiatric diagnosis, he makes use of various measures that cut across such diagnoses, relate more clearly to genetic makeup, and ultimately provide a better way of analytically describing various forms of psychopathology.

Sheri L. Johnson, Daniel Fulford, and Lori Eisner discuss in chapter 3 the problem of integrating biological and behavioral mechanisms by noting that "for decades, psychosocial researchers all but abandoned the study of bipolar disorder, assuming that the genetic roots of disorder implied the irrelevance of behavioral mechanisms" (p. 77) This regrettable development in psychopathology research stems from the assumption that disorders with predominant underlying biological mechanisms require exclusively biological treatments, thus making the psychological bases of etiological theories and treatment seem irrelevant or extraneous (Miller & Keller, 2004). In some circumstances, as Miller and Keller (2004) suggested, reframing the mechanism involved as psychological rather than biological admits psychological or psychosocial manipulations or interventions.

This notion of psychological relevance has been borne out by recent advances in behavioral mechanisms associated with bipolar illness. Johnson et al., for example, suggest in their chapter that development of mania is tied to elevations in reward responsivity and emotional reactivity realized in the dopamine system. They note that vulnerability to mania may be due to at-risk individuals' elevations in sensitivity to reward and greater cognitive shifts after receipt of the reward. In general, Johnson and coauthors note that the risk of mania appears tied to the trait of intense focus on the pursuit of extrinsically reinforcing life goals. In terms of emotional reactivity, individuals with bipolar disorder appear to experience extremes of emotion more frequently, and negative environments seem tied to the course of the disorder. However, evidence for this hypothesis has not been strong. The authors speculate that mood symptoms might moderate the extent of emotional reactivity observed among persons with bipolar disorder—that is, reactivity to negative stimuli might increase during periods of depression. Similarly, many behavioral mechanisms implemented in neurological circuitry have resulted in successful psychological intervention strategies. In his seminal book, *Madness Explained*, Richard Bentall (2003) expertly summarized many behavioral mechanisms implicated in the development of delusional and paranoid thought, hallucinations, negative symptoms, and thought disorder, and he described various psychology-based interventions developed and successfully implemented on the basis of these mechanisms.

In chapter 2, Deanna M. Barch and Todd S. Braver combine neurocognitive and behavioral views to promote the notion that individuals with schizophrenia experience a deficit in the ability to represent and maintain context. Building on the immediacy hypothesis (Salzinger, 1984; Salzinger & Serper, 2004) and the pioneering work (as they say) of "individuals such as Shakow, Salzinger, Hemsley, and Gray" (p. 41), the authors suggest that contextual processing deficits may be a key component of many of the symptoms of schizophrenia. The authors frame their proposed mechanism in a computational model that permits testable predictions about the pattern of deficits to be expected under different conditions. They note, however, that their mechanism needs further elucidation. An understanding of how context-processing deficits contribute to difficulties in everyday life of patients with schizophrenia needs to be elaborated, yet, overall, Barch and Braver provide convincing evidence that contextual processing deficits mediate, at least in part, much psychopathology exhibited by individuals with schizophrenia.

To return to one of our original questions about behavioral mechanisms, we should note that since the time of the influential writings of Aaron Beck and Albert Ellis in the 1960s and 1970s, behavioral mechanism research has been predominantly cognitive in nature; hence, many authors in this volume conceptualize dysfunction in terms of cognitive etiological mechanisms. Lauren B. Alloy, Lyn Y. Abramson, David Grant, and Richard Liu present in chapter 4 a comprehensive cognitive mechanism for the origins of suicidality and vulnerability of unipolar depressive disorders based on empirical findings from the Temple–Wisconsin Cognitive Vulnerability to Depression (CVD) Project. The CVD Project uses a prospective behavioral high-risk design to test the mechanisms underlying hopelessness and Beck's theories of depression. The authors of this chapter examined individuals' cognitive styles, the occurrence of negative life events, and the occurrence of both depressive symptoms and clinically significant depressive episodes over the course of their CVD enrollment. They found that cognitive risk for depression involves a combination of factors, including a negative inferential style, dysfunctional attitudes, rumination, negative self-referential processing, and stressful life events, imparting vulnerability, especially for hopelessness depression. However, the authors note that it is still unknown whether nondepressed individuals at high cognitive risk are more likely than low-risk individuals to develop depression only when they experience stressful life events or whether cognitive risk may confer vulnerability to depression even in the absence of negative life events.

Similarly, Simon A. Rego, Katherine L. Muller, and William C. Sanderson in chapter 5 emphasize cognitive dysfunction as a core psychopathological mechanism underlying anxiety disorders. Attributions related to the perception and response to danger constitute a core mechanism underlying all anxiety disorders. Specifically, the authors note that disturbances in anxious apprehension (expressed by biases in information processing), fear and panic (expressed by false alarms), and avoidance behaviors constitute three primary mechanisms mediating all anxiety disorders. Although in the past various anxiety disorders were studied in isolation, the focus on a key cognitive mechanism has resulted in the study of common characteristics of all anxiety disorders as well as in the development of unified approaches to treatment.

As can be seen from the chapters that make up this volume, significant advances in the behavioral mechanisms that increase our understanding of psychopathology and provide a roadmap for treatment have been formulated. However, as noted earlier, unanimity concerning biology-based causes of dysfunction has made proponents of psychological sciences increasingly concerned about the division in the field and the viability of psychology as a scholarly discipline. As Timothy Melchert (2007) noted, the field of psychology

> has been heavily marked by internecine conflict between camps and schools. The competition and antagonism between the various camps and the "dogma eat dogma" (Larson, 1980, p. 19) environment that characterized much of our history might have subsided somewhat in recent years, but the deep divisions that became evident during the controversy surrounding recovered memories of child abuse and the ongoing contention between those espousing positivist and postmodern viewpoints suggest that the competition and divisions have not yet been resolved. (p. 34)

The lack of understanding of behavioral mechanisms, as Janet Polivy and C. Peter Herman point out in chapter 6, leaves us with little theoretical structure for studying certain types of psychopathology. They question the "core psychopathology" that constitutes eating disorders (EDs) and note that researchers have had difficulty distinguishing the importance between risk factors for EDs and the actual agreed-on symptoms of the disorder. They note that the "failure to distinguish between risk factors for a disorder and symptoms of the disorder itself has implications for treatment and prevention of disorders" (p. 193) and tends to fracture the field. Elsewhere, they say that despite decades of research, "our lack of understanding of the causal mechanisms underlying EDs leaves us with little conceptual framework for investigating them" (p. 186).

One solution to the fragmentation of psychological theory noted by Melchert (2007) is the ongoing process advanced by the American Psychological Association of replacing unsupported theoretical models with science-based paradigms of mental illness. Along these lines, in chapter 7, Clara M. Bradizza and Paul R. Stasiewicz note the fragmentation of theory-based etiological models for drug dependence. They integrate existing models of drug dependence by demonstrating the behavioral mechanisms that contribute to the initiation and maintenance of drug dependence. They maintain that the development of an integrative model based on operant conditioning capable of incorporating findings from diverse theoretical perspectives may reduce fragmented approaches to existing research and improve drug treatment intervention programs. Bradizza and Stasiewicz conclude that negative and positive reinforcement models provide convincing behavioral mechanisms of the process by which individuals make the transition from nonproblem substance use to drug and alcohol addiction.

The drive for empirically supported treatments has quickly become the predominant approach to guiding mental health treatment and has become the hot topic in the field of mental health. Models backed by research evidence regarding the effectiveness of assessment and treatment have the great potential of uniting psychological science and providing effective treatments for various mental disorders. The cornerstone of this approach is the generation of behavioral mechanisms that fuel our assessment and guide our treatment approaches.

It remains for us to comment on the nature of behavioral mechanisms described in this book. The term *cognitive mechanism* in no way excludes behavior. Thus, Rego et al.'s (chap. 5) concept of *cognitive vigilance* does not exclude the behavior of looking around or thinking about (verbally considering) the significance of events. Their concept of bias in the patient's attention processes (i.e., looking out for slights or impending danger) would be no more nonbehavioral than looking out for a sniper when told that one is around or when one's reinforcement history has proved that looking around pays off—that is, the behavior is negatively reinforced. The more controversial point is whether this bias causes the anxiety disorder or whether that is simply what it is. Beck (1991) alluded to this point when he wrote, "To conclude that cognitions cause depression is analogous to asserting that delusions cause schizophrenia" (p. 371). In other words, despite their great explanatory potential, behavioral mechanisms often simply describe the nature of the malady, such as the neural circuit that causes too rapid a response or the stressful life event that deprives the individual of positive reinforcement. Thus, in the former case, schizophrenic speech may be the result of the speaker responding to only part of what the speaker hears because the speaker is responding too fast, and in the latter case, that kind of emotional behavior may be caused by extinction.

Behavioral mechanisms fundamentally elucidate the nature of the psychopathology. As the pages of this book reveal, behavioral mechanisms are multifaceted and allow the clinician and the researcher to reveal even more links in the chain of psychological functions that explain how—and, more important, why—psychopathology is produced.

REFERENCES

American Psychiatric Association. (2000). *Diagnostic and statistical manual of mental disorders* (4th ed., text revision). Washington, DC: Author.

Andreasen, N. (2001). *Brave new brain: Conquering mental illness in the era of the genome*. New York: Oxford University Press

Beck, A. T. (1991). Cognitive therapy: A 30-year retrospective. *American Psychologist, 46*, 368–375.

Bentall, R. (2003). *Madness explained: Psychosis and human nature*. London: Penguin Books.

Larson, D. (1980). Therapeutic schools, styles, and schoolism: A national survey. *Journal of Humanistic Psychology, 20*, 3–20.

Melchert, T. P. (2007). Strengthening the scientific foundations of professional psychology: Time for the next steps. *Professional Psychology: Research and Practice, 38*, 34–43.

Miller, G. A., & Keller, J. (2004). Psychology and neuroscience: Making peace. In T. F. Oltmanns & R. E. Emery (Eds.), *Current directions in abnormal psychology* (pp. 3–9). Upper Saddle River, NJ: Pearson/Prentice Hall.

Moore, J. (2003). Explanation and description in traditional neobehaviorism, cognitive psychology, and behavior analysis. In K. A. Lattal & P. N. Chase (Eds.), *Behavior theory and philosophy* (pp. 13–39). New York: Kluwer Academic.

Salzinger, K. (1980). The behavioral mechanism to explain abnormal behavior. In F. L. Denmark (Ed.), *Annals of the New York Academy of Sciences: Vol. 340. Psychology: The leading edge* (pp. 66–87). New York: New York Academy of Sciences.

Salzinger, K. (1984). The immediacy hypothesis in a theory of schizophrenia. In W. D. Spaulding & J. K. Cole (Eds.), *Nebraska Symposium on Motivation: Vol. 31. Theories of schizophrenia and psychosis* (pp. 231–282). Lincoln: University of Nebraska Press.

Salzinger, K. (1992). Connections: A search for bridges between behavior and the nervous system. In D. Friedman & G. Bruder (Eds.), *Annals of the New York Academy of Sciences: Vol. 658. Psychophysiology and experimental psychopathology: A tribute to Samuel Sutton* (pp. 276–286). New York: New York Academy of Sciences.

Salzinger, K., & Serper, M. (2004). Schizophrenia: The immediacy mechanism. *International Journal of Psychology and Psychological Therapy, 4*, 397–409.

1

ENDOPHENOTYPES IN PSYCHIATRIC RESEARCH: FOCUS ON SCHIZOPHRENIA

ASSEN JABLENSKY

The concept of *endophenotype* (related terms include *intermediate phenotype*, *elementary phenotype*, and *subclinical trait*) refers to "measurable components, unseen by the unaided eye, along the pathway between disease and distal genotype" (Gottesman & Gould, 2003, p. 1). Endophenotypes are objectively measurable, biologically anchored heritable traits that cosegregate with clinical illness in pedigrees and may also be expressed in clinically unaffected members. They are likely to be more proximal to the primary biological defect and hence more sensitive to the "genetic signal" than the complex clinical phenotype (Almasy & Blangero, 2001). The term *endophenotype* has its origins in early 20th-century plant and insect genetics and was introduced into psychiatric genetics as long ago as the early 1970s by Gottesman and Shields (1972), primarily with reference to schizophrenia, to fill the gap between the search for causative genes and the elusive disease process. Biological traits matching the endophenotype definition have been widely and successfully used in biomedical research into the genetics of other complex, multifactorial diseases (e.g., excessive serum iron in idiopathic hemochromatosis; long QT interval in ischemic heart disease; electroencephalography abnormality in juvenile myoclonic epilepsy). However, it was not until the late 1990s that the concept gained currency in psychiatric research, with a rapidly growing number of publications appearing in the last 5 years. The surge of interest in endophenotypes was largely influenced by the limited success of the first generation of genetic linkage and association studies, which had been almost exclusively predicated on clinical diagnosis (based on criteria listed in the *Diagnostic and Statistical Manual of Mental Disorders* [4th ed.; *DSM–IV*, American Psychiatric Association, 1994], and the *International Classification of Diseases* [10th ed.; *ICD–10*, World Health Organization, 1994]) as *the* phenotype. Although a number of different psychiatric disorders have been examined in recent years from the vantage point of endophenotype-based strategies—for example, bipolar disorder (Cannon & Keller, 2006), autism (Viding & Blakemore, 2007), and attention-deficit/hyperactivity disorder (Waldman, 2005)—the greatest stakes for this novel approach have been placed on the genetics of schizophrenia.

WHY FOCUS ON SCHIZOPHRENIA?

With a lifetime risk of approximately 1% and onset in adolescence or early adulthood (Jablensky, 2000), schizophrenia affects profoundly a person's cognition and abilities to navigate adaptively through the complex social and emotional demands of everyday life. More than 50% of individuals affected by the disorder develop chronic disabilities, and nearly all experience a diminished quality of life. Schizophrenia is one of the genetically complex disorders, with broad heritability at approximately 80% and likely multifactorial etiology involving multiple genes of small to moderate effect, as well as a host of environmental influences for which a common denominator has yet to be established. Despite the current availability of powerful techniques of genetic analysis, such as whole-genome association studies, the basic problem of credibly "connecting phenotype with the genotype" (Botstein & Risch, 2003) in schizophrenia remains unresolved, largely because of excessive phenotypic variation, unknown composition of study samples, and limited application of a systems biology approach to the study of genotype–phenotype relationships. Phenotypic variation in schizophrenia points to likely etiological heterogeneity underlying the clinical diagnostic phenotype. Not unlike other genetically complex disorders, the syndrome of schizophrenia could represent an amalgamation of several distinct, or only partially overlapping, disease variants with pathophysiologies that should be amenable to dissection using the tools of neuroscience, genomics, and systems biology. Recent reviews and meta-analyses of genetic linkage and association findings point to multiple chromosomal regions that may harbor susceptibility genes, and to an ever-increasing number of candidate genes, for which supportive evidence has been only partially replicated or not replicated at all (Harrison & Weinberger, 2005). No causative allele, or a genetic mutation, has to date been unequivocally demonstrated, and further progress in the field increasingly appears to be constrained by a "second level of complexity" (Fanous & Kendler, 2005) related to the extreme individual variation in all phenotypic domains of the disorder, from neuroanatomy to neuropsychology.

ENDOPHENOTYPES: ORIGINS AND RATIONALE

Early research involving specific endophenotypes included a study of twins discordant for schizophrenia (Matthysse, Holzman, & Lange, 1986), who were tested for smooth-pursuit eye movements (SPEM). An unexpected finding was the nearly perfect concordance in monozygotic twins for SPEM dysfunction, whereas only 50% of dizygotic twins were concordant, suggestive of Mendelian dominant transmission of the trait. Proceeding from these findings, Holzman (1987) elaborated a model postulating a genetically transmitted latent trait that causes either schizophrenia, poor eye tracking, or both. The latent trait was thought to be associated with a disease process in the brain that independently invades one region or another, giving rise to diverse symptoms. Analysis of apparently divergent manifestations, such as SPEM and clinical schizophrenia, may point toward a common etiology, as in neurology (e.g., Friedreich's ataxia and hereditary cerebellar ataxia were found to be parts of the same pathological process, affecting differentially anatomically distinct regions but resulting in similar dysfunction). Similar reasoning should apply to psychiatric disorders, by parsing behaviors into the simplest components that could be studied biologically (Holzman, 1994). In a similar vein, Cromwell (1993) argued that clinical diagnosis is not the ideal phenotype for genetic investigation of schizophrenia and that cognitive, biobehavioral, and other markers might account for more of the genetic variance than does the clinical diagnosis. He provided a list of "things to do before the geneticist arrives," which included identification of *schizophrenia-related variants*: variables known to be associated with schizophrenia, but not necessarily part of its diagnosis; variables that emerge earlier than schizophrenia symptoms, being also vulnerability markers; and variables found among mentally healthy first-degree relatives and other relatives. The proposed schizophrenia-related variants included lexical priming (resistance, in patients with schizophrenia and in their biological relatives, to the normally occurring interference from an incongruent priming word) and the paradigm of reaction time crossover (the amount of slowing in reaction time when longer preparatory intervals are presented consecutively at the same length).

Probably the most significant theoretical framework, in which the endophenotype idea was implicitly embedded, was provided by Paul Meehl's (1990) concept of *schizotaxia*. Meehl regarded schizophrenia as a "loose syndrome," a cluster of seemingly unrelated phenomena, and postulated at its basis a genetically determined, generalized integrative defect in the central nervous system, a "slippage at the synapse," which he termed *schizotaxia*. As quantitative indicators of schizotaxia, he proposed soft neurological signs and minor physical anomalies; neurophysiological tests, such as SPEM and the P50 potential; attentional measures of signal-to-noise ratio; and syntactical and semantic aberrations. The model predicted functional impairments in domains involving relatively distant subsystems (e.g., more than three synapses away), domains requiring complex integration of inputs (e.g., from multiple sensory modalities), domains demanding finely tuned control by their subsystems, and domains in which the external reinforcement schedule is highly stochastic:

> Whatever is wrong with the schizotaxic [central nervous system] is ubiquitous, a functional aberration present throughout, operating everywhere from the sacral cord to the frontal lobes . . . a *functional parametric aberration of the synaptic control system* . . . an integrative defect analogous to dyslexia. (Meehl, 1990, p. 14)

SHORTCOMINGS OF THE DIAGNOSTIC CATEGORY AS A PHENOTYPE FOR BIOLOGICAL RESEARCH

Since the time of the inception of the concept, and into the present, schizophrenia has been diagnosed by analysis of the subjective symptoms reported by patients; the history and course of those symptoms; observation of behavior, affect, and speech; and (to a lesser extent) evaluation of premorbid development, personality traits, and family background. The diagnostic criteria of *DSM–IV* and *ICD–10* were conceived with a view to achieving three fundamentally different goals: (a) to identify groups of patients with broadly similar clinical presentation and prognosis, (b) to facilitate early diagnosis and choice of treatment, and (c) to define a homogeneous heritable diagnostic category for genetic etiological research. Although the first two goals have been largely achieved, as regards clinical utility of the criteria, the third has not been attained. Despite high estimated heritability of schizophrenia (approximately 80%, based on twin studies; Sullivan et al., 2003), there are hardly any robustly replicated findings pointing to causal genes in studies using the diagnostic category as the phenotype. The inconsistency of the results suggests extensive locus and allelic heterogeneity as well as an admixture of phenotypically varied clinical populations.

Despite the reasonable level of interrater agreement that can be achieved on the categorical diagnosis, the symptoms of schizophrenia span a wide range of psychopathology and display an extraordinary amount of interindividual variability and temporal inconstancy. Because no symptom is pathognomonic or necessary, although variable subsets of symptoms can be sufficient for the diagnosis, patients may be allocated to the diagnostic category of schizophrenia without having a single symptom in common. Moreover, symptoms may actually reflect compensatory behaviors (Gur et al., 2007) and vary across the course of the illness and its treatments. As a consequence, the phenomenological similarity of patients, selected for genetic and other biological research by the current criteria, is modest at best, or disconcertingly low at worst. This is part of the reason for the limited capacity of the diagnosis to predict accurately which biological or behavioral attributes will be shared by the majority of individuals allocated to the diagnostic category or to draw "zones of rarity" (Kendell & Jablensky, 2003) that clearly demarcate schizophrenia from other disorders. Such flaws raise doubts about the capacity of the broad clinical definition of schizophrenia to carve out biologically homogeneous clinical populations for genetic analysis. As Ginsburg et al. (1996) pointed out, inattention to the discrepancy between diagnoses, which may include more than one phenotype, and the diversity of their genetic underpinnings, continues to be an impediment to the uncovering of the genetic bases of behavioral disorders. Although in Mendelian diseases genotypes are usually strongly indicative of phenotypes, this reciprocal relationship does not exist in diseases with complex genetics, where it is the interactions among genotype, environment, and epigenetic factors that shape the phenotype. Further complexity arises from the great variety of morphometric, biochemical, and epigenetically regulated cell phenotypes in the brain, which calls for "more optimally reduced measures of neuropsychiatric functioning (more elementary phenomena) . . . than behavioural 'macros' " (Gottesman & Gould, 2003, p. 2).

HOW HETEROGENEOUS IS SCHIZOPHRENIA?

There is compelling evidence that schizophrenia, as defined by the current diagnostic criteria, is phenotypically heterogeneous, not only in its clinical phenomenology but also at the level of cognitive functioning (Joyce & Roiser, 2007). A major question, rarely addressed directly in schizophrenia research, is how to model the inherent phenotypic heterogeneity of the disorder. Two alternative (though not entirely irreconcilable) concepts are (a) the view of schizophrenia as a *unitary* disorder and (b) the hypothesis that the diagnostic category is a collection of *multiple* disease variants or subtypes. According to the unitary view, schizophrenia is best conceptualized as one neurodevelopmental disorder in which clinical heterogeneity is due to variable rates of progression ("pathological shift," according to Heinrichs, 2004) along multiple dimensions of brain structure and function. The alternative model of a composite disease entity, originally foreshadowed by Bleuler (1920/ 1976), posits several variant disorders, each underpinned by a relatively distinct etiology and/or pathophysiology but all sharing a broad, common final pathway of clinical phenotype expression (this model has salient counterparts in mental retardation, dementia, and epilepsy). Clinical samples, selected solely according to diagnostic category, are predicted by this model to contain an admixture of different disorders, and the corollary is that parsing such samples into component subtypes will reduce biological heterogeneity. Substantial indirect support for this model is provided by the successful application of "splitting" strategies in the unraveling of the genetics of other complex diseases, such as Type 2 diabetes (Hanis et al., 1996) or breast cancer (Ford et al., 1998). The inherent heterogeneity, which was built into the original concept of schizophrenia but became obfuscated in modern diagnostic classifications (*DSM–IV* and *ICD–10*), is now coming back to center stage as a working biological model. Examples include the tentative delineation of a "deficit syndrome" in schizophrenia (Kirkpatrick, Buchanan, McKenney, Alphs, & Carpenter, 1989), based on selected negative symptoms presumed to be primary, or of subtypes defined by particular cognitive dysfunctions (Heinrichs, 2004). These approaches, based on modest sample sizes, have until recently remained relatively isolated from the mainstream of genetic research in schizophrenia.

ENDOPHENOTYPE CRITERIA

Amid growing doubts about the capacity of the broad diagnostic category to serve as the sole biologically meaningful phenotype for gene discovery, the concept of endophenotype offers a novel perspective on parsing the complexity of schizophrenia that could be either an alternative or a complement to symptom-based phenotypes. This is where the endophenotype concept begins to be translated into research strategies, calling for explicit standard criteria for what constitutes an endophenotype. The following checklist is an amalgamation of the original criteria first proposed by Gottesman and Shields (1972) and subsequently revised (Gottesman & Gould, 2003); additional versions have been proposed by Almasy and Blangero (2001); Bearden and Freimer (2006); and Snitz, MacDonald, and Carter (2006). There are also recent reviews by Gur et al. (2007) and Turetsky et al. (2007) on behalf of the Consortium on the Genetics of Schizophrenia.

Endophenotypes must meet the following criteria:

- Have an association with illness in the general population and (desirably) correlation with illness severity. The association should vary continuously in the general population (ideally, as a normally distributed trait).
- Have an association with causes of the disorder, not with its consequences, such as effects of medication or degeneration due to disease progression.

- Have a modest to large effect size of the endophenotype prevalence in affected individuals as compared with healthy control individuals.
- Be cosegregated with illness within families.
- Have heritable variation in the endophenotype distribution within pedigrees.
- Have a stable, state-independent characteristic (observable regardless of the patient's clinical status of acute illness or remission), reflected in acceptable test–retest reliability, reproducibility, and concurrent validity.
- Present at a higher rate in nonaffected family members than in the general population (high relative risk ratio, λ_r).
- Possess good psychometric properties and be analyzable on a quantitative scale.
- Be related to known or plausibly suspected neurobiological substrate (latent endophenotype constructs should relate to reasonably well-characterized neural systems models).
- Involve homologies of expression across species to enable development of animal models.
- Allow practicality of administration of the relevant test measures.

It is notable that the current consensus on endophenotype criteria leaves out entirely some of the earlier desiderata, such as endophenotypes having a simpler genetic architecture than the illness phenotype, or being attributable to the effects of a single major gene. There is no doubt that the genetic basis of some endophenotypes may be as complex as the genetics of the disease itself and that multiple genes may be involved. Although endophenotypes can provide useful trait markers, they may not be any easier to dissect at a genetic level than the disorders to which they are related (Flint & Munafo, 2007). Furthermore, the requirement that any endophenotype should be specifically, or preferably, linked to schizophrenia (as defined by *DSM* criteria) and not to other disorders has been gradually abandoned. It is now increasingly clear that overlaps exist in genetic susceptibility across the traditional binary classification of psychosis (Owen, Craddock, & Jablensky, 2007).

COGNITIVE ENDOPHENOTYPES

Cognitive deficit, as a salient feature of schizophrenia, was part of Kraepelin's (1919/1971) original definition of *dementia praecox* as essentially characterized by "weakening of the mainsprings of volition, lowered mental efficiency, unsteadiness of attention, inability to sift, arrange and correct ideas, and to accomplish mental grouping of ideas" (p. 25). Meta-analytic or systematic reviews of the evidence (Gur et al., 2007; Heinrichs, 2004) suggest that, in regard to the criteria of effect sizes and consistency of reported findings, cognitive dysfunction in schizophrenia is a prime candidate for the endophenotype domain. Compromised higher cognitive function (low IQ) prior to the onset of disease has been shown to be a risk factor for schizophrenia in two large, population-based studies (Davidson et al., 1999; Zammit et al., 2004). There is remarkable agreement in the literature that deficits in multiple cognitive domains predate the onset of clinical symptoms, are not attributable to antipsychotic medications, persist over the course of the illness, are unrelated to its duration, occur in nonpsychotic relatives, are specific to schizophrenia as compared with other psychotic disorders, and behave like a stable trait. Cognitive deficits are thus likely to be a core feature of schizophrenia (not an epiphenomenon of the illness) and meet the criteria for an endophenotype. This conclusion is underscored by Heinrichs and Zakzanis's (1998) meta-analysis of 204 studies published between 1980 and 1994 (with a total of 7,420 schizophrenia patients and 5,865 control individuals) in which effect sizes (Cohen's d) and the U statistic (degree of nonoverlap) were calculated for 22 neurocognitive test variables ranging from IQ, verbal memory, and attention to executive function and language. Neurocognitive deficit was found to be a reliable and well-replicated finding in schizophrenia, although no single test or cognitive construct was capable of perfectly separating schizophrenia patients from control participants. Seven widely used measures achieved effect sizes greater than 1.0 (60%–70% nonoverlap between the patients and control participants): (a) global verbal memory (1.41), (b) bilateral motor skills (1.30), (c) performance IQ (1.26), (d) the continuous performance task (1.16), (e) word fluency (1.15), (f) the Stroop task (1.11), and (g) the Wechsler Adult Intelligence Scale—Revised (1981) IQ (1.10). Although a subset of approximately 50% of patients had nearly normal performance, significant cognitive impairment was common in schizophrenia and exceeded the deficits found in some neurological disorders, justifying the view that "schizophrenia is a neurological disorder that manifests itself in behaviour" (Heinrichs & Zakzanis, 1998, p. 437).

Cognitive deficits in schizophrenia are heterogeneous, however (Joyce & Roiser, 2007). They range from pervasive, generalized dysfunction, through patchy focal disorders, to mild focal deficits or nearly normal performance. Yet amid seemingly extensive heterogeneity, converging evidence points to specific deficits in verbal declarative memory (mainly in the early encoding stage) and in working memory as major sources of variance (Cirillo & Seidman, 2003). This observation has prompted attempts at delineating particular profiles or subtypes. Whereas conventional cluster analyses tend to distribute individuals into subgroups of severely compromised, intermediate, and mildly affected performance, classical fine-grained neuropsychological analyses (case studies of individual profiles instead of group means; delineation of generalized/ differential deficits; the search for double dissociations) have identified subtypes and patterns of dysfunction that to some extent parallel the amnestic syndromes in coarse brain disease, such as Huntington's, Parkinson's, or Alzheimer's. Thus, Paulsen et al. (1995) elicited from approximately 50% of schizophrenia patients a subcortical (striatal, Huntington's/Parkinson's-type) memory profile combining prominent retrieval deficit with absence of storage deficits (rapid forgetting). Another 15% had a cortical (hippocampal–thalamic, Alzheimer's-type) profile (primary encoding and storage impairment, with an excess of irrelevant word intrusions on free and cued recall), and the profiles of the remaining 35% did not deviate significantly from those of the control individuals. These findings were replicated by Turetsky et al. (2002) and supported by neuroimaging data suggesting ventricular enlargement with preserved temporal lobe gray matter in the subcortical group and left-hemisphere temporal and frontal volume reduction in the cortical group. Dickinson, Iannone, Wilk, and Gold (2004) estimated that more than 30% of the variance in cognitive test performance by patients with schizophrenia could be explained by a large-effect g factor, affecting the integration of multiple intermodal brain functions into core cognitive operations such as concept formation and reasoning skills. Further variance, however, can be explained by a number of independent, small-effect variables selectively affecting specific functions, such as processing speed and visual memory.

Promising as they are, these approaches to "splitting" schizophrenia are limited by sample size as well as by insufficient efforts to integrate multidomain data (e.g., neuroimaging and neurophysiological measurements) that might increase their capacity to parse the deficits characterizing schizophrenia. With a few exceptions (e.g., Bilder et al., 2002; Egan et al., 2001; Hallmayer et al., 2005; Paunio et al., 2004), cognitive deficits have not yet been systematically tested as endophenotypes in molecular genetic studies.

The relevant cognitive indicators with moderate to high effect sizes, which meet the criteria of endophenotypes and have recently been reviewed for the Consortium on the Genetics of Schizophrenia (Gur et al., 2007), include attention, verbal declarative memory, working memory, face memory, and emotion processing. The salient characteristics of these measures are summarized in Table 1.1. It is, however, likely that most cognitive measures available today assess interrelated facets of complex interactive neural networks rather than isolated processing modules and should be investigated jointly.

NEUROPHYSIOLOGICAL/PSYCHOPHYSIOLOGICAL ENDOPHENOTYPES

Five potential endophenotypes in the domain of neuro- and psychophysiology have been extensively characterized in a number of clinical studies, although for the majority, relatively little is known at present regarding their genetic underpinnings.

TABLE 1.1

Synopsis of Selected Characteristics of Candidate Endophenotypes in Schizophrenia Research

Domain/tests	Association with disorder	Effect size	Trait stability/state independence	Heritability/segregation within families	Underlying neurobiology/genetics
		Cognition			
Attention: Continuous performance task (CPT) Identical pairs (CPT–IP): working memory load Degraded stimulus (CPT–DS): perceptual disambiguation	Schizophrenia (SZ) patients consistently worse than controls (C). CPT–IP associated with negative symptoms; CPT–DS associated with cognitive disorganization.	CPT–IP $d = 1.51$ CPT–DS $d = 1.29$ (WAFSS)	Test–retest: CPT–IP $r = .56$ (SZ); .73 (C) CPT–DS $r = .65$ SZ); .72 (C) Both stable across clinical states.	Twin studies: CPT–IP $h^2 = .39–.49$ (C) CPT–DS $h^2 = .51–.57$ (C) CPT–DS $\lambda_r = 9$ (siblings); $\lambda_r = 12$ (parents)	Linkage to 6p24 (WAFSS). Association with the 22q11 deletion syndrome.
Verbal declarative memory (VDM): WMS–III LM CVLT RAVLT	The most consistently found deficit in SZ patients. VDM deficits related to negative symptoms.	$d = 1.41–2.39$	Test–retest: $rs = .62–.64$ (SZ), .74–.88 (C)	Twin studies: $h^2s = .47–.63$ (C), .21–.49 (SZ) Mild deficits in unaffected family members.	VDM deficits associated with decreased volume of hippocampus; association with DISC1 reported.
Working memory (WM): Online maintenance of information: Spatial delayed response Digits forward	Consistently found deficits in SZ patients.	LNS > 1.4 SD (SZ vs. controls) LNS $d = 0.66$ (unaffected family members vs. controls)	Constancy over time; minimal correlation with positive symptoms; moderate correlation with negative symptoms.	Twin studies: $h^2s = .43–.49$ (C), .36–.42 (SZ)	WM deficits associated with DLPFC and posterior parietal dysfunction. Likely role of COMT val158met polymorphism and DISC1.

Endophenotype/task	Findings in schizophrenia	Stability	Heritability (twin/family studies)	Neurobiology/associations
Maintenance + manipulation: N-back tasks, Digits backward, Letter–number sequencing (LNS)		No published data.		
Face memory and emotion processing: Face recognition tasks, Emotion recognition tasks	Frequently found deficits in SZ patients.	Possibly stable trait; more data required.	Twin studies: h^2s = .33 (faces), .37 (emotion). Mild deficits in unaffected family members.	Associations (fMRI): Faces: right fusiform gyrus and frontotemporal circuitry. Emotion: amygdala and hippocampus. Genetic association not known.
Sensory gating: P50 event-related potential (suppression ratio and amplitude difference)	SZ patients fail to attenuate response to second (test) stimulus.	Neurophysiology/psychophysiology Test–retest: r = .66–.73. Suppression deficit present in both acutely psychotic and stabilized patients. Clozapine reduces deficit. Amplitude: $d = 0.78$ Suppression ratio: $d = 0.54$ (WAFSS)	Twin studies: h^2 = .53–.68. Unaffected relatives and high-risk individuals show less suppression than controls, but data are inconsistent.	Cholinergic activation of hippocampal CA3/CA4 interneurons inhibits the firing of pyramidal neurons. Involvement of temporoparietal and prefrontal circuits likely. Association with the CHRNA7 gene coding for the α-7 subunit of the nicotinic receptor. *(continues)*

TABLE 1.1

Synopsis of Selected Characteristics of Candidate Endophenotypes in Schizophrenia Research *(Continued)*

Domain/tests	Association with disorder	Effect size	Trait stability/ state independence	Heritability/ segregation within families	Underlying neurobiology/ genetics
Failure of automatic inhibition: Prepulse inhibition of startle reflex (PPI)	SZ patients are deficient in automatic inhibition of startle. The response is influenced by atypical antipsychotics and nicotine. DA agonists reduce, NMDA antagonists increase, PPI.		Test–retest: $r > .90$ Longitudinal stability of PPI across clinical states has been little investigated.	Twin studies: $h^2 > .50$ PPI deficits found in unaffected family members. Males produce greater PPI than females. PPI in Asians > Caucasians.	PPI regulated by a limbic cortico–striato–pallido–pontine circuit interacting with the primary startle circuit at the pons reticular nucleus. PPI is abnormal in the 22q11 deletion syndrome. Possible role of the D2-like receptor G-protein and hippocampal $\alpha5$ subunit of the $GABA_A$ receptor.
Stimulus deviance detection: Mismatch negativity (MMN). Formation of an early (preattentive) auditory memory trace; automatic comparison process. MMN tests the integrity of the primary auditory memory network.	Deficit is present in the majority of SZ patients (not ameliorated by atypical antipsychotics). Presence of MMN deficit in first-episode patients uncertain.	$d \sim 1.0$ (meta-analysis), 0.74 (WAFSS)	Test–retest: $rs = .78$ (duration MMN), .53 (frequency MMN). Intraclass $r = .9$ over 1 year.	No formal h^2 estimates available. Abnormality is present in a proportion of unaffected family members.	MMN is reduced in the 22q11 deletion syndrome. Possible association with the COMT val158met polymorphism.

Endophenotype	Findings	Effect size	Reliability	Heritability	Comments
Working memory updating/stimulus salience evaluation: Auditory P300 event-related potential Composite of P3a (frontal), P3b (parietal)	Amplitude decrement and increased latency in SZ patients: one of the most consistent findings in the disorder.	Meta-analysis: $d = 0.89$ (amplitude) $d = 0.59$ (latency) WAFSS: $d = 0.91$ (amplitude)	Test–retest: $rs = .81$–$.91$ (2 weeks), $.59$–$.61$ (1–2 years).	Twin studies: $h^2 = .60$ Unaffected family members similar to probands. Familial deficit most evident for P3a.	Amplitude decrement correlated with smaller left superior temporal gyrus. Genetic linkage to 6p24. Possible association with DISC1 and the DRD2 receptor.
Saccadic dysfunction: Antisaccade task: inhibition of reflexive prosaccade; performance of antisaccade to a mirror location.	SZ patients: increased error rate; longer latencies to correct antisaccade task performance; reduced spatial accuracy	$d = 0.99$ (patients vs. C, WAFSS) $d = 0.99$ (relatives vs. C)	Test–retest: $r = .87$ (2 years) COGS intersite study: $r = .77$–$.96$ Deficit stable across clinical states	Twin studies: $h^2 = 0.57$ Error rate in unaffected family members: inconsistent data	Sensorimotor reprogramming; DLPFC, lateral interparietal area, supplementary eye field neurons. Linkage to 22q11–12 (COMT effect?)

Neuroimaging

Endophenotype	Findings	Effect size	Reliability	Heritability	Comments
Three-dimensional computational cortical surface mapping: Reduced hippocampal volumes	Hippocampal volumes: Probands < unaffected co-twins < healthy participants. Decrease in hippocampal size associated with cognitive deficit (memory dysfunction)			Twin studies: $h^2 = .42$	Hippocampal volume is environment and activity dependent. Possible role of DISC1, BDNF and TRAX genes.

(continues)

ENDOPHENOTYPES IN PSYCHIATRIC RESEARCH

TABLE 1.1
Synopsis of Selected Characteristics of Candidate Endophenotypes in Schizophrenia Research *(Continued)*

Domain/tests	Association with disorder	Effect size	Trait stability/ state independence	Heritability/ segregation within families	Underlying neurobiology/ genetics
Corpus callosum morphology	Vertical (upward) displacement			Present in both affected and unaffected family members. Putative neuro-anatomical marker of biological vulnerability for SZ.	Genetic/neuro-developmental origin likely.
fMRI response to working memory tasks	Exaggerated activation in right DLPFC in unaffected family members. Inefficient WM processing, similar to deficit in SZ patients.				Possible role of COMT val158met polymorphism.

Note. Empty cells indicate there are no applicable data available. WAFSS = Western Australian Family Study of Schizophrenia; WMS–III LM = Working Memory Span; CVLT = California Verbal Learning Test; RAVLT = Rey's Auditory Verbal Learning Test; DISC1 = Disrupted in Schizophrenia (gene); DLPFC = Dorsolateral prefrontal cortex; COMT = Catechol-O-methyltransferase; fMRI = functional magnetic resonance imaging; P50 = sensory gating potential; DA = Dopamine; NMDA = *N*-methyl-*D*-aspartate; DRD2 = Dopamine receptor D2; COGS = Cognition in Schizophrenia Consortium; BDNF = Brain-derived neurotrophic factor; TRAX = Translin-associated protein partner; WM = Working memory.

The P50 Component

The *P50 component* of an early (preattentive) event-related potential (ERP) has been systematically investigated as a measure of auditory sensory gating (Freedman, Adler, & Leonard, 1999; Freedman et al., 1996; Freedman, Waldo, Bickford-Wimer, & Nagamoto, 1991). P50 is a positive deflection occurring upon the presentation of a pair of clicks with a 500-milliseconds interstimulus interval. The P50 wave generated to the second (test) click is normally suppressed relative to the P50 response to the first (conditioning) click, likely because of the activation by the first click of cholinergic and GABA-ergic inhibitory neural circuitry in the hippocampus. Impaired suppression of P50 is present in the majority of patients with schizophrenia as well as in a proportion of their unaffected first-degree relatives. P50 is largely uninfluenced by typical antipsychotic drugs, although amelioration of the deficit may occur with administration of atypical antipsychotics. Genetic linkage has been found to a region on chromosome 15q13-14 and subsequently association with the CHRNA7 gene within that region, coding for the α-7 subunit of the nicotinic receptor (Leonard & Freedman, 2006).

Prepulse Inhibition of Startle

Prepulse inhibition of startle (PPI) is an operational measure of sensorimotor gating in which weak acoustic prestimuli presented at brief intervals before a startle-eliciting stimulus reduce the magnitude of the blink reflex component of the startle response (Cadenhead, Swerdlow, Shafer, Diaz, & Braff, 2000). It is a stable neurobiological marker that has been investigated extensively in both animal models and human studies, and it has been reproduced reliably in multi-site studies (Swerdlow et al., 2007). PPI is mediated by circuitry involving the limbic cortex, striatum, pallidum, and pontine tegmentum, interacting with the primary startle circuit at the level of the brain stem (the caudal reticular nucleus of the pons). In patients with schizophrenia, PPI is deficient in the sense that inhibition of the startle fails and the brain remains responsive to the second stimulus. In humans, PPI is significantly heritable, as shown by twin studies (Anokhin et al., 2003), and the inhibitory deficit tends to be present in first-degree relatives of schizophrenia patients (Cadenhead et al., 2000).

Mismatch Negativity

Mismatch negativity (MMN) is a negative ERP component, recorded as a response to low-probability deviant sounds in a sequence of standard acoustic stimuli while the subject's attention is directed elsewhere (Näätanen, 1992). The stimulus deviance can be designed to be either one of pitch or of duration. The MMN is a response to the detection by the auditory system of a deviation from an established pattern of acoustic stimulation in primary sensory memory. Reduction in amplitude is observed in the majority of schizophrenia patients (Catts et al., 1995) and in a proportion of their unaffected first-degree relatives (Michie, Innes-Brown, Todd, & Jablensky, 2002). The MMN deficit is likely to be specific to schizophrenia (Umbricht et al., 2003), but whether it is present in the early stages of the disorder or appears only with disease progression remains uncertain.

P300

P300 is a group of ERP components related to frontal (P3a) and parietal (P3b) generators. It has been extensively studied in schizophrenia and a range of other disorders. P300 is generated in an auditory oddball paradigm in response to attended infrequent target stimuli requiring an overt (effortful) reaction. P300 reflects several different cognitive processes, including attention, contextual updating of working memory, and attribution of salience to a deviant stimulus (Turetsky et al., 2007). Reduced amplitude of the oddball P300 response is a robust abnormality, observed in the majority of schizophrenia patients (see meta-analysis in Jeon & Polich, 2003). As a trait abnormality, the P300 amplitude decrement is independent of medication effects, length of illness, or severity of symptoms, and it can be elicited in clinically unaffected first-degree relatives of schizophrenia patients (Turetsky, Colbath, & Gur, 2000).

Antisaccade Task

The *antisaccade (AS) task* is an oculomotor paradigm, assessing inhibitory capacity, in which a fixation cue appears unpredictably in an eccentric location. The individual is instructed to inhibit the reflexive prosaccade response and instead make a volitional saccade in the opposite, mirror image direction. Errors are recorded if the saccade is in the wrong direction or is dysmetric. Patients with schizophrenia produce increased error rates, reduced accuracy of antisaccades, and longer latencies to correct response (Curtis, Calkins, & Iacono, 2001). The AS task is not influenced by the clinical state of the patient, and the effects of antipsychotic medication, if any, tend to be in the direction of mild improvement. The data on deficits in AS performance among unaffected first-degree relatives are not entirely consistent, with some studies reporting increased AS error rates (Clementz, McDowell, & Zisook, 1994) and others failing to find such a deficit (Brownstein et al., 2003).

Neuroimaging Endophenotypes

Imaging genetics is an emerging strategy for mapping neural structures and brain activity as a function of genotype (Meyer-Lindenberg & Weinberger,

2006). Evolving powerful techniques for three-dimensional cortical surface mapping as well as novel functional neuroimaging methods are certain to have a profound impact on the whole field of endophenotype research into schizophrenia, ultimately leading to future whole genome–full brain association studies. For the time being, however, the applications of imaging endophenotypes to the genetics of complex psychiatric disorders are limited by problems of reliability and reproducibility, risk of spurious findings, and lack of high-dimensional analytical methods that would control for Type I error (Bearden, van Erp, Thompson, Toga, & Cannon, 2007; Glahn, Thompson, & Blangero, 2007).

AN ILLUSTRATIVE EXAMPLE OF ENDOPHENOTYPE APPLICATION: THE WESTERN AUSTRALIAN FAMILY STUDY OF SCHIZOPHRENIA

The Western Australian Family Study of Schizophrenia (WAFSS; Jablensky, 2006) was one of the first research endeavors to apply a systematic endophenotyping approach to the search for the genetic basis of schizophrenia. A core aim of the WAFSS since its inception in 1996 was to address the problem of heterogeneity in schizophrenia. The research design endorsed the hypothesis that the syndrome of schizophrenia comprises several subtypes that could be delineated by objective endophenotype measurements of brain function and by exploring their genetic underpinnings. By the end of 2006, the study population comprised 895 individuals who had donated blood samples, including 473 members (157 affected with schizophrenia or schizophrenia spectrum disorder) of 126 nuclear families, 195 additional patients with schizophrenia, and 161 unrelated healthy control individuals. Clinical assessment included standardized diagnostic interviews, developmental history (detailed maternal interviews and case notes), and treatment documentation (from the Western Australian psychiatric case register). Best-estimate diagnoses (*ICD–10* and *DSM–IV*) were established by two senior clinicians. Participants completed a comprehensive neurocognitive assessment. Because abnormalities in cognitive performance in schizophrenia had been shown to be prevalent and robustly replicable, the core battery of tasks focused on a range of relatively independent (though interactive) cognitive domains: general ability (premorbid and current IQ); verbal learning and memory; sustained attention; speed of information processing; behavioral lateralization; and psychometric measures of schizotypy, temperament, and character. The tests selected were required to have prior evidence of reliability, subsequently confirmed on subsets of participants across all tests assessed. The cognitive evaluation of the phenotype was complemented by electrophysiological measures (event-related brain potentials, ERP, and an antisaccade task) in

145 individuals and structural magnetic resonance imaging in 70 individuals (see Figure 1.1).

In the analysis of the endophenotypes assessed, the various neurocognitive and personality measures were aggregated into a limited number of quantitative traits, using *grade of membership analysis* (Manton, Woodbury, & Tolley, 1994; Woodbury, Clive, & Garson, 1978), a version of latent structure analysis that defines latent groups (*pure types* [PTs]) and allows individuals to resemble each PT to a quantifiable degree, thus yielding a set of quantitative traits for use as covariates in genetic analysis. Two PTs represented >90% of

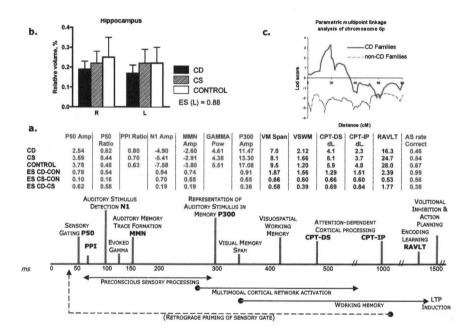

	P50 Amp	P50 Ratio	PPI Ratio	N1 Amp	MMN Amp	GAMMA Pow	P300 Amp	VM Span	VSWM	CPT-DS dL	CPT-IP dL	RAVLT	AS rate Correct
CD	2.54	0.62	0.80	-4.90	-2.60	4.61	11.47	7.0	2.12	4.1	2.3	16.3	0.46
CS	3.59	0.44	0.70	-5.41	-2.91	4.38	13.30	8.1	1.66	5.1	3.7	24.7	0.54
CONTROL	3.78	0.48	0.63	-7.58	-3.80	5.51	17.08	9.5	1.20	5.9	4.8	28.0	0.67
ES CD-CON	0.78	0.54		0.94	0.74		0.91	1.87	1.56	1.29	1.51	2.39	0.99
ES CS-CON	0.10	0.16		0.70	0.55		0.65	0.66	0.60	0.66	0.60	0.53	0.56
ES CD-CS	0.62	0.58		0.19	0.19		0.36	0.58	0.39	0.69	0.84	1.77	0.38

Figure 1.1. Neurocognitive, neurophysiological, and neuroimaging features of the cognitive deficit (CD) and cognitively spared (CS) subtypes, compared with healthy control individuals (CON). A tentative mapping of key neurocognitive and electrophysiological features onto a virtual timeline of brain information processing is depicted. Panel A: Electrophysiological and neurocognitive tests. Panel B: Structural magnetic resonance imaging volumetry of hippocampus. Panel C: Genetic analysis revealed a CD-specific locus on chromosome 6p25-24. P50 = sensory gating potential, amplitude (Amp) and attenuation ratio; ES = effect size (Cohen's *d*); PPI = prepulse inhibition, attenuation ratio; N1 = auditory event-related negative potential; MMN = mismatch negativity potential associated with the formation of an early auditory memory trace; Pow = power; GAMMA = waves in the gamma band (~40 Hz), associated with conscious perception; P300 = event-related potential evoked by a stimulus demanding attention; VM = visual memory; VSWM = visuospatial working memory; CPT = continuous performance task, DS = degraded stimulus, IP = identical pairs; RAVLT = Rey's Auditory Verbal Learning Test; AS = antisaccade task; LTP = long-term potentiation; R = right hemisphere; L = left hemisphere; Lod score = logarithm of odds.

the patients with schizophrenia and 23% of their unaffected first-degree relatives, whereas another two comprised control individuals without schizophrenia and clinically healthy relatives with age-related cognitive deficits. The two schizophrenia PTs presented sharply contrasting cognitive patterns: one of generalized cognitive deficit (labeled the *CD subtype*) and one cognitively spared (*CS subtype*).

A tentative mapping of key neurocognitive and electrophysiological features onto a virtual timeline of brain information processing is presented in Figure 1.1. The CD phenotype displays pervasive deficit across the majority of cognitive domains. The most affected functions are the following: encoding in verbal memory (with 98% of CD cases scoring ≥ 1 *SD* below the performance level of control participants), current IQ (with 91% scoring ≥ 1 *SD* below control participants), sustained attention/working memory (with 90% scoring ≥ 1 *SD* below control participants), and verbal memory delayed recall (with 87% scoring ≥ 1 *SD* below control participants). Comparable deficits arise in visual memory span and visuospatial working memory (Badcock, Badcock, Read, & Jablensky, 2008). Memory impairment is present at very short delay (immediate recall), is stable with increasing delay intervals, and points to compromised encoding rather than retention/forgetting. Note that 12.7% of the clinically unaffected first-degree relatives of CD participants exhibited similar deficits, although of attenuated severity. Most of the CS patients performed within 1 standard deviation of the control levels on all functions. The electrophysiological data (see Panel A of Figure 1.1) reveal further significant deficits in the CD subtype relative to both CS patients and control individuals: reduced P50 amplitude and ratio, abnormal PPI, low amplitudes of N1 component of the auditory event-related potential and P300, and high error rates and low self-correction rates on the AS task. Coherence of ERP-evoked gamma band oscillations is within normal range, but power is reduced in both CD and CS. Effect sizes (Cohen's *d*) are shown for the following comparisons: CD–control participants, CS–control participants, and CD–CS. The largest effect size, 2.39, is associated with immediate memory recall. On structural magnetic resonance imaging, CD individuals have volume reductions in the medial temporal lobes and the hippocampi, particularly on the left (see Panel B), whereas reduction in the frontal lobes is minimal.

Following a whole-genome scan (380 microsatellites at an average distance of 9.81 centi-Morgan (cM), linkage analysis (see Panel C, Figure 1.1) identified a CD-specific locus on 6p25-24 (Hallmayer et al., 2005). The phenotypic data clearly depict cognitive deficit, particularly in encoding in verbal memory, as the core feature of a homogeneous group of CD patients who represent a *dysmnesic* subtype of schizophrenia, reminiscent of Kraepelin's (1909/1971) dementia praecox. The CD subtype was also associated with an increased risk of pregnancy complications. The history of early development—

typically characterized by learning difficulties, marked shyness, and social withdrawal—and the higher incidence of schizophrenia in the pedigrees of CD probands define the CD subtype as a likely neurodevelopmental disorder, in which both genetic susceptibility and adverse prenatal events may play a role. Although positive psychotic symptoms do not differentiate between the CD and CS subtypes, CD patients consistently display more negative symptoms, in particular, poverty of speech, poor nonverbal communication, and diminished social drive. In my own studies (based on consecutive admissions or referrals), the CD subtype accounts for approximately 40% of all schizophrenia patients.

The cognitive and electrophysiological responses of CD patients suggest impaired synaptic function at the early stages of sensory encoding with a cascade effect along the timeline of information processing and a likely anatomical locus in the left medial temporal lobe. Impaired verbal memory in schizophrenia is consistently supported by meta-analyses of cognitive studies (Aleman, Hijman, de Haan, & Kahn, 1999; Cirillo & Seidman, 2003; Heinrichs & Zakzanis, 1998; Trandafir, Meary, Schurhoff, Leboyer, & Szoke, 2006), and recent research evidence underscores the involvement of the hippocampal formation in key memory and perceptual functions affected in schizophrenia (Harrison, 2004; Meyer-Lindenberg et al., 2005; Sim et al., 2006), providing a conceptual link to synaptic plasticity and its genetic regulation. Linkage analysis of the WAFSS sample (Hallmayer et al., 2005) has produced evidence for a distinct genetic basis of the CD subtype, and the genetic association data point to the involvement of different categories of postsynaptic proteins (some participating in the early reaction to excitatory stimulation, others in the delayed response leading to synaptic modification) in conferring susceptibility to the CD endophenotype. In sum, the WAFSS data furnish a link between CD and synaptic plasticity and warrant a systematic examination of the molecular network involved and the potential contribution of multiple interacting proteins.

DECONSTRUCTING SCHIZOPHRENIA?

Phenotypic variability has been confounding the search for the causes of schizophrenia since the inception of the diagnostic category. The inconsistent and poorly replicated results of genetic linkage and association studies using the diagnostic category as the sole schizophrenia phenotype are kindling discontent with the current nosology of schizophrenia. Schizophrenia geneticists are facing a particularly difficult situation as they seek to discover specific genes contributing to an overinclusive diagnostic category for which no specific biological substrate has yet been identified—most likely because of extensive genetic heterogeneity and an admixture of different underlying disease subtypes. The genetic polymorphisms and neurobiological deficits underlying schizophrenia are multiple, varied, and partly shared with predisposition to other disorders, although they primarily express a common final pathway within the schizophrenia spectrum. Such polymorphisms and deficits need not be intrinsically pathological and may represent extreme variants of normal structure and function. Above a certain density threshold, their additive or nonlinear interaction could give rise to the diagnostic symptoms in probands, but subclinical manifestations as endophenotype traits will be detectable in otherwise-healthy people, with a higher relative risk in biological relatives of probands.

Although reasoning along such lines is increasingly common among researchers, the approaches proposed to deal with the phenotype bottleneck in schizophrenia research differ substantially. On the one hand, there are proposals to abandon the Kraepelinian dichotomy of schizophrenic and affective disorders in favor of a psychosis-spectrum illness. On the other hand, there is an emerging "splitting" agenda, seeking narrowly constrained phenotypes that may tag distinct variants or subtypes of schizophrenia and resolve part of its etiological heterogeneity. Candidate endophenotypes, or markers of pathogenetic processes affecting cognition, brain morphology, and neurophysiology, constitute the mainstay of this approach. Genetic linkage and association studies using such endophenotypes have produced promising results that set a high priority for replication. Subtyping strategies are supported by mounting evidence that sample stratification, particularly using quantitative endophenotype traits as covariates, can reduce heterogeneity and substantially increase power. This approach has scored successes in the genetics of other complex diseases, and its application to schizophrenia genetics will bring the disorder into the mainstream of current research on the common genetic diseases.

In contrast to otherwise-powerful but hypothesis-free approaches, such as whole-genome association studies, which are not predicated on prior neurobiological information, endophenotype-guided studies enable the simultaneous use of molecular biology and neurobiology in identifying specific brain dysfunction that might be caused by functional clusters of genetic polymorphisms (Braff, Freedman, Schork, & Gottesman, 2007).

There are, however, several important caveats and unknowns to consider. First, a cognitive or neurophysiological variable meeting most of the stipulated endophenotype criteria may not be causally involved in the clinical phenomenology of the disorder. In schizophrenia (as in many other psychiatric disorders), we are still facing an explanatory gap between objectively measurable neurocognitive dysfunction and subjectively experienced symptoms, such as primary delusions, passivity experiences, or third-person auditory hallucinations. Second, genes influencing neurocognitive or neuroanatomical endophenotypes may selectively exert their effects only at early developmental stages (*in utero* or in early infancy), whereas their expression in later life would be altered by epigenetic modification due to environmental stress, substance use, or medication. Third, we do not have at present any validated simple, relatively low-cost covariate measure of a large effect size, analogous to the QT interval, glucose tolerance index, or serum iron level, that would enable the splitting of the clinical phenotype along genetic fault lines. Instead, endophenotype-based studies of schizophrenia (or any other psychiatric disorder, for that matter) will require comprehensive measurement of multiple variables, thus constraining and underpowering the effective sample size. Strategies preempting such methodological pitfalls should include concerted efforts to achieve proper standardization of evidence-based endophenotype testing batteries comprising a core of well-established standard tests as a reference point but allowing for additional experimental, custom-designed applications. As Gerlai (2002) proposed, such batteries should be organized hierarchically, starting from broader, less specific tests that cover major domains of cognition and are sensitive to multiple deficits, and then proceeding to increasingly focused tests (e.g., for specific mechanisms of memory). It would be desirable to increase the information density of the tests (i.e., the number of measures that can be obtained from a single test), as well as their flexibility, because this would allow researchers to tap into a broader spectrum of brain functions.

What kind of data would constitute supportive evidence for distinct component disorders or subtypes within schizophrenia? Converging evidence from endophenotype-based studies suggests that measures of neurocognitive dysfunction provide the largest effect sizes and increases in relative risk to relatives among a host of candidate endophenotypes and are cost-efficient for phenotyping large samples. In particular, several patterns of short-term and working memory impairment against a background of generalized cognitive deficit have been replicated across studies and are present in a substantial proportion (approximately 50%) of schizophrenia patients. Because many of the neurocognitive tests tap into several component processes, composite endophenotypes, integrating multiple neurocognitive measures, are more likely than single-feature endophenotypes to capture variation that is genetically influenced. The subtypes generated by such approaches should be capable of classifying individuals rather than variables, and the resulting classification is likely to be *polythetic* (based on subsets of correlated features rather than on the presence of all defining attributes). Whether subtypes are discrete taxa (i.e., identifiable by marked areas of discontinuity with other subtypes); dimensional, representing continua with fuzzy boundaries; or hybrid (class quantitative, with dimensions superimposed on discrete categories) is testable with taxometric methods common in biological classifications. In the context of genetic research, the most significant criterion of a subtype's validity will be the gain in predictive power and process understanding, in the sense of mechanistic explanation of disease phenomena.

The dissection of the syndrome of schizophrenia into modular endophenotypes with specific neurocognitive or neurophysiological underpinnings is beginning to be perceived as a promising approach in schizophrenia genetics. The current evidence is neither final nor static and needs to be reexamined as new concepts and technologies—coming from molecular genetics, neuroscience, cognitive science, or brain imaging—bring forth new perspectives on disease causation and brain function. This must be complemented by a refined, reliable, and valid phenotyping not only at the level of symptoms but also involving correlated neurobiological features. The study of endophenotypes cutting across the conventional diagnostic boundaries may reveal unexpected patterns of associations with symptoms, personality traits, or behavior. The mapping of clinical phenomenology onto specific brain dysfunction and genetics may in the future substantially recast the present nosology of psychiatric disorders.

REFERENCES

Aleman, A., Hijman, R., de Haan, E. H., & Kahn, R. S. (1999). Memory impairment in schizophrenia: A meta-analysis. *American Journal of Psychiatry, 156*, 1358–1366.

Almasy, L., & Blangero, J. (2001). Endophenotypes as quantitative risk factors for psychiatric disease: Rationale and study design. *American Journal of Medical Genetics (Neuropsychiatric Genetics), 105*, 42–44.

American Psychiatric Association. (1994). *Diagnostic and statistical manual of mental disorders* (4th ed.). Washington, DC: Author.

Anokhin, A. P., Heath, A. C., Myers, E., Ralano, A., & Wood, S. (2003). Genetic influences on prepulse inhibition of startle reflex in humans. *Neuroscience Letters, 353*, 45–48.

Badcock, J. C., Badcock, D. R., Read, C., & Jablensky, A. (2008). Examining encoding imprecision in spatial working memory in schizophrenia. *Schizophrenia Research, 100*, 144–152.

Bearden, C. E., & Freimer, N. B. (2006). Endophenotypes for psychiatric disorders: Ready for primetime? *Trends in Genetics, 22*, 306–313.

Bearden, C. E., van Erp, T. G. M., Thompson, P. M., Toga, A. W., & Cannon, T. D. (2007). Cortical mapping of genotype–phenotype relationships in schizophrenia. *Human Brain Mapping, 2*, 519–532.

Bilder, R. M., Volavka, J., Czobor, P., Malhotra, A. K., Kennedy, J. L., Ni, X., et al. (2002). Neurocognitive correlates of the COMT val158met polymorphism in chronic schizophrenia. *Biological Psychiatry, 52*, 701–707.

Bleuler, E. (1976). *Textbook of psychiatry* (A. A. Brill, Trans.). New York: Arno Press. (Original work published 1920)

Botstein, D., & Risch, N. (2003). Discovering genotypes underlying human phenotypes: Past successes for Mendelian disease, future approaches for complex disease. *Nature Genetics, 33*(Suppl.), 228–237.

Braff, D., Freedman, R., Schork, N. J., & Gottesman, I. I. (2007). Deconstructing schizophrenia: An overview of the use of endophenotypes in order to understand a complex disorder. *Schizophrenia Bulletin, 33,* 21–32.

Brownstein, J., Krastoshevsky, O., McCollum, C., Kundamal, S., Matthysse, S., Holzman, P. S., et al. (2003) Antisaccade performance is abnormal in schizophrenia patients but not in their biological relatives. *Schizophrenia Research, 63,* 13–25.

Cadenhead, K. S., Swerdlow, N. R., Shafer, K. M., Diaz, M., & Braff, D. L. (2000). Modulation of the startle response and startle laterality in relatives of schizophrenic patients and in subjects with schizotypal personality disorder: Evidence of inhibitory deficit. *American Journal of Psychiatry, 157,* 1660–1668.

Cannon, T. D., & Keller, M. C. (2006) Endophenotypes in the genetic analysis of mental disorders. *Annual Review of Clinical Psychology, 2,* 267–290.

Catts, S. V., Shelley, A. M., Ward, P. B., Liebert, B., McConaghy, N., Andrews, A., et al. (1995). Brain potential evidence for an auditory sensory memory deficit in schizophrenia. *American Journal of Psychiatry, 152,* 213–219.

Cirillo, M. A., & Seidman, L. J. (2003). Verbal declarative memory dysfunction in schizophrenia: From clinical assessment to genetics and brain mechanisms. *Neuropsychology Review, 13,* 43–77.

Clementz, B. A., McDowell, J. E., & Zisook, S. (1994). Saccadic system functioning among schizophrenia patients and their first-degree biological relatives. *Journal of Abnormal Psychology, 103,* 277–287.

Cromwell, R. L. (1993). Schizophrenia research: Things to do before the geneticist arrives. In R. L. Cromwell & C. R. Snyder. (Eds.), *Schizophrenia: Processes, treatments, and outcome* (pp. 51–61). New York: Oxford University Press.

Curtis, C. E., Calkins, M. E., & Iacono, W. G. (2001). Saccadic disinhibition in schizophrenia patients and their first-degree biological relatives: A parametric study of the effects of increasing inhibitory load. *Experimental Brain Research, 137,* 228–236.

Davidson, M., Reichenberg, A., Rabinowitz, J., Weiser, M., Kaplan, Z., & Mark, M. (1999). Behavioral and intellectual markers for schizophrenia in apparently healthy male adolescents. *American Journal of Psychiatry, 156,* 1328–1335.

Delis, D. C., Kramer, J. H., Kaplan, E., & Ober, B. A. (1983). *California Verbal Learning Test (CVLT)—Adult Version.* San Antonio, TX: Psychological Corporation.

Dickinson, D., Iannone, V. N., Wilk, C. M., & Gold, J. M. (2004). General and specific cognitive deficits in schizophrenia. *Biological Psychiatry, 55,* 826–833.

Egan, M. F., Goldberg, T. E., Kolachana, B. S., Callicott, J. H., Mazzanti, C. M., Straub, R. E., et al. (2001). Effect of COMT val108/158met genotype on frontal lobe function and risk for schizophrenia. *Proceedings of the National Academy of Sciences, 98,* 6917–6922.

Fanous, A. H., & Kendler, K. S. (2005). Genetic heterogeneity, modifier genes, and quantitative phenotypes in psychiatric illness: Searching for a framework. *Molecular Psychiatry, 10,* 6–13.

Flint, J., & Munafo, M. R. (2007). The endophenotype in psychiatric genetics. *Psychological Medicine, 37,* 163–180.

Ford, D., Easton, D. F., Strattom, M., Narod, S., Goldgar, D., Devilee, P., et al. (1998). Genetic heterogeneity and penetrance analysis of the BRCA1 and BRCA2 genes in breast cancer families. *American Journal of Human Genetics, 62,* 676–689.

Freedman, R., Adler, L. E., & Leonard, S. (1999). Alternative phenotypes for the complex genetics of schizophrenia. *Biological Psychiatry, 45,* 551–558.

Freedman, R., Adler, L. E., Myles-Worsley, M., Nagamoto, H. T., Miller, C., Kisley, M., McRae, K., et al. (1996). Inhibitory gating of an evoked response to repeated auditory stimuli in schizophrenic and normal subjects: Human recordings, computer simulation, and an animal model. *Archives of General Psychiatry, 53,* 1114–1121.

Freedman, R., Waldo, M., Bickford-Wimer, P., & Nagamoto, H. (1991). Elementary neuronal dysfunctions in schizophrenia. *Schizophrenia Research, 4,* 233–243.

Gerlai, R. (2002). Phenomics: Fiction or the future? *Trends in Neurosciences, 25,* 506–509.

Ginsburg, B. E., Werick, T. M., Escobar, J. I., Kugelmass, S., Treanor, J. J., & Wendtland, L. (1996). Molecular genetics of psychopathologies: A search for simple answers to complex problems. *Behavior Genetics, 26,* 325–334.

Glahn, D. C., Thompson, P. M., & Blangero, J. (2007). Neuroimaging endophenotypes: Strategies for finding genes influencing brain structure and function. *Human Brain Mapping, 28,* 488–501.

Gottesman, I. I., & Gould, T. D. (2003). The endophenotype concept in psychiatry: Etymology and strategic intentions. *American Journal of Psychiatry, 160,* 636–645.

Gottesman, I. I., & Shields, J. (1972). *Schizophrenia and genetics: A twin study vantage point.* New York: Academic Press.

Gur, R. E., Calkins, M. N., Gur, R. C., Horan, W. P., Nuechterlein, K. H., Seidman, L. J., & Stone, W. S. (2007). The Consortium on the Genetics of Schizophrenia: Neurocognitive endophenotypes. *Schizophrenia Bulletin, 33,* 49–68.

Hallmayer, J. F., Kalaydjieva, L., Badcock, J., Dragovic, M., Howell, S., Michie, P. T., et al. (2005). Genetic evidence for a distinct subtype of schizophrenia characterized by pervasive cognitive deficit. *American Journal of Human Genetics, 77,* 468–476.

Hanis, C. L., Boerwinkle, E., Chakraborty, R., Ellsworth, D. L., Concannon, P., Stirling, B., et al. (1996). A genome-wide search for human non-insulin–dependent (type 2) diabetes genes reveals a major susceptibility locus on chromosome 2. *Nature Genetics, 13,* 161–166.

Harrison, P. J. (2004). The hippocampus in schizophrenia: A review of the neuropathological evidence and its pathophysiological implications. *Psychopharmacology, 174,* 151–162.

Harrison, P. J., & Weinberger, D. R. (2005). Schizophrenia genes, gene expression, and neuropathology: On the matter of their convergence. *Molecular Psychiatry, 10*, 40–68.

Heinrichs, R. W. (2004). Meta-analysis and the science of schizophrenia: Variant evidence or evidence of variants? *Neuroscience and Biobehavioral Reviews, 28*, 379–394.

Heinrichs, R. W., & Zakzanis, K. K. (1998). Neurocognitive deficit in schizophrenia: A quantitative review of the evidence. *Neuropsychology, 12*, 426–445.

Holzman, P. S. (1987) Genetic latent structure models: Implications for research on schizophrenia. *Psychological Medicine, 17*, 271–274.

Holzman, P. S. (1994). The role of psychological probes in genetic studies of schizophrenia. *Schizophrenia Research, 13*, 1–9.

Jablensky, A. (2000). Epidemiology of schizophrenia: The global burden of disease and disability. *European Archive of Psychiatry and Clinical Neuroscience, 250*, 274–285.

Jablensky, A. (2006). Subtyping schizophrenia: Implications for genetic research. *Molecular Psychiatry, 11*, 815–836.

Jeon, Y. W., & Polich, J. (2003). Meta-analysis of P300 and schizophrenia: Paradigms and practical applications. *Psychophysiology, 40*, 684–701.

Joyce, E. M., & Roiser, J. P. (2007). Cognitive heterogeneity in schizophrenia. *Current Opinion in Psychiatry, 20*, 268–272.

Kendell, R., & Jablensky, A. (2003). Distinguishing between the validity and utility of psychiatric diagnoses. *American Journal of Psychiatry, 160*, 4–12.

Kirkpatrick, B., Buchanan, R. W., McKenney, P. D., Alphs, L. D., & Carpenter, W. T. (1989). The Schedule for the Deficit Syndrome: An instrument for research in schizophrenia. *Psychiatry Research, 30*, 119–123.

Kraepelin, E. (1971). *Psychiatrie. 8 Auflage* [Dementia praecox and paraphrenia]. Huntington, NY: Krieger Publishing. (Original work published 1909)

Leonard, S., & Freedman, R. (2006). Genetics of chromosome 15q13–q14 in schizophrenia. *Biological Psychiatry, 15*, 115–122.

Manton, K. G., Woodbury, M. A., & Tolley, D. H. (1994). *Statistical applications using fuzzy sets.* New York: Wiley.

Matthysse, S., Holzman, P. S., & Lange, K. (1986). The genetic transmission of schizophrenia: Application of Mendelian latent structure analysis to eye tracking dysfunction in schizophrenia and affective disorder. *Journal of Psychiatric Research, 20*, 57–65.

Meehl, P. E. (1990). Toward an integrated theory of schizotaxia, schizotypy, and schizophrenia. *Journal of Personality Disorders, 4*, 1–99.

Meyer-Lindenberg, A. S., Olsen, P. K., Kohn, P. D., Brown, T., Egan, M. F., Weinberger, D. R., & Berman, K. F. (2005). Regionally specific disturbance of dorsolateral prefrontal–hippocampal functional connectivity in schizophrenia. *Archives of General Psychiatry, 62*, 379–386.

Meyer-Lindenberg, A., & Weinberger, D. R. (2006). Intermediate phenotypes and genetic mechanisms of psychiatric disorders. *Nature Review of Neuroscience, 7,* 818–827.

Michie, P. T., Innes-Brown, H., Todd, J., & Jablensky, A. (2002). Duration mismatch negativity in biological relatives of patients with schizophrenia spectrum disorders. *Biological Psychiatry, 52,* 749–758.

Näätanen, R. (1992). *Attention and brain function.* Hillsdale, NJ: Erlbaum.

Owen, M. J., Craddock, N., & Jablensky, A. (2007). The genetic deconstruction of psychosis. *Schizophrenia Bulletin, 33,* 905–911.

Paulsen, J. S., Heaton, P. K., Sadek, J. R., Perry, W., Delis, D. C., Braff, D., et al. (1995). The nature of learning and memory impairments in schizophrenia. *Journal of the International Neuropsychology Society, 1,* 88–99.

Paunio, T., Tuulio-Henriksson, A., Hiekkalinna, T., Perola, M., Varilo, T., Partonen, T., et al. (2004). Search for cognitive trait components of schizophrenia reveals a locus for verbal learning and memory on 4q and for visual working memory on 2q. *Human Molecular Genetics, 13,* 1693–1702.

Schmidt, M. (1996). *Rey Auditory and Verbal Learning Test: A Handbook.* Los Angeles: Western Psychological Services.

Sim, K., DeWitt, I., Ditman, T., Zalesak, M., Greenhouse, I., Goff, D., et al. (2006). Hippocampal and parahippocampal volumes in schizophrenia: A structural MRI study. *Schizophrenia Bulletin, 32,* 332–340.

Snitz, B. E., MacDonald A. W., & Carter, C. S. (2006). Cognitive deficits in unaffected first-degree relatives of schizophrenia patients: A meta-analytic review of putative endophenotypes. *Schizophrenia Bulletin, 32,* 179–194.

Sullivan, P. F., Kendler, K. S., & Neale, M. C. (2003). Schizophrenia as a complex trait: Evidence from a meta-analysis of twin studies. *Archives of General Psychiatry, 60,* 1187–1192.

Swerdlow, N. R., Sprock, J., Light, G. A., Cadenhead, K., Calkins, M. E., Dobie, D. J., et al. (2007). Multi-site studies of acoustic startle and prepulse inhibition in humans: Initial experience and methodological considerations based on studies by the Consortium on the Genetics of Schizophrenia. *Schizophrenia Research, 92,* 237–251.

Trandafir, A., Meary, A., Schurhoff, F., Leboyer, M., & Szoke, D. (2006). Memory tests in first-degree adult relatives of schizophrenia patients: A meta-analysis. *Schizophrenia Research, 81,* 217–226.

Turetsky, B. I., Calkins, M. E., Light, G. A., Olincy, A., Radant, A. D., & Swerdlow, N. R. (2007). Neurophysiological endophenotypes in schizophrenia: The viability of selected candidate measures. *Schizophrenia Bulletin, 33,* 69–94.

Turetsky, B. I., Colbath, E. A., & Gur, R. E. (2000). P300 subcomponent abnormalities in schizophrenia: III. Deficits in unaffected siblings of schizophrenic probands. *Biological Psychiatry, 47,* 380–390.

Turetsky, B. I., Moberg, P. J., Mozley, L. H., Moelter, S. T., Agrin, R. N., Gur, R. C., et al. (2002). Memory-delineated subtypes of schizophrenia: Relationship to clinical, neuroanatomical, and neurophysiological measures. *Neuropsychology,* *16,* 481–490.

Umbricht, D., Koller, R., Schmid, L., Skrabo, A., Grubel, C., Huber, T., et al. (2003). How specific are deficits in mismatch negativity generation to schizophrenia? *Biological Psychiatry, 47,* 1120–11.

Viding, E., & Blakemore, S. J. (2007). Endophenotype approach to developmental psychopathology: Implications for autism research. *Behavioral Genetics, 37,* 51–60.

Waldman, I. D. (2005). Statistical approaches to complex phenotypes: Evaluating neuropsychological endophenotypes for attention-deficit/hyperactivity disorder. *Biological Psychiatry, 57,* 1347–1356.

Woodbury, M. A., Clive, J., & Garson, A. (1978). Mathematical typology: A grade of membership technique for obtaining disease definition. *Computers in Biomedical Research, 11,* 277–298.

World Health Organization. (1994). *International classification of diseases* (10th ed.). Geneva, Switzerland: Author.

Zammit, S., Allebeck, P., David, A. S., Dalman, C., Hemmingsson, T., Lundberg, I., & Lewis, G. (2004). A longitudinal study of premorbid IQ score and risk of developing schizophrenia, bipolar disorder, severe depression, and other non-affective psychoses. *Archives of General Psychiatry, 61,* 354–360.

2

CONTEXT, GOALS, AND BEHAVIORAL REGULATION IN SCHIZOPHRENIA: PSYCHOLOGICAL AND NEURAL MECHANISMS

DEANNA M. BARCH AND TODD S. BRAVER

In this chapter, we lay out the framework of a theory regarding one set of behavioral mechanisms that may contribute to a number of the cognitive and other symptomatic deficits experienced by individuals with schizophrenia. We argue that a deficit in the ability to represent and maintain context in order to guide behavior is a key component of many of the behavioral abnormalities demonstrated by individuals with schizophrenia. Our theory is not the first to put forth such a framework, and we build on the groundbreaking work of individuals such as Shakow, Salzinger, Hemsley, and Gray. However, we try to expand on this prior work by embedding it in a computational framework that allows us to make specific testable predictions about the pattern of impairments that should be expected under different conditions. Furthermore, this connectionist framework allows us to incorporate hypotheses about the neurobiological mechanisms that normally support context-processing functions and the ways in which disturbances in these mechanisms may give rise to the difficulties present in individuals with schizophrenia. Although we think this continues to be a promising avenue of research, we also acknowledge that much work remains to be done. For example, it is not yet clear how our conceptualizations of context map onto other conceptualizations of context, such as those put forth by J. A. Gray (1998) and Phillips and Silverstein (2003). Empirical and computation work centered on this topic would help us understand the degree to which these conceptualizations converge on a common set of phenomena or mechanisms, or represent complementary or alternative accounts. Furthermore, much work is still needed in terms of understanding how context-processing deficits may contribute to the difficulties in everyday life function experienced by individuals with schizophrenia. The influence of context on language production and social cognition may be a natural starting point for such investigations because these are clear areas of translational potential.

CONTEXT, GOALS, AND BEHAVIORAL REGULATION IN SCHIZOPHRENIA: PSYCHOLOGICAL AND NEURAL MECHANISMS

Traditional clinical conceptualizations of schizophrenia have typically focused on symptoms such as hallucinations, delusions, and disorganized speech, which are often considered the hallmark features of this disorder. This focus is understandable because these are often the most glaringly obvious symptoms of this debilitating disorder and often the phenomena that bring individuals to the attention of the mental health system. However, clinicians, researchers, and theorists have long noted that individuals with schizophrenia also commonly suffer from disturbances in a number of other aspects of behavior, including memory, attention, and the control of cognition and emotion. Importantly, a growing body of research suggests that impairments in behavioral control and cognitive function may be more important for understanding impairments in social and occupational functioning in individuals with schizophrenia than is the severity of symptoms such as hallucinations and delusions (M. F. Green, Kern, & Heaton, 2004). Although research on cognitive and behavioral abnormalities in schizophrenia has a long and venerable history, such findings on the relevance of cognition for functional outcomes has shone a new spotlight on the importance of understanding behavior and function in this illness. In some ways, this emphasis is ironic because many professionals have considered the past 2 decades to be the purview of biologically focused research in schizophrenia. There has been an explosion of studies focusing on molecular genetics, neurotransmitter function, and neuroanatomy in schizophrenia, often with little explicit connection to behavior or symptoms (DeLisi & Fleischhaker, 2007; Lewis & Mirnics, 2006; Lipska et al., 2006). As such, the evidence that cognitive function is critical for understanding functional abilities and outcomes in this disorder reiterates the importance of including behavior and cognition in the equation as the glue that will link molecular level studies to the phenomenology of the disorder itself (Ross, Margolis, Reading, Pletnikov, & Coyle, 2006).

A close examination of the types of behaviors and cognitive disturbances displayed by individuals with schizophrenia suggests that many of these disturbances appear to reflect an inability to control or regulate their cognitive and emotional states. In this chapter, we review the evidence that one of the core cognitive disturbances in schizophrenia is a deficit in one or more components of executive function, which leads to disturbances in the ability to appropriately regulate thoughts and behavior in accordance with internal goals and with stimuli that may not be present in the current external environment. More specifically, we suggest that individuals with schizophrenia experience a disturbance in a specific type of executive control process that we refer to as the ability to represent and maintain context (Barch, Carter, et al., 2001; Braver, Barch, & Cohen, 1999a; Braver & Cohen, 1999; Cohen & Servan-Schreiber, 1992), due to a disturbance in the function of dopamine (DA) in the dorsolateral prefrontal cortex (DLPFC). It is important to note that these ideas regarding context processing are not unique in terms of conceptualizing schizophrenia and, as we discuss in more detail later in this chapter, build on the work of researchers such as Shakow, Salzinger, Hemsley, and Gray.

One of the challenges to developing theories as to the nature and source of behavioral and cognitive deficits in schizophrenia is the ability to make explicit and testable predictions that differentiate one theory from another. Furthermore, although a focus on behavior is important in and of itself, it is also clear that to fully understand the nature and causes of schizophrenia, we need to understand how behavioral and cognitive disturbances arise from a set of neurobiological impairments. Thus, it is also critical to explicitly link behavioral mechanisms to biologically plausible mechanisms. To accomplish these goals, we have used computational modeling as a tool for specifying the processes by which context influences ongoing behavior, the biological mechanisms that support context processing (e.g., DLPFC and the DA system), and how specific disturbances to these mechanisms lead to cognitive impairments (Braver, 1997; Braver, Barch, & Cohen, 1999a, 1999b; Braver & Cohen, 1999; Braver, Cohen, & McClelland, 1997; Braver, Cohen, & Servan-Schreiber, 1995; Cohen & Servan-Schreiber, 1992). These models have been constructed within the *parallel distributed processing*, or *neural network framework*, allowing the quantitative simulation of human performance in cognitive tasks using principles of processing that are similar to those believed to apply in the brain (McClelland, 1993; Rumelhart & McClelland, 1986). The nature of these models and the results of simulations have been discussed in detail elsewhere (Braver, 1997; Braver & Cohen, 1999; Braver et al., 1995, 1997, 1999a, 1999b).

Context Processing

The ability to regulate behavior by means of internal goals and stimuli that are no longer present in the current environment requires the maintenance of internal representations over time and the ability to detect, adjust, and respond to changing contingencies and feedback in the environment. This is not a unitary process, and it requires the coordinated action of a number of different functions and mechanisms. In our own work, we have focused on several such mechanisms that we think are important for cognitive and behavioral control, including context representation, context maintenance, context updating, conflict detection, and subgoal processing (Barch, Braver, et al., 2001; Barch, Carter, et al., 2001; Botvinick, Braver, Barch, Carter, & Cohen, 2001; Braver & Bongiolatti, 2002; Braver, Cohen, & Barch, 2002; Braver et al., 1999a; O'Reilly, Noelle, Braver, & Cohen, 2002). Furthermore, we have argued that deficits in the representation, maintenance, and updating of context may be central to understanding cognitive and behavioral dysregulation in schizophrenia (see Table 2.1). Before we describe our model of how context processing operates and its relationship to neural substrates, it is important to make clear what we mean by *context*.

As Hemsley (2005) aptly noted, the term *context* has been applied in many different environments, often to mean many different things. For example, Hemsley argued that "context may be seen to influence the processing of target stimuli by drawing on patterns of predictive behavior" (p. 44). We think this definition of context does capture an elemental property of most

TABLE 2.1
Behavioral Mechanisms in Schizophrenia

Mechanism	Definition	References
Context processing	The ability to internally represent and maintain information about prior stimuli or processing outcomes that can be used to guide upcoming behavior.	Barch et al. (2003); Cohen et al. (1999); Cohen and Servan-Schreiber (1992)
Response selection	Selecting material for optimal response on the basis of the current or preceding context.	Shakow (1962)
Immediacy	The tendency to respond to stimuli (both external and response produced) that are close in time and space, at the expense of more remote stimuli.	Salzinger (2006); Salzinger et al. (1970)
Associative learning	The ability to learn an association between a particular stimulus and specific response.	J. A. Gray et al. (1991)

definitions and uses of the term *context*—namely, that there is some stimulus or set of stimuli that carries information about how to respond to other stimuli and that this information must be stored or available to the organism in some way. However, the nature and temporal dynamics of this information vary widely across different uses of this term. Specifically, the term *context* is often used to refer to visual–spatial information and relationships (Knierim, Lee, & Hargreaves, 2006; Silverstein, Kovacs, Corry, & Valone, 2000), temporal relationships (J. A. Gray et al., 1995), and even social–emotional information (M. J. Green, Waldron, & Coltheart, 2007). Our definition of context shares an emphasis on stored information that can predict behavior. However, our definition of context information focuses much more strongly on internal representations that must be actively held online in a form that allows them to be used to mediate task-appropriate behavior. In many ways, our use of the term *context* is much more analogous to the use of the term *goal*, in that we emphasize the need for the active internal maintenance of derived representations, even if these abstracted representations were developed from prior externally available stimuli.

In our models, representations of context are used specifically to support task-relevant information against sources of interference that can occur solely as a function of time (e.g., noise accumulating in the system) or because of specific competing processes or information (e.g., the need to process other stimuli, distractions). Context representations can comprise a variety of different types of information, such as a specific prior stimulus; the result of processing a sequence of prior stimuli; or more abstract information, such as task instructions or goals. One domain in which the use of context makes intuitive sense is in language processing. Take as an example the following sentence: "In order to keep pigs, you need a pen." In this sentence, the first clause serves as context that biases you toward the appropriate meaning of the word *pen* (a fenced enclosure) for this sentence rather than the more common meaning of the word *pen* (a writing instrument). This is a case in which the result of processing the first part of the sentence (e.g., a sequence of prior stimuli) creates a contextual representation that can bias future behavior (e.g., semantic interpretation of the word *pen*). As another example, consider a task-switching paradigm in which a cue tells you which task to perform on letter stimuli. One cue might indicate that the task is to decide whether the letters are vowels or consonants. A different cue might indicate that the task is to decide whether the letters are from the first or second half of the alphabet. In the absence of such a cue, the participant would not know what task to complete because the same class of stimuli is used for both tasks. However, in this case, the cue (a specific prior stimulus) serves as context that allows the person to determine what response to make. As yet another example, take the well-known Stroop task. In one condition of this task, participants are shown color words written in different colors (e.g., the word *RED* written in blue). In the absence of any other information, a participant's natural response is to read the word rather than to name the color because this is what one typically does when presented with verbal stimuli. In other words, reading the word instead of naming the color is the prepotent response. However, in the Stroop task, participants are given the instruction to ignore the word and instead to name the color. We would argue that in this situation, the task instructions serve as a context that allows the participant to inhibit the prepotent response tendency to read the word.

One important lesson we have learned from our work is that the use of computational models to simulate context-processing functions has demonstrated how a single underlying mechanism, operating under different task conditions, might support three cognitive functions that are often treated as independent: (a) *attention,* or the selection and support of task-relevant information for processing; (b) *active memory,* or the online maintenance of such task-relevant information; and (c) *inhibition,* or the suppression of task-irrelevant information. When a task involves a delay between a cue and a later contingent response, it is usually assumed that a working memory function is involved. However, there is no dedicated mechanism for this function in our model. Rather, the mechanism used to represent context information is used to maintain task-relevant information against the interfering, and cumulative, effects of noise over time. When a task involves competing, task-irrelevant processes (as in the Stroop task, task switching, and Flanker tasks), it is often assumed that a special inhibitory function is in charge of directly suppressing or overriding these irrelevant processes. However, in our model, there is no separate dedicated mechanism for inhibition. Rather, context representations accomplish the same effect by providing top-down support for task-relevant processes, allowing these to compete effectively against irrelevant ones. Thus, both for tasks that tap inhibition and for those that tap working memory, the same mechanism is involved; it is simply a matter of the behavioral conditions under which it operates (i.e., the source of interference) that lead us to label it as having an "inhibitory" or a "working memory" function. Furthermore, attentional functions can be supported by context representations under both types of conditions. This is because such context representations allow the individuals to select and focus on task-relevant information for processing over other potentially competing sources of information. Thus, in all circumstances, the same context-processing mechanism is involved. We hypothesize that this context-processing mechanism is impaired in schizophrenia. Consequently, we suggest that disturbances in context processing may form a common basis for many of the deficits observed across multiple cognitive domains in schizophrenia, including attention, inhibition, working memory, and language processing.

One task that we have used in numerous studies is a version of the classic Continuous Performance Test (Rosvold, Mirsky, Sarason, Bransome, & Beck, 1956) known as the *AX-CPT* (Cohen, Barch, Carter, & Servan-Schreiber, 1999; Servan-Schreiber, Cohen, & Steingard, 1996), which has been specifically designed as a measure of context representation and maintenance. An illustration of this task is presented in Figure 2.1. Participants (see Panel A of the figure) are presented with cue–probe pairs and told to make a target response to an X (probe), but only when it follows an A (cue), and to make a nontarget response otherwise. A correct response to X depends on maintaining the context provided by the cue (A or not-A). The standard version of the AX-CPT often has used a low percentage of target trials, usually in the range of 10%. One difficulty with such versions is that it hard to know whether errors of omission reflect a failure to use context or simple lack of attention to the task. Thus, we increased the frequency of target (AX) trials so that they occur with a high frequency (70%; see Panel C of Figure 2.1), with the remaining 30% of trials distributed across three types of nontarget trials (BX, AY, and BX, where *B* refers to any non-A cue and Y refers to any

The AX-CPT (Continuous Performance Test)

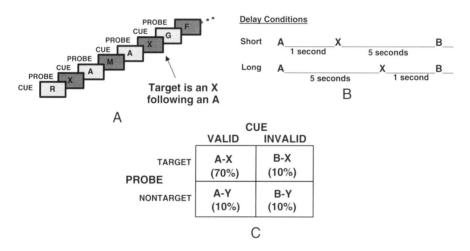

Figure 2.1. The AX-CPT (a version of the Continuous Performance Test). Panel A: Schematic of stimuli presentation across time in the AX-CPT. Panel B: Illustration of the timing of the stimuli in task conditions of the AX-CPT with either a short or a long delay between the cue and the probe. Panel C: Illustration of relative frequencies of different trial types in the AX-CPT. From "Selective Deficits in Prefrontal Cortex Function in Medication-Naive Patients With Schizophrenia," by D. M. Barch, C. S. Carter, T. S. Braver, F. W. Sabb, A. MacDonald III, D. C. Noll, and J. D. Cohen, 2001, *Archives of General Psychiatry, 58,* pp. 280–288. Copyright 2001 by American Medical Association. Adapted with permission.

non-X probe). This creates two types of bias that can occur, allowing one to specifically probe integrity of context processing and to distinguish context-processing deficits from a failure to attend to the task. The first bias, or *prepotent response*, caused by the high percentage of targets is that participants expect to make a target response when they see an X probe because this is the correct response on most of the trials (87.5% of trials in which an X is presented). On BX trials, participants have to use to the context provided by the B cue to inhibit this bias to respond "target" to an X (which would lead to a false alarm). Thus, impaired context representations will lead to poor performance on BX trials because the context provided by the B cue would not be available to override the tendency to want to response "target" to the X. The second bias is that participants expect to make a "target" response after they see an A cue because most of the time an X follows the A cue (87.5% of A-cue trials). However, on trials in which the A is not followed by an X, use of the context provided by the A to predict the occurrence of the X actually *creates* the tendency to give a false-alarm response. Thus, counterintuitively, having active and intact representations of context will actually lead to worse performance on AY trials, because context induces an invalid expectancy, leading to worse AY than BX performance. In contrast, individuals with impaired context representations should show worse BX than AY performance. In other words, individuals with impaired context representations (i.e., individuals with schizophrenia) should show worse BX performance, but better AY performance, than individuals with intact context representations.

We can also include a second manipulation in the AX-CPT that lets us examine the maintenance of context information as well as the initial representation of context, by manipulating the delay between the cue and probe (see Panel B of Figure 2.1). When the interval or delay between the cue and the probe is lengthened from, for example, 1 second to 5 or 10 seconds, context must be actively maintained within *working memory* (supported by the prefrontal cortex [PFC] in this and other theories of working memory function; see "The Neurobiology of Context Processing"). Our context-processing theory predicts that performance on AY and BX trials will vary as a function of delay (Braver et al., 1995, 1999a, 2002). When individuals can actively maintain context over a delay, the strength of context representations should stay the same or even increase with delay. If it does, then BX performance should stay the same or even get better with longer delays because there is more time for context information to prepare the person to inhibit an incorrect response to the X. In contrast, AY performance should stay the same or get worse with delay because there is more time for context representations to induce the participant to prepare for a target response, which must be inhibited when a Y rather than an X occurs. In contrast, if context maintenance is impaired, then BX performance should get worse with delay, but AY performance should actually improve.

We and a number of other groups have conducted studies using this AX-CPT task to study context processing in individuals with schizophrenia. This work has shown that context-processing deficits are present in both medicated and unmedicated individuals and at both acute and chronic stages of the illness (Barch, Carter, et al., 2001; Barch, Carter, & Cohen, 2003; Cohen et al., 1999; Holmes et al., 2005; Javitt, Shelley, Silipo, & Lieberman, 2000; Lee & Park, 2006; MacDonald & Carter, 2003; Servan-Schreiber et al., 1996; Stratta, Daneluzzo, Bustini, Casacchia, & Rossi, 1998; Stratta, Daneluzzo, Bustini, Prosperini, & Rossi, 2000). An illustration of the pattern of behavior seen in individuals with schizophrenia on AX-CPT type tasks is provided in Figure 2.2. This particular data set comes from a study in first-episodic neuroleptic naive individuals with schizophrenia. As shown in Figure 2.2, in regard to percentage errors, the individuals with schizophrenia made significantly more BX errors (or context-failure errors) than did healthy control individuals. In contrast, the individuals with schizophrenia made significantly fewer AY errors (context-induced errors), particularly at the longer delay. Taken together, this pattern of both impaired and enhanced performance suggests that context representations are less available or less able to influence processing in individuals with schizophrenia, leading to fewer predictive errors to nontargets following the occurrence of an A and more failures to override the prepotent tendency to respond target to X on BX trials.

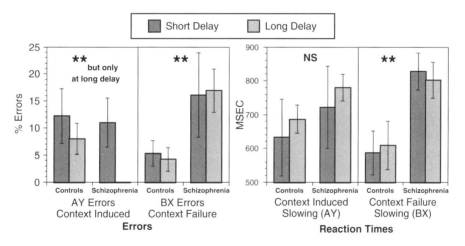

Figure 2.2. Left panel: BX and AY errors in the AX-CPT task in participants from (Barch, Carter, et al., 2001). Right panel: BX and AY reaction times from the same participants. CPT = Continuous Performance Test; NS = not significant. **p < .05. From "Selective Deficits in Prefrontal Cortex Function in Medication-Naive Patients With Schizophrenia," by D. M. Barch, C. S. Carter, T. S. Braver, F. W. Sabb, A. MacDonald III, D. C. Noll, and J. D. Cohen, 2001, *Archives of General Psychiatry, 58,* pp. 280–288. Copyright 2001 by American Medical Association. Reprinted with permission.

These context-processing deficits are apparent in the pattern of reaction times (RTs) as well as errors. As shown for reaction times in Figure 2.2, the individuals with schizophrenia were significantly slower than control individuals on correct BX trials, suggesting that the context provided by the B cue was less available to override the prepotent response tendency. Of importance, however, individuals with schizophrenia were not significantly slower than control individuals on AY trials. This is important because AY trials were the slowest trials for control individuals, and a generalized deficit in performance might have predicted that patients should show the most slowing on these AY trials. However, the slowing in control individuals on AY trials reflects the predictive use of context, which is less apparent in the individuals with schizophrenia, leading them to actually experience less of a context-induced interference effect.

There is consistent evidence across studies that people with schizophrenia show an inability to use or represent context in a way that allows them to bias ongoing processing. However, it is much less clear whether this deficit interacts with delay, such that their behavioral deficits are exacerbated with a longer delay between the cue and the probe. A number of studies have found that context-processing deficits are worse at a long compared with a short delay in individuals with schizophrenia (Cohen et al., 1999; Elvevåg, Duncan, & McKenna, 2000; Holmes et al., 2005; Javitt et al., 2000; Servan-Schreiber et al., 1996; Stratta et al., 1998, 2000). However, a number of other studies have found equal impairments at a short and a long delay (Barch, Carter, et al., 2001; Barch et al., 2003; Javitt, Rabinowicz, Silipo, & Dias, 2007; Lee & Park, 2006; MacDonald, Carter, et al., 2005; Perlstein, Dixit, Carter, Noll, & Cohen, 2003). At least two factors may be influencing the variability in results across studies. The first is whether the patients are early in the course of illness (i.e., first episode) or more chronic. The few studies with first-episodic patients have not found significant increases in BX errors or RTs at the long compared with the short delay (Barch, Carter, et al., 2001; Barch et al., 2003; MacDonald, Carter, et al., 2005), or have at least found smaller increases as a function of delay than in studies with patients with chronic schizophrenia (Javitt et al., 2000). This suggests that early in the course of illness patients with schizophrenia experience deficits in the initial representation of context, but not further deficits in the maintenance of context. In contrast, several studies of patients with chronic schizophrenia have reported significant increases in BX error or RTs at a long compared with a short delay (Cohen et al., 1999; Elvevåg et al., 2000; Javitt et al., 2000; Servan-Schreiber et al., 1996; Stratta et al., 1998, 2000), or that AY errors are reduced at the long delay in patients. If this pattern holds up, it would suggest that deficits in context maintenance might emerge as the illness continues. However, not all such studies with chronic-schizophrenia patients show this increase at the long delay (Javitt et al., 2007; Lee & Park, 2006).

The second factor that may be influencing the presence or absence of increased delay-related deficits in context processing in patients with schizophrenia is the performance of control participants. In some studies with chronic patients, the control participants also showed an increase in BX errors or RTs from the short to the long delay, making it difficult to detect a differentially greater increase in patients (Cohen et al., 1999; Javitt et al., 2000, 2007). At this point it is not entirely clear why some healthy control individuals show reductions in context processing at the long versus short delay, although it is possible that this may be related to some changes in the ability to represent and/or maintain context that occurs with age (Braver et al., 2001) or that can vary as a function of factors such as fluid intelligence (Burgess & Braver, 2008) or even genetic factors (MacDonald, Carter, Flory, Ferrell, & Manuck, 2007). More research that directly addresses all of these factors clearly is needed to clarify the nature, course, and timing of deficits in context representation and maintenance in schizophrenia.

Are Context-Processing Deficits Specific to Schizophrenia?

Many psychiatric disorders involve various types of cognitive deficits. To understand the specific role of such deficits in the pathophysiology of schizophrenia, it is important to clarify the degree to which such deficits are specific to schizophrenia. If context-processing deficits are present in a range of putatively unrelated disorders, this may suggest that they are more generally related to the experience of having a psychiatric illness rather than playing a fundamental role in the development of schizophrenia. Early work on this question revealed that individuals with nonpsychotic major depression did not show any evidence of context-processing deficits (Cohen et al., 1999). This finding was subsequently replicated in a separate sample of individuals with nonpsychotic depression (Holmes et al., 2005). Such results suggest that context-processing deficits are specific to schizophrenia compared with having any type of psychiatric illness. In a recent study, patients with schizophrenia showed clearly more severe context-processing deficits compared with euthymic and currently nonpsychotic patients with bipolar disorder (Brambilla et al., 2007). However, such results do not clarify the issue of specificity of context-processing deficits to schizophrenia compared with other forms of psychosis. To address this question, we compared AX-CPT task performance in first-episodic neuroleptic naive individuals with schizophrenia to first-episodic neuroleptic naive individuals with other psychotic disorders (bipolar disorder, psychotic depression, delusional disorders). We found that at baseline, all individuals with psychosis showed similar deficits in context processing. Of interest, however, is that this pattern diverged across time, such that context processing improved at 4 weeks in the nonschizophrenia psychotic disorder but stayed stable in schizophrenia.

This was despite the fact that both groups showed similar improvement in symptomatology. Such results suggest that although context-processing deficits may be present in both schizophrenia and nonschizophrenia psychotic disorders, they may play different roles. Specifically, in schizophrenia context-processing deficits may show more evidence of reflecting trait-like vulnerability factors but show more state-related episode indicators in other disorders (Barch et al., 2003).

Are Context-Processing Deficits Part of the Liability to Schizophrenia?

The growing evidence for the importance of cognitive deficits in understanding schizophrenia has led many researchers to examine whether cognitive deficits might serve as endophenotypic markers of risk for schizophrenia liability (Gottesman & Hanson, 2005). If at least some cognitive functions have an identifiable link to neurobiological and genetic mechanisms (as recent cognitive neuroscience and functional genomics research suggests), then cognitive deficits may serve as promising endophenotypic markers in the search for the etiology of schizophrenia (Cannon, van Erp, & Glahn, 2002; Sitskoorn, Aleman, Ebisch, Appels, & Kahn, 2004; Snitz, MacDonald, & Carter, 2006). One way to examine whether context-processing deficits may represent endophenotypic markers is to determine whether they are present in populations thought to share vulnerability to schizophrenia but who do not have the manifest illness. As such, a number of studies have examined whether context-processing deficits are present in the first-degree relatives of individuals with schizophrenia, who presumably share liability for this disorder. For example, MacDonald, Pogue-Geile, Johnson, and Carter (2003) showed that nonpsychotic siblings of patients with schizophrenia show a performance pattern on the AX-CPT similar to that found in schizophrenia patients, demonstrating increased BX errors and RTs, as well as decreased AY errors and no difference in AY RTs. In addition, MacDonald, Goghari, et al. (2005) found a similar result in a variant of the AX-CPT called the *dot pattern expectancy task,* showing that the first-degree relatives of patients with schizophrenia showed increased errors on the dot pattern expectancy task condition that was the equivalent of BX trials. We have also recently found evidence that the siblings of individuals with schizophrenia show increased BX errors and RT compared with control participants, particularly at the long delay (Delawalla, Csernansky, & Barch, 2008). This finding is illustrated in Figure 2.3 using a composite score that combines both error and RT information into a single measure. As can be seen in the figure, siblings and control individuals do not differ in AY performance, but siblings show a significant decrement in BX performance.

We have also examined context-processing deficits in individuals with schizotypal personality disorder, which is thought to share genetic lia-

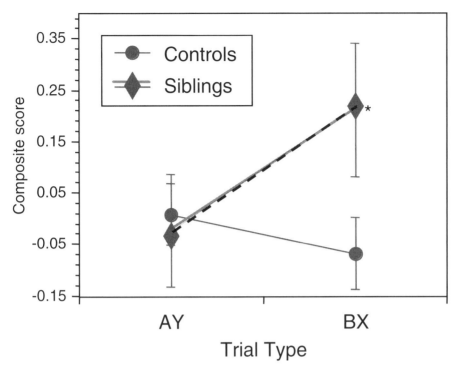

Figure 2.3. Differences between healthy control individuals and siblings of individuals with schizophrenia on a composite measure of errors and reaction times for AY and BX trials. From "Prefrontal Cortex Function in Nonpsychotic Siblings of Individuals with Schizophrenia," by Z. Delawalla, J. G. Csernansky, and D. Barch, 2008, *Biological Psychiatry, 63,* pp. 490–497. Copyright 2008 by Elsevier. Reprinted with permission.

bility with schizophrenia. Like individuals with schizophrenia, individuals with schizotypal personality disorder displayed increased BX errors, but not AY errors, combined with increased BX RTs but not with AY RTs. However, none of these effects were significantly exacerbated with delay in the individuals with schizotypal personality disorder. These results suggest that individuals with schizotypal personality disorder also have difficulty utilizing contextual information to govern behavioral responding but that increasing the delay over which such information must be maintained does not worsen this deficit. Taken together, these results with the siblings of patients with schizophrenia and individuals with schizotypal personality disorder are consistent with the hypothesis that deficits in context processing may represent an endophenotypic marker of risk for schizophrenia. However, much more work in this area is needed because there are a number of other criteria that an endophenotypic marker must meet that have not yet been examined in relationship to context processing (Gottesman & Hanson, 2005).

Other Measures of Context Processing in Schizophrenia

A number of studies using tasks other than the AX-CPT have also provided evidence for deficits in context processing in schizophrenia. For example, a growing number of studies suggest that deficits in context processing can be observed in the domain of language comprehension and production, harkening back to the early suggestions of Salzinger and colleagues (Salzinger, Portnoy, & Feldman, 1966; Salzinger, Portnoy, Pisoni, & Feldman, 1970). In a behavioral sense, a number of studies have used variants of priming tasks to examine the degree to which individuals with schizophrenia are able to use context to bias their processing of verbal stimuli that are inherently ambiguous, either because they have several different interpretations (e.g., two meanings of the word *pen*) or different completions (e.g., missing-letter tasks). For example, Cohen et al. (1999) demonstrated that patients with schizophrenia were less able to use the preceding context to bias their production of a subordinate versus dominant word completion. More ecologically valid results come from studies using contextual violation paradigms, in which people are asked to process sentences and act on words that are either consistent with the preceding context or violate the preceding context. For example, Kuperberg and her colleagues (Kuperberg, Kreher, Goff, McGuire, & David, 2006; Kuperberg, McGuire, & David, 1998) found that individuals with schizophrenia and thought disorders were less disrupted by the presence of context-dependent linguistic violations. In other work, Titone, Levy, and Holzman (2000) found results suggesting that language-processing impairments in schizophrenia reflected a deficit in using context to inhibit task-irrelevant meanings rather than a deficit in using context to facilitate task-relevant meetings. As shown in Panel A of Figure 2.4, Titone used homonyms with both subordinate (less frequently used meaning) and dominant interpretations (more frequent meaning) embedded in sentences that should predict or bias the subordinate interpretations. She then examined priming to visual targets associated with either the subordinate or dominant meaning. As shown in Panel B of Figure 2.4, Titone found that patients did not differ from control participants in priming of the targets related to the subordinate meaning (i.e., in using context to facilitate processing of subordinate meaning). However, patients showed significantly more priming of targets related to the dominant meaning, suggesting that they were unable to use context to inhibit the context-inappropriate, but prepotent, meaning of the homonym.

Additional evidence for linguistic deficits in context processing in schizophrenia comes from studies examining an event-related potential component called *the* N400. The N400 is a negative going component of an event-related potential waveform that occurs approximately 400 milliseconds after the onset of the stimulus of interest. The N400 is thought to index the degree of consistency or relatedness between a stimulus (e.g., word) and the preceding

A

Moderately Biasing Sentence

Because it was extremely loud, we really enjoyed the jam.

BAND (subordinate meaning target)

JELLY (dominant meaning target)

Strongly Biasing Sentence

Because the musicians were great, we really enjoyed the jam.

BAND (subordinate meaning target)

JELLY (dominant meaning target)

B

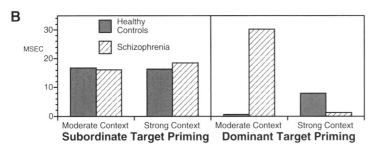

Figure 2.4. Panel A: Illustration of the sentence stimuli used by Titone et al. (2000) to bias processing of the subordinate meaning of words. Panel B: The pattern of dominant and subordinate meaning priming in the control individuals and individuals with schizophrenia in Titone et al. (2000). From "Contextual Insensitivity in Schizophrenic Language Processing: Evidence From Lexical Ambiguity," by D. Titone, D. L. Levy, and P. S. Holzman, 2000, *Journal of Abnormal Psychology, 109,* pp. 761–767. Copyright 2001 by the American Psychological Association.

context (a single word, a sentence, or an entire discourse; Brown & Hagoort, 1993; Kutas & Hillyard, 1980). In healthy control participants, words that are not consistent with the preceding context elicit a larger N400 than words that are consistent with the preceding context. A number of different paradigms have been used in N400 studies to examine linguistic processing in schizophrenia. For example, Condray, Steinhauer, Cohen, van Kammen, and Kasparek (1999) used a lexical decision task in which pairs of words were presented that were either semantically related or semantically unrelated (for related studies, see Grillon, Ameli, & Glazer, 1991; Kostova, Passerieux, Laurent, & Hardy-Bayle, 2003, 2005; Kostova, Passerieux, Laurent, et al., 2003). Control participants demonstrated a significant priming effect in N400s, as evidenced by larger N400s to unrelated compared with related words. In contrast, drug-free individuals with schizophrenia did not show an N400 priming effect. This suggests that patients were unable to use the context provided the first word to facilitate processing of the second word. Salisbury, O'Donnell, McCarley, Nestor, and Shenton (2000) used a sentence-constraint paradigm in which they presented four-word sentences to participants. Each sentence was of the form "THE *NOUN* WAS *ADJECTIVE/VERB*," and the final adjective/verb was always consistent with the noun. Salisbury et al. examined N400s to the initial noun and the sentence final adjective/verbs and found that control participants showed significantly reduced N400s to the sentence final adjective/verbs compared with the nouns presented earlier in the sentence. They interpreted this result as consistent with the idea that the control participants used the noun to generate contextual representations that can help facilitate processing of consistent semantic information. However, the patients with schizophrenia did not show any reduction in N400 to the sentence-final words compared with the nouns, suggesting that patients were unable to either develop or use such contextual representations.

In other work, Sitnikova, Salisbury, Kuperberg, and Holcomb (2002) examined N400s in a clever paradigm involving two clause sentences. The first clause ended with a homograph that had asymmetrical meanings (a dominant meaning and a subordinate meaning). The second clause started with a strong semantic associate of the dominant meaning of the homograph that ended the preceding clause. On half the trials, the first clause biased the subordinate meaning of the homograph (so that the second clause should be inconsistent and should elicit an N400). On the other half of the trials, the first clause biased the dominant meaning of the homograph (so that the second clause should be consistent and should not elicit an N400). Compared with the consistent-clause condition (i.e., first clause biased dominant meaning, second clause starting with dominant associate), the control participants demonstrated larger N400s in the inconsistent second clause condition. This suggests that control participants were able to use the context in the first clause to facilitate processing of the subordinate meaning of the homograph, and to suppress the dominant meaning. In contrast, the patients showed clear evidence of being unable to use the context provided by the sentence to bias their processing. Specifically, the patients with schizophrenia showed a significantly smaller N400 than control participants to the dominant meaning of the homograph when it followed a context that should have biased the subordinate meaning. Furthermore, the individuals with schizophrenia did not show any differences in the magnitude of the N400 to consistent and inconsistent second clauses (for related studies, see Adams et al., 1993; Niznikiewicz et al., 1997; Ohta, Uchiyama, Matsushima, & Toru, 1999; Olichney, Iragui, Kutas, Nowacki, & Jeste, 1997; Strandburgh et al., 1997; Titone, Holzman, & Levy, 2002; Titone, Levy, & Holzman, 2000). Taken together, these studies on linguistic processing in schizophrenia provide converging evidence for context-processing deficits in schizophrenia that influence verbal behavior.

Studies using a number of other cognitive tasks besides the AX-CPT have also been cited as evidence for deficits in context processing. However, we should note that the interpretation of these studies is less clear because the tasks were not specifically designed to measure context processing, and their results are open to alternative interpretations. Nonetheless, the results of many of these studies are consistent with the predictions of the context-processing model. An example of one such task in the color–word Stroop task, in which participants are presented with color words written in different colors (e.g., the word *BLUE* written in red) and asked to ignore the word and name the color. As described earlier, the context-processing theory suggests that task instructions in the Stroop task serve as context representations that should bias processing in favor of color naming over word reading. As such, a deficit in context processing should lead individuals with schizophrenia to be less able to ignore the word information. Consistent with this prediction, numerous studies have found that individuals with schizophrenia are less able to inhibit the prepotent response to read the word, as evidenced by increased errors in the incongruent condition (color and word conflict) or by an increase in the total Stroop effect in RT (Barch, Carter, Hachten, & Cohen, 1999; Barch, Carter, Perlstein, et al., 1999; Carter, Robertson, & Nordahl, 1992; Chen, Wong, Chen, & Au, 2001; Cohen et al., 1999; Elvevåg et al., 2000; Henik et al., 2002; Taylor, Kornblum, & Tandon, 1996). Furthermore, in recent work we have used the process dissociation techniques developed by Jacoby (1991) to estimate the contributions of both word naming and color reading to Stroop performance in schizophrenia, finding that color reading estimates are reduced while word reading estimates increased (Barch, Carter, & Cohen, 2004). Another task used recently to assess context processing is called the *preparing to overcome prepotency task*. In this task, participants are signaled by one cue (green) to make a response to a rightward-pointing arrow with their right hand (compatible), and to another cue (red) to respond to a rightward-pointing arrow with their left hand (incompatible). In this latter case, the cue provides context that should allow them to overcome their prepotent response to use a compatible hand. Cho, Konecky, and Carter (2006) found that patients with schizophrenia made more errors in the incompatible condition, which is consistent with a deficit in the use of context.

Silverstein and colleagues have suggested that deficits in context processing and contextual integration among individuals with schizophrenia extend even to the level of basic perceptual processing (Silverstein et al., 2000). For example, Silverstein and other researchers have shown deficits in various perceptual integration tasks that they describe as reflecting the use of context (Silverstein et al., 2006; Uhlhaas, Phillips, Mitchell, & Silverstein, 2006). These tasks involved Gestalt processing, contour integration, and other visual context paradigms. However, it is not yet clear whether the type of contextual processing measured in these paradigms is the same as that measured in tasks such as AX-CPT. However, such results raise the intriguing possibility that deficits in context processing account for deficits among individuals with schizophrenia both on high-level cognitive tasks as well as in more basic sensory and perceptual domains.

Context Processing, Symptoms, and Life Function in Schizophrenia

If deficits in context processing are a core cognitive deficit in schizophrenia, then it is important to ask whether these cognitive deficits contribute to the behavioral and symptomatic manifestations of this illness. As we noted earlier, one of the ecologically valid areas in which context use is most apparent is in language processing. Furthermore, one of the core symptoms of schizophrenia is disorganized language production, often referred to as *formal thought disorder*. As such, a number of theorists have suggested that deficits in the representation and use of context in schizophrenia may most directly contribute to deficits in coherent language production, and potentially language comprehension (Barch et al., 1996; Cohen, Targ, Servan-Schreiber, & Spiegel, 1992; Kerns, Cohen, Stenger, & Carter, 2004; Kuperberg, Deckersbach, Holt, Goff, & West, 2007; Kuperberg, Ditman, Kreher, & Goldberg, in press; Kuperberg et al., 1998). More specifically, the hypothesis is that both within and between sentences, patients with schizophrenia are less able to use either the global discourse goals, or the preceding sentences, as context that constrains the choice and production of subsequent sentences. If so, this would explain why patients can produce sentences that seem unconnected to the preceding sentences, or to the global topic of the discourse, often wandering off track during conversation (Barch & Berenbaum, 1996). Consistent with this hypothesis, a number of studies have shown that deficits in context processing seem to be particularly associated with the presence of formal thought disorder in schizophrenia, or disorganization symptoms more generally (Barch, Carter, Hachten, & Cohen, 1999; Barch, Carter, Perlstein, et al., 1999; Barch et al., 2003; Cohen et al., 1999; Kerns & Berenbaum, 2002, 2003; Kostova et al., 2005; Kuperberg et al., 1998; Stratta et al., 2000; Uhlhaas et al., 2006). Such findings are interesting in light of research suggesting that representations of context information are important for guiding coherent ongoing language production (Levelt, 1989).

Most of the research on context processing influences on disorganization and formal thought disorder in schizophrenia has focused on disorganization in the language domain. However, individuals with schizophrenia can also show disorganized behavior in other domains, including social behavior, dress, and affect. Although the links to context processing are not as clear as in the language domain, one can imagine that such deficits might relate to a deficit in the ability to use information about the social context to guide behavior. This is a more global use of the term *context* than we have used in our models, and it is not clear that the same mechanisms are at play integrating social context as operating in specific tasks contexts. Nonetheless, there is recent intriguing evidence that individuals with schizophrenia show impaired use of emotional context when judging affective faces (M. J. Green et al., 2007), a problem that could in theory contribute to social–cognitive impairments.

THE NEUROBIOLOGY OF CONTEXT PROCESSING

One can understand and appreciate the influence of context-processing deficits on behavior in schizophrenia without necessarily understanding the neurobiology of such deficits. However, in our work we have viewed understanding a specific link to specific neurobiological mechanisms as an important goal that will help to further our understanding of the causes and treatments of this illness. In particular, we have postulated that representations of context information are supported by the DLPFC and actively maintained there when task demands require such active maintenance (O'Reilly, Braver, & Cohen, 1999). Furthermore, we have hypothesized that the DA projections to the DLPFC regulate the access to such context information, insulating this information from the interfering effects of noise over intervals in which the information must be sustained while at the same time allowing for the appropriate updating of such context information when needed (Braver & Cohen, 2000). These hypotheses are consistent with the broader neuroscience literature, in which active maintenance in the service of control is a function commonly ascribed to the PFC (Fuster, 1989; Goldman-Rakic, 1987; Miller & Cohen, 2001), and the DA system is widely held to modulate the active maintenance properties of the PFC (Cohen, Braver, & Brown, 2002; M. Luciana, Collins, & Depue, 1998; Sawaguchi, Matsumura, & Kubota, 1990; Seamans & Yang, 2004; Williams & Goldman-Rakic, 1995). In our model, the context-processing functions of cognitive control critically depend on DLPFC–DA system interactions. As a consequence, the model predicts that individuals and populations with impairments in either or both DLPFC or the DA system should demonstrate specific patterns of impaired cognitive control related to the processing of context.

Role of the Prefrontal Cortex

Many different functional neuroimaging studies have demonstrated that the prefrontal cortex is activated when individuals have to maintain information in working memory (Wager & Smith, 2003). However, most of these studies did not use tasks specifically designed to selectively measure context processing. We and our colleagues have conducted a number of neuroimaging studies using tasks, such as the AX-CPT and the switching Stroop, that were specifically designed to measure context processing. These studies have consistently demonstrated that regions of the DLPFC are activated by the need to represent and maintain context (Barch et al., 1997; Braver & Cohen, 2001; Kerns et al., 2004; MacDonald, Cohen, Stenger, & Carter, 2000). Furthermore, we have demonstrated that this response of the DLPFC is specific to context-processing demands compared with general task difficulty or conflict demands (Barch et al., 1997; MacDonald et al., 2000). To gain further insight into the role that the DLPFC plays in context processing, we also examined how behavior and DLPFC activity is altered in healthy individuals when context processing is disrupted. For example, we developed a version of the AX-CPT in which participants are presented with distractor items during the delay between the cue and the probe. Our hypothesis was that if deficits on the AX-CPT among individuals with schizophrenia were due to disturbances in the ability to maintain context information, then disturbing the ability to maintain context information in healthy adults should elicit the same types of task deficits as found in individuals with schizophrenia. Consistent with this hypothesis, we found that adding distractors during the delay between the cue and the probe in the long delay conditions of the AX-CPT increased the number of BX errors (and slowed BX RTs) that healthy participants made, but decreased the number of AY errors, which is consistent with a reduced ability to use context information. In a subsequent functional neuroimaging study using the same task design, we found that the addition of distractions and impairments in task performance were accompanied by a selective decrease in dorsolateral PFC activity (but no change or even an increase in ventrolateral PFC activity; Braver & Cohen, 2001). The results of this study and others have provided some clues about the different contributions that the dorsolateral versus ventrolateral PFC play in context processing. More specifically, we have argued that ventrolateral regions of the PFC may serve a more general role in phonological processing or rehearsal that may in no way be selective or specific to context representations (an idea put forth by many other researchers as well). In contrast, it may be that DLPFC may be more specifically involved in the development and/or maintenance of context representations.

We have also examined the patterns of brain activity found in individuals with schizophrenia during the performance of tasks such as the AX-CPT. These studies have demonstrated fairly consistently that individuals with schizophrenia showed altered activity in DLPFC during tasks that tap context processing (Barch, Carter, 2001; Cho et al., 2006; MacDonald & Carter, 2003; MacDonald, Carter, et al., 2005; Perlstein et al., 2003; Snitz et al., 2005). Furthermore, recent research suggests that such DLPFC deficits are specific to individuals with schizophrenia compared with individuals with other psychotic disorders, who show a different pattern of potentially increased DLPFC activity (MacDonald, Carter, et al., 2005). Of importance, several studies have now demonstrated that the first-degree relatives of individuals with schizophrenia also show impaired activity in DLPFC during context-processing tasks, although the impairments are not necessarily as severe as those found in ill individuals with schizophrenia (Delawalla et al., 2008; MacDonald, Becker, & Carter, 2006). For example, as shown in Figure 2.5, the siblings of individuals with schizophrenia show enhanced DLPFC activity compared with control individuals at a short delay, but reduced activity compared with

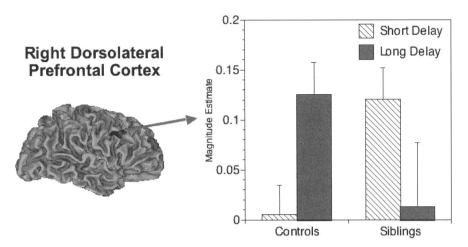

Figure 2.5. The pattern of activity in the right dorsolateral prefrontal cortex during the short- and long-delay trials of the AX-CPT task in control individuals and the siblings of individuals with schizophrenia. The figure of the brain illustrates regions that showed Group × Delay interactions. CPT = Continuous Performance Test. From "Prefrontal Cortex Function in Nonpsychotic Siblings of Individuals with Schizophrenia," by Z. Delawalla, J. G. Csernansky, and D. Barch, 2008, *Biological Psychiatry, 63*, pp. 490–497. Copyright 2008 by Elsevier. Reprinted with permission.

control individuals at a long delay. This suggests that they may need to recruit more DLPFC resources for representing context even for a short period of time and that these DLPFC resources may not be sufficient for maintenance of context over longer delays.

Role of Dopamine

As described earlier, our models also postulate a central role for DA in context processing and hypothesize that impaired DA function in DLPFC contributes to context-processing deficits. This hypothesis is consistent with a wealth of evidence in nonhuman primates and humans suggesting that DA plays an important role in working memory more generally (Arnsten, Cai, Murphy, & Goldman-Rakic, 1994; Barch & Carter, 2005; Brozoski, Brown, Rosvold, & Goldman, 1979; Cai & Arnsten, 1997; Castner, Williams, & Goldman-Rakic, 2000; de Sonneville, Njiokiktjien, & Bos, 1994; Goldman-Rakic, 1995; Kimberg & D'Esposito, 2003; Kimberg, D'Esposito, & Farah, 1997; Luciana & Collins, 1997; Luciana, Collins, & Depue, 1995; Luciana, Depue, Arbisi, & Leon, 1992; Luciana et al., 1998; Mattay et al., 1996, 2000, 2003; Mehta et al., 2000; Mehta, Swainson, Gogilvie, Sahakian, & Robbins, 2001; Mintzer & Griffiths, 2003; Muller, von Cramon, & Pollmann, 1998; Sawaguchi & Goldman-Rakic, 1994; Williams & Goldman-Rakic, 1995). In the context of schizophrenia, there is evidence that nonspecific DA agonists, such as amphetamine, can improve working memory and other cognitive control functions in medicated patients with schizophrenia (Barch & Carter, 2005; Daniel et al., 1991; Goldberg, Bigelow, Weinberger, Daniel, & Kleinman, 1991). Furthermore, research has also shown that changes in D1 receptor availability in DLPFC are associated with working memory impairment in schizophrenia (Abi-Dargham et al., 2002). We also have some preliminary data suggesting that dopamine may play a role in context processing in humans, in that the administration of oral amphetamine can help reverse interference induced decrements in context processing (Barch & Braver, 2005).

RELATIONSHIP TO OTHER BEHAVIORAL THEORIES

As we have noted, the term *context* has been used to refer to a number of related but dissociable phenomena. In addition, we are not the first to notice the importance of context impairments in the behavior of individuals with schizophrenia. For example, in his early work, Shakow (1962; see Table 2.1) suggested that

> we see particularly the various difficulties created by context. . . . It is as if, in the scanning process which takes place before the response to a stimulus is made, the schizophrenic is unable to select out the material relevant for optimal response. (p. 4)

Relatedly, Salzinger et al. (1970) coined the term *immediacy hypothesis* (see Table 2.1) to refer to the fact that individuals with schizophrenia "tend to respond to stimuli (both external and response produced) that are close in time and space, at the expense of more remote stimuli" (p. 74; see also Salzinger, 2006). We owe much of the impetus for the development of our own ideas from this preceding work and do not lay claim to fundamental differences in some of the basic components of the hypothesis. However, we do view our work as building on these earlier theories through instantiation in formal model development and explicit links to neurobiological mechanisms, as described earlier.

Although we view our theory as describing many of the same phenomena alluded to by Shakow (1962) and Salzinger (1966), there are two other related theories of behavioral impairments in schizophrenia from which we do think our model differs in fundamental ways. One such theory is the influential work of Jeffrey Gray (Gray, Feldon, Rawlins, Hemsley, & Smith, 1991), who integrated his work on neuroanatomy with the psychological theories of Hemsley (1993) to suggest that positive psychotic symptoms in schizophrenia reflect a deficit in the ability to use stored information about past regularities to influence ongoing information processing, due to a deficit in the input of the hippocampus to the nucleus accumbens. Gray (1998) argued that this deficit leads to a "functional imbalance equivalent to hyper activity in the mesolimbic dopamine pathway" (p. 250) and that this in turn leads individuals with schizophrenia to experience stimuli as novel that in fact are not. There are two major distinctions between our theory and Gray's theory. At the cognitive or behavioral level, the emphasis in Gray's theory is on what we would refer to as more passive storage mechanisms or associative learning mechanisms (see Table 2.1), including episodic or long-term memory functions (hence the emphasis on the hippocampus). For example, one of the paradigms on which Gray and his colleagues depend to test these predictions is *latent inhibition*, in which preexposure to a stimulus with no consequence makes it more difficult to subsequently learn an association to the preexposed stimuli (for a review, see Lubow, 2005). In contrast, our theory much more strongly emphasizes the importance of context representations that need to be activity maintained and used by the individual to guide ongoing behavior.

A second difference between our theory and Gray's is the nature of the presumed neurobiological deficits. Both of our theories share an emphasis on the important role of the DA system in modulating contextual influences on ongoing processing. However, Gray's theory emphasizes abnormalities in limbic function characterize by disturbed hippocampus inputs in to the basal ganglia, leading to functional hyperdopaminergic states in the basal ganglia. Furthermore, the empirical work on latent inhibition in schizophrenia suggests that it is more impaired in acute unmedicated states and that treatment improves latent inhibition, putatively by means of reducing hyperdopaminergic states (N. S. Gray & Snowden, 2005; Lubow, 2005). In contrast, our theory emphasizes abnormal DLPFC function, related to reduced DA function (Braver et al., 2002). Our work has suggested that the types of context-processing deficits studied in our models are present in both the acute and chronic stages and are not clearly ameliorated by treatment with antipsychotic medications (Barch et al., 2003; Cohen et al., 1999). Although we are emphasizing here the differences between our theory and Gray's, it is important to note that there may actually be more similarities than differences and that both sets of mechanisms may be contributing to the panoply of "context-processing" deficits found in schizophrenia. In future work, it would be important to have more empirical attempts to compare, contrast, and even reconcile the theories, using both behavioral and neurobiological methods. For example, it would be important to know whether deficits in latent inhibition are related to deficits in the types of context-processing tasks used in our models and whether any covariation among deficits varies as a function of illness stage, symptom manifestation, and treatment status.

A second related theory is the work of Phillips and Silverstein (2003), who have argued that context-processing deficits in schizophrenia reflect impaired cognitive coordination due to N-methyl-D-aspartate (NMDA) receptor hypofunction. More specifically, Phillips and Silverstein argued that context effects in information processing can occur through modulation of the strength and salience of neuronal responses, in a way that does not necessarily change the meaning of signals. As evidence for this hypothesis, Phillips and Silverstein outlined the studies that have shown that NMDA-antagonist administration in humans can elicit deficits in a number of cognitive domains that may reflect context processing (e.g., Stroop test, auditory and visual context processing). Furthermore, Phillips and Silverstein pointed out that administration of NMDA antagonists can also elicit a number of symptoms similar to those found in schizophrenia, both those that can be easily construed as reflecting context-processing deficits (e.g., conceptual disorganization) and those that may not be as easily understood in this framework (e.g., withdrawal). One major difference between our theory as outlined here and that of Phillips and Silverstein is the distinction between *representational specificity* and *processing specificity*. Our theory posits that context effects in many domains are mediated by specific types of representations supported by particularly neurobiological mechanisms (e.g., DLPFC and DA). In contrast, Phillips and Silverstein suggested that context effects are mediated not by specific types of representations but rather by specific types of processing (e.g., synaptic interactions modulated by NMDA). An important area of future research will be to compare and contrast these mechanisms computationally and experimentally to determine whether they might actually reflect complementary mechanisms that give rise to different classes of context effects.

Context Processing and Learning in Schizophrenia

This chapter has been devoted to describing a specific theory regarding the mechanisms contributing to a range of cognitive and functional deficits in schizophrenia, as well as related theories. A critical question to ask at this point is whether these types of cognitive deficits in schizophrenia can be modified, either by pharmacological or behavioral means. In regard to pharmacological pathways, there is growing evidence that antipsychotic medications (both typical and atypical) can lead to modest improvement in a range of cognitive functions that may (or may not) include context processing (Keefe, Bilder, et al., 2007; Keefe, Sweeney, et al., 2007). Little work has specifically examined context-processing functions in schizophrenia. However, as described earlier, there is some preliminary evidence that amphetamine, an indirect DA agonist, can enhance context processing in stable medicated individuals with schizophrenia (Barch & Carter, 2005).

A growing body of work has also examined whether cognitive function can be improved in schizophrenia through rehabilitation approaches (Pfammatter, Junghan, & Brenner, 2006). In other words, this work has examined whether individuals with schizophrenia can learn to improve cognitive function in a way that may lead to more sustained improvement than found with medications (at least, once they are discontinued) and that may contribute to improved functional outcomes. The approaches taken to improving cognition in these studies have varied widely. For example, one approach involves extensive training on computerized cognitive tasks taking a drill-and-practice approach, often with a progressive increase in difficulty as the individual improves his or her performance on the trained tasks (e.g., Bell, Bryson, Greig, Corcoran, & Wexler, 2001; Fiszdon, Whelahan, Bryson, Wexler, & Bell, 2005; Kurtz, Seltzer, Shagan, Thime, & Wexler, 2007; e.g., Silverstein et al., 2005). Another series of studies has also used computerized cognitive training, but included more explicit instruction on beneficial strategies to use during information processing (e.g., Penades et al., 2006; e.g., Wykes, Newton, et al., 2007; Wykes, Reeder, et al., 2007). In addition, work by Hogarty et al. (2004) has demonstrated the effectiveness of an approach that combines training on special cognitive tasks with social cognition groups focused on higher level aspects of cognitive remediation.

A critical question is the degree to which these training approaches lead to sustained gains in cognitive function and/or lead to changes in life function. A number of studies have now addressed this question, showing that these gains are maintained out to 6 months (e.g., Fiszdon, Bryson, Wexler, & Bell, 2004; e.g., Wykes et al., 2003), and at least one study has shown that these gains can be maintained for as long as 24 months (e.g., Hogarty et al., 2004). Furthermore, a number of studies have shown that these improvements in cognitive function are associated with improvements in social functioning (Hogarty et al., 2004; Pfammatter et al., 2006) and occupational function (e.g., McGurk, Mueser, Feldman, Wolfe, & Pascaris, 2007). Such results suggest that improvements in cognitive function through a rehabilitation approach can have real and positive consequences for individuals with schizophrenia. Furthermore, these results demonstrate that at least some aspects of learning are clearly intact among individuals with schizophrenia and can be harnessed to enhance a range of cognitive impairments in this disorder.

CONCLUSION

The evidence that individuals with schizophrenia experience cognitive impairments has been present for many decades, but the search for the precise mechanisms leading to this impairment, at both a psychological and neural level, still continues. Of importance, the insights provided by early researchers in this area (e.g., Shakow, Salzinger) about the nature of cognitive impairment in schizophrenia are still providing a major guiding framework for the cognitive and cognitive neuroscience research being conducted in this era. Understanding context processing in schizophrenia is clearly critical to elucidating the source and nature of cognitive and functional impairment in this disorder as well as to elucidating the neurobiological mechanisms that contribute to the pathophysiology of this disorder. At the same time, recent research on cognitive remediation in schizophrenia provides hope that we will be able to ameliorate these cognitive impairments in a way that can lead to real functional improvement. The process of developing the most effective cognitive remediation strategies will clearly be aided by a full understanding of the nature of the primary deficits because this will, we hope, allow us to develop and hone targeted intervention strategies.

REFERENCES

Abi-Dargham, A., Mawlawi, O., Lombardo, I., Gil, R., Martinez, D., Huang, Y., et al. (2002). Prefrontal dopamine D_1 receptors and working memory in schizophrenia. *Journal of Neuroscience, 22,* 3708–3719.

Adams, J., Fauz, S. F., Nestor, P. G., Shenton, M. E., Marcy, B., Smith, S. R., et al. (1993). ERP abnormalities during semantic processing in schizophrenia. *Schizophrenia Research, 10,* 247–257.

Arnsten, A. F., Cai, J. X., Murphy, B. L., & Goldman-Rakic, P. S. (1994). Dopamine D_1 receptor mechanisms in the cognitive performance of young adult and aged monkeys. *Psychopharmacology, 116,* 143–151.

Barch, D. M., & Berenbaum, H. (1996). Language production and thought disorder in schizophrenia. *Journal of Abnormal Psychology, 105,* 81–88.

Barch, D. M., & Braver, T. S. (2005). Cognitive control and schizophrenia: Psychological and neural mechanisms. In R. W. Engle, G. Sedek, U. von Hecker, & A. M. McIntosh (Eds.), *Cognitive limitations in aging and psychopathology* (pp. 122–159). New York: Cambridge University Press.

Barch, D. M., Braver, T. S., Akbudak, E., Conturo, T., Ollinger, J., & Snyder, A. V. (2001). Anterior cingulate cortex and response conflict: Effects of response modality and processing domain. *Cerebral Cortex, 11,* 837–848.

Barch, D. M., Braver, T. S., Nystom, L. E., Forman, S. D., Noll, D. C., & Cohen, J. D. (1997). Dissociating working memory from task difficulty in human prefrontal cortex. *Neuropsychologia, 35,* 1373–1380.

Barch, D. M., & Carter, C. S. (2005). Amphetamine improves cognitive function in medicated individuals with schizophrenia and in healthy volunteers. *Schizophrenia Research, 77,* 43–58.

Barch, D. M., Carter, C. S., Braver, T. S., McDonald, A., Sabb, F. W., Noll, D. C., et al. (2001). Selective deficits in prefrontal cortex regions in medication naive schizophrenia patients. *Archives of General Psychiatry, 50,* 280–288.

Barch, D. M., Carter, C. S., & Cohen, J. D. (2003). Context processing deficit in schizophrenia: Diagnostic specificity, 4-week course, and relationships to clinical symptoms. *Journal of Abnormal Psychology, 112*, 132–143.

Barch, D. M., Carter, C. S., & Cohen, J. D. (2004). Factors influencing Stroop performance in schizophrenia. *Neuropsychology, 18*, 477–484.

Barch, D. M., Carter, C. S., Hachten, P. C., & Cohen, J. (1999). The "benefits" of distractibility: The mechanisms underlying increased Stroop effects in schizophrenia. *Schizophrenia Bulletin, 24*, 749–762.

Barch, D. M., Carter, C., Perlstein, W., Baird, J., Cohen, J., & Schooler, N. (1999). Increased Stroop facilitation effects in schizophrenia are not due to increased automatic spreading activation. *Schizophrenia Research, 39*, 51–64.

Barch, D. M., Cohen, J. D., Servan-Schreiber, D., Steingard, S. S., Steinhauer, S., & van Kammen, D. (1996). Semantic priming in schizophrenia: An examination of spreading activation using word pronunciation and multiple SOAs. *Journal of Abnormal Psychology, 105*, 592–601.

Bell, M., Bryson, G., Greig, T., Corcoran, C., & Wexler, B. E. (2001). Neurocognitive enhancement therapy with work therapy: Effects on neuropsychological test performance. *Archives of General Psychiatry, 58*, 763–768.

Botvinick, M. M., Braver, T. S., Barch, D. M., Carter, C. S., & Cohen, J. C. (2001). Conflict monitoring and cognitive control. *Psychological Review, 108*, 624–652.

Brambilla, P., Macdonald, A. W. III, Sassi, R. B., Johnson, M. K., Mallinger, A. G., Carter, C. S., et al. (2007). Context processing performance in bipolar disorder patients. *Bipolar Disorders, 9*, 230–237.

Braver, T. S. (1997). *Mechanisms of cognitive control: A neurocomputational model.* Unpublished doctoral dissertation, Carnegie Mellon University, Pittsburgh, PA.

Braver, T. S., Barch, D. M., & Cohen, J. D. (1999a). Cognition and control in schizophrenia: A computational model of dopamine and prefrontal function. *Biological Psychiatry, 46*, 312–328.

Braver, T. S., Barch, D. M., & Cohen, J. D. (1999b). *Mechanisms of cognitive control: Active memory, inhibition, and the prefrontal cortex* (Technical Rep. No. PDP. CNS.99.1). Pittsburgh PA: Carnegie Mellon University.

Braver, T. S., Barch, D. M., Keys, B. A., Carter, C. S., Cohen, J. D., Kaye, J. A., et al. (2001). Context processing in older adults: Evidence for a theory relating cognitive control to neurobiology in healthy aging. *Journal of Experimental Psychology: General, 130*, 746–763.

Braver, T. S., & Bongiolatti, S. R. (2002). The role of the frontopolar prefrontal cortex in subgoal processing during working memory. *NeuroImage, 15*, 523–536.

Braver, T. S., & Cohen, J. D. (1999). Dopamine, cognitive control, and schizophrenia: The gating model. *Progress in Brain Research, 121*, 327–349.

Braver, T. S., & Cohen, J. D. (2000). On the control of control: The role of dopamine in regulating prefrontal function and working memory. In S. Monsell & J. Driver (Eds.), *Attention and performance XVIII* (pp. 713–738). Cambridge, MA: MIT Press.

Braver, T. S., & Cohen, J. D. (2001). Working memory, cognitive control, and the prefrontal cortex: Computational and empirical studies. *Cognitive Processing, 2,* 25–55.

Braver, T. S., Cohen, J. D., & Barch, D. M. (2002). The role of the prefrontal cortex in normal and disordered cognitive control: A cognitive neuroscience perspective. In D. T. Stuss & R. T. Knight (Eds.), *Principles of frontal lobe function* (pp. 428–448). Oxford, England: Oxford University Press.

Braver, T. S., Cohen, J. D., & McClelland, J. L. (1997). An integrated computational model of dopamine function in reinforcement learning and working memory. *Society for Neuroscience Abstracts, 23,* 775.

Braver, T. S., Cohen, J. D., & Servan-Schreiber, D. (1995). Neural network simulations of schizophrenic performance in a variant of the CPT-AX: A predicted double dissociation. *Schizophrenia Research, 15,* 110.

Brown, C., & Hagoort, P. (1993). The processing nature of the n400: Evidence from masked priming. *Journal of Cognitive Neuroscience, 5,* 34–44.

Brozoski, T. J., Brown, R. M., Rosvold, H. E., & Goldman, P. S. (1979, August 31). Cognitive deficit caused by regional depletion of dopamine in prefrontal cortex of rhesus monkey. *Science, 205,* 929–931.

Burgess, G. C., & Braver, T. S. (2008). *Proactive interference effects on working memory can be modulated by expectancy: Evidence for dual mechanisms of cognitive control.* Manuscript submitted for publication.

Cai, J. X., & Arnsten, A. F. T. (1997). Dose-dependent effects of the dopamine D1 receptor agonists a77636 or skf81297 on spatial working memory in aged monkeys. *Journal of Pharmacology and Experimental Therapeutics, 283,* 183–189.

Cannon, T. D., van Erp, T. G., & Glahn, D. C. (2002). Elucidating continuities and discontinuities between schizotypy and schizophrenia in the nervous system. *Schizophrenia Research, 54,* 151–156.

Carter, C. S., Robertson, L. C., & Nordahl, T. E. (1992). Abnormal processing of irrelevant information in schizophrenia: Selective enhancement of Stroop facilitation. *Psychiatry Research, 41,* 137–146.

Castner, S. A., Williams, G. V., & Goldman-Rakic, P. S. (2000, March 17). Reversal of antipsychotic induced working memory deficits by short term dopamine D1 receptor stimulation. *Science, 287,* 2020–2022.

Chen, E. Y. H., Wong, A. W. S., Chen, R. Y. L., & Au, J. W. Y. (2001). Stroop interference and facilitation effects in first-episode schizophrenia patients. *Schizophrenia Research, 48,* 29–44.

Cho, R. Y., Konecky, R. O., & Carter, C. S. (2006). Impairments in frontal cortical gamma synchrony and cognitive control in schizophrenia. *Proceedings of the National Academy of Sciences, 103,* 19878–19883.

Cohen, J. D., Barch, D. M., Carter, C., & Servan-Schreiber, D. (1999). Context-processing deficits in schizophrenia: Converging evidence from three theoretically motivated cognitive tasks. *Journal of Abnormal Psychology, 108,* 120–133.

Cohen, J. D., Braver, T. S., & Brown, J. W. (2002). Computational perspectives on dopamine function in prefrontal cortex. *Current Opinion in Neurobiology, 12,* 223–229.

Cohen, J. D., & Servan-Schreiber, D. (1992). Context, cortex and dopamine: A connectionist approach to behavior and biology in schizophrenia. *Psychological Review, 99*, 45–77.

Cohen, J. D., Targ, E., Servan-Schreiber, D., & Spiegel, D. (1992). The fabric of thought disorder: A cognitive neuroscience approach to disturbances in the processing of context in schizophrenia. In D. J. Stein & J. E. Young (Eds.), *Cognitive science and clinical disorders* (pp. 101–127). New York: Academic Press.

Condray, R., Steinhauer, S. R., Cohen, J. D., van Kammen, D. P., & Kasparek, A. (1999). Modulation of language processing in schizophrenia: Effects of context and haloperidol on the event-relate potential. *Biological Psychiatry, 45*, 1336–1355.

Daniel, D. G., Weinberger, D. R., Jones, D. W., Zigun, J. R., Coppola, R., Handel, S., et al. (1991). The effect of amphetamine on regional cerebral blood flow during cognitive activation in schizophrenia. *Journal of Neuroscience, 11*, 1907–1917.

Delawalla, Z., Csernansky, J. G., & Barch, D. M. (2008). Prefrontal cortex function in non-psychotic siblings of individuals with schizophrenia. *Biological Psychiatry, 63*, 490–497.

DeLisi, L. E., & Fleischhaker, W. (2007). Schizophrenia research in the era of the genome, 2007. *Current Opinions in Psychiatry, 20*, 109–110.

de Sonneville, L. M., Njiokiktjien, C., & Bos, H. (1994). Methylphenidate and information processing: Part 1: Differentiation between responders and nonresponders; Part 2: Efficacy in responders. *Journal of Clinical and Experimental Neuropsychology, 16*, 877–897.

Elvevåg, B., Duncan, J., & McKenna, P. J. (2000). The use of cognitive context in schizophrenia: An investigation. *Psychological Medicine, 30*(4), 885–897.

Fiszdon, J. M., Bryson, G. J., Wexler, B. E., & Bell, M. D. (2004). Durability of cognitive remediation training in schizophrenia: Performance on two memory tasks at 6-month and 12-month follow-up. *Psychiatry Research, 125*, 1–7.

Fiszdon, J. M., Whelahan, H., Bryson, G. J., Wexler, B. E., & Bell, M. D. (2005). Cognitive training of verbal memory using a dichotic listening paradigm: Impact on symptoms and cognition. *Acta Psychiatrica Scandinavica, 112*, 187–193.

Fuster, J. M. (1989). *The prefrontal cortex* (2nd ed.). New York: Raven Press.

Goldberg, T. E., Bigelow, L. B., Weinberger, D. R., Daniel, D. G., & Kleinman, J. E. (1991). Cognitive and behavioral effects of the coadministration of dextroamphetamine and haloperidol in schizophrenia. *American Journal of Psychiatry, 148*, 78–84.

Goldman-Rakic, P. S. (1987). Circuitry of primate prefrontal cortex and regulation of behavior by representational memory. In F. Plum & V. Mountcastle (Eds.), *Handbook of physiology—The nervous system* (Vol. 5, pp. 373–417). Bethesda, MD: American Physiological Society.

Goldman-Rakic, P. S. (1995). Cellular basis of working memory. *Neuron, 14*, 477–485.

Gottesman, I. I., & Hanson, D. R. (2005). Human development: Biological and genetic processes. *Annual Review of Psychology, 56*, 263–286.

Gray, J. A. (1998). Integrating schizophrenia. *Schizophrenia Bulletin, 24*, 249–266.

Gray, J. A., Feldon, J., Rawlins, J. N. P., Hemsley, D. R., & Smith, A. D. (1991). The neuropsychology of schizophrenia. *Behavioral and Brain Sciences, 14*, 1–84.

Gray, J. A., Joseph, M. H., Hemsley, D. R., Young, A. M., Warburton, E. C., Boulenguez, P., et al. (1995). The role of mesolimbic dopaminergic and retro-hippocampal afferents to the nucleus accumbens in latent inhibition: Implications for schizophrenia. *Behavior and Brain Research, 71*, 19–31.

Gray, N. S., & Snowden, R. J. (2005). The relevance of irrelevance to schizophrenia. *Neuroscience and Biobehavioral Reviews, 29*, 989–999.

Green, M. F., Kern, R. S., & Heaton, R. K. (2004). Longitudinal studies of cognition and functional outcome in schizophrenia: Implications for matrics. *Schizophrenia Research, 72*, 41–51.

Green, M. J., Waldron, J. H., & Coltheart, M. (2007). Emotional context processing is impaired in schizophrenia. *Cognitive Neuropsychiatry, 12*, 259–280.

Grillon, C., Ameli, R., & Glazer, W. M. (1991). N400 and semantic categorization in schizophrenia. *Biological Psychiatry, 29*, 467–480.

Hemsley, D. R. (1993). A simple (or simplistic?) cognitive model for schizophrenia. *Behavior Research Therapy, 31*, 633–645.

Hemsley, D. R. (2005). The schizophrenic experience: Taken out of context? *Schizophrenia Bulletin, 31*, 43–53.

Henik, A., Carter, C. S., Salo, R., Chaderjian, M., Kraft, L., Nordahl, T. E., et al. (2002). Attentional control and word inhibition in schizophrenia. *Psychiatry Research, 110*, 137–149.

Hogarty, G. E., Flesher, S., Ulrich, R., Carter, M., Greenwald, D., Pogue-Geile, M., et al. (2004). Cognitive enhancement therapy for schizophrenia: Effects of a 2-year randomized trial on cognition and behavior. *Archives of General Psychiatry, 61*, 866–876.

Holmes, A. J., MacDonald, A. III, Carter, C. S., Barch, D. M., Andrew Stenger, V., & Cohen, J. D. (2005). Prefrontal functioning during context processing in schizophrenia and major depression: An event-related fMRI study. *Schizophrenia Research, 76*, 199–206.

Jacoby, L. L. (1991). The process dissociation framework: Separating automatic from intentional uses of memory, *Journal of Memory and Language, 30*, 513–541.

Javitt, D. C., Rabinowicz, E., Silipo, G., & Dias, E. C. (2007). Encoding vs. retention: Differential effects of cue manipulation on working memory performance in schizophrenia. *Schizophrenia Research, 91*, 159–168.

Javitt, D. C., Shelley, A., Silipo, G., & Lieberman, J. A. (2000). Deficits in auditory and visual context-dependent processing in schizophrenia. *Archives of General Psychiatry, 57*, 1131–1137.

Keefe, R. S., Bilder, R. M., Davis, S. M., Harvey, P. D., Palmer, B. W., Gold, J. M., et al. (2007). Neurocognitive effects of antipsychotic medications in patients with chronic schizophrenia in the Catie trial. *Archives of General Psychiatry, 64*, 633–647.

Keefe, R. S., Sweeney, J. A., Gu, H., Hamer, R. M., Perkins, D. O., McEvoy, J. P., et al. (2007). Effects of olanzapine, quetiapine, and risperidone on neurocognitive function in early psychosis: A randomized, double-blind 52-week comparison. *American Journal of Psychiatry, 164,* 1061–1071.

Kerns, J. G., & Berenbaum, H. (2002). Cognitive impairments associated with formal thought disorder in people with schizophrenia. *Journal of Abnormal Psychology, 111,* 211–224.

Kerns, J. G., & Berenbaum, H. (2003). The relationship between formal thought disorder and executive functioning component processes. *Journal of Abnormal Psychology, 112,* 339–352.

Kerns, J. G., Cohen, J. D., Stenger, V. A., & Carter, C. S. (2004). Prefrontal cortex guides context-appropriate responding during language production. *Neuron, 43,* 283–291.

Kimberg, D. Y., & D'Esposito, M. (2003). Cognitive effects of the dopamine receptor agonist pergolide. *Neuropsychologica, 41,* 1020–1027.

Kimberg, D. Y., D'Esposito, M., & Farah, M. J. (1997). Effects of bromocriptine on human subjects depend on working memory capacity. *NeuroReport, 8,* 381–385.

Knierim, J. J., Lee, I., & Hargreaves, E. L. (2006). Hippocampal place cells: Parallel input streams, subregional processing, and implications for episodic memory. *Hippocampus, 16,* 755–764.

Kostova, M., Passerieux, C., Laurent, J. P., & Hardy-Bayle, M. C. (2003). An electrophysiologic study: Can semantic context processes be mobilized in patients with thought-disordered schizophrenia? *Canadian Journal of Psychiatry, 48,* 615–623.

Kostova, M., Passerieux, C., Laurent, J. P., & Hardy-Bayle, M. C. (2005). N400 anomalies in schizophrenia are correlated with the severity of formal thought disorder. *Schizophrenia Research, 78,* 285–291.

Kostova, M., Passerieux, C., Laurent, J. P., Saint-Georges, C., & Hardy-Bayle, M. C. (2003). Functional analysis of the deficit in semantic context processes in schizophrenic patients: An event-related potentials study. *Neurophysiological Clinics, 33,* 11–22.

Kuperberg, G. R., Deckersbach, T., Holt, D. J., Goff, D., & West, W. C. (2007). Increased temporal and prefrontal activity in response to semantic associations in schizophrenia. *Archives of General Psychiatry, 64,* 138–151.

Kuperberg, G., Ditman, T., Kreher, D. A., & Goldberg, T. (in press). Approaches to understanding language dysfunction in neuropsychiatric disorders: Insights from the study of schizophrenia. In S. Wood, N. Allen, & C. Pantelis (Eds.), *Handbook of neuropsychology of mental illness.* Cambridge, England: Cambridge University Press.

Kuperberg, G. R., Kreher, D. A., Goff, D., McGuire, P. K., & David, A. S. (2006). Building up linguistic context in schizophrenia: Evidence from self-paced reading. *Neuropsychology, 20,* 442–452.

Kuperberg, G. R., McGuire, P. K., & David, A. S. (1998). Reduced sensitivity to linguistic context in schizophrenic thought disorder: Evidence from on-line monitoring for words in linguistically anomalous sentences. *Journal of Abnormal Psychology, 107*, 423–434.

Kurtz, M. M., Seltzer, J. C., Shagan, D. S., Thime, W. R., & Wexler, B. E. (2007). Computer-assisted cognitive remediation in schizophrenia: What is the active ingredient? *Schizophrenia Research, 89*, 251–260.

Kutas, M., & Hillyard, S. A. (1980, January 11). Reading senseless sentences: Brain potentials reflect semantic incongruity. *Science, 207*, 203–205.

Lee, J., & Park, S. (2006). The role of stimulus salience in CPT-AX performance of schizophrenia patients. *Schizophrenia Research, 81*, 191–197.

Levelt, W. J. M. (1989). *Speaking: From intention to articulation.* Cambridge, MA: MIT Press.

Lewis, D. A., & Mirnics, K. (2006). Transcriptome alterations in schizophrenia: Disturbing the functional architecture of the dorsolateral prefrontal cortex. *Progress in Brain Research, 158*, 141–152.

Lipska, B. K., Mitkus, S. N., Mathew, S. V., Fatula, R., Hyde, T. M., Weinberger, D. R., et al. (2006). Functional genomics in postmortem human brain: Abnormalities in a DISC1 molecular pathway in schizophrenia. *Dialogues in Clinical Neuroscience, 8*, 353–357.

Lubow, R. E. (2005). Construct validity of the animal latent inhibition model of selective attention deficits in schizophrenia. *Schizophrenia Bulletin, 31*, 139–153.

Luciana, M., & Collins, P. F. (1997). Dopamine modulates working memory for spatial but not object cues in normal humans. *Journal of Cognitive Neuroscience, 4*, 58–68.

Luciana, M., Collins, P. F., & Depue, R. A. (1995, March). *DA and 5-ht influences on spatial working memory functions of prefrontal cortex.* Paper presented at the Second Annual Meeting of the Cognitive Neuroscience Society, San Francisco.

Luciana, M., Collins, P. F., & Depue, R. A. (1998). Opposing roles for dopamine and serotonin in the modulation of human spatial working memory functions. *Cerebral Cortex, 8*, 218–226.

Luciana, M., Depue, R. A., Arbisi, P., & Leon, A. (1992). Facilitation of working memory in humans by a D_2 dopamine receptor agonist. *Journal of Cognitive Neuroscience, 4*, 58–68.

MacDonald, A. W. III, Becker, T. M., & Carter, C. S. (2006). Functional magnetic resonance imaging study of cognitive control in the healthy relatives of schizophrenia patients. *Biological Psychiatry, 60*, 1241–1249.

MacDonald, A. W. III, & Carter, C. S. (2003). Event-related fMRI study of context processing in dorsolateral prefrontal cortex of patients with schizophrenia. *Journal of Abnormal Psychology, 112*, 689–697.

MacDonald, A. W. III, Carter, C. S., Flory, J. D., Ferrell, R. E., & Manuck, S. B. (2007). COMT val158met and executive control: A test of the benefit of specific deficits to translational research. *Journal of Abnormal Psychology, 116*, 306–312.

MacDonald, A., Carter, C. S., Kerns, J. G., Ursu, S., Barch, D. M., Holmes, A. J., et al. (2005). Specificity of prefrontal dysfunction and context processing deficits to schizophrenia in a never medicated first-episode psychotic sample. *American Journal of Psychiatry, 162,* 475–484.

MacDonald, A. W. III, Cohen, J. D., Stenger, V. A., & Carter, C. S. (2000, June 9). Dissociating the role of the dorsolateral prefrontal and anterior cingulate cortex in cognitive control. *Science, 288,* 1835–1838.

MacDonald, A. W. III, Goghari, V. M., Hicks, B. M., Flory, J. D., Carter, C. S., & Manuck, S. B. (2005). A convergent–divergent approach to context processing, general intellectual functioning, and the genetic liability to schizophrenia. *Neuropsychology, 19,* 814–821.

MacDonald, A. W., Pogue-Geile, M. F., Johnson, M. K., & Carter, C. S. (2003). A specific deficit in context processing in the unaffected siblings of patients with schizophrenia. *Archives of General Psychiatry, 60,* 57–65.

Mattay, V. S., Berman, K. F., Ostrem, J. L., Esposito, G., Van Horn, J. D., Bigelow, L. B., et al. (1996). Dextroamphetamine enhances "neural network-specific" physiological signals: A positron-emission tomography rCBF study. *Journal of Neuroscience, 15,* 4816–4822.

Mattay, V. S., Callicott, J. H., Bertolino, A., Heaton, I., Frank, J. A., Coppola, R., et al. (2000). Effects of dextroamphetamine on cognitive performance and cortical activation. *NeuroImage, 12,* 268–275.

Mattay, V. S., Goldberg, T. E., Fera, F., Hariri, A. R., Tessitore, A., Egan, M. F., et al. (2003). Catechol O-methyltransferase val158-met genotype and individual variation in the brain response to amphetamine. *Proceedings of the National Academy of Sciences, 100,* 6186–6191.

McClelland, J. L. (1993). Toward a theory of information processing in graded, random, and interactive networks. In D. E. Meyer & S. Kornblum (Eds.), *Attention and performance XIV: Synergies in experimental psychology, artificial intelligence, and cognitive neuroscience* (pp. 655–688). Cambridge, MA: MIT Press.

McGurk, S. R., Mueser, K. T., Feldman, K., Wolfe, R., & Pascaris, A. (2007). Cognitive training for supported employment: 2–3 year outcomes of a randomized controlled trial. *American Journal of Psychiatry, 164,* 437–441.

Mehta, M. A., Owen, A. M., Sahakian, B. J., Mavaddat, N., Pickard, J. D., & Robbins, T. W. (2000). Methylphenidate enhances working memory by modulating discrete frontal and parietal lobe regions in the human brain. *Journal of Neuroscience, 20,* 1–6.

Mehta, M. A., Swainson, R., Gogilvie, A. D., Sahakian, B. J., & Robbins, T. W. (2001). Improved short-term spatial memory but impaired reversal learning following the dopamine D_2 agonist bromocriptime in human volunteers. *Psychopharmacology, 159,* 10–20.

Miller, E. K., & Cohen, J. D. (2001). An integrative theory of prefrontal cortex function. *Annual Review of Neuroscience, 21,* 167–202.

Mintzer, M., & Griffiths, R. R. (2003). Triazolam–amphetamine interaction: Dissociation of effects of memory versus arousal. *Journal of Pharmacology, 17,* 17–29.

Muller, U., von Cramon, Y., & Pollmann, S. (1998). D_1-versus D_2-receptor modulation of visuospatial working memory in humans. *Journal of Neuroscience, 18,* 2720–2728.

Niznikiewicz, M. A., O'Donnell, B. F., Nestor, P. G., Smith, L., Law, S., Karapelou, M., et al. (1997). ERP assessment of visual and auditory language processing in schizophrenia. *Journal of Abnormal Psychology, 106,* 85–94.

Ohta, K., Uchiyama, M., Matsushima, E., & Toru, M. (1999). An event-related potential study in schizophrenia using Japanese sentences. *Schizophrenia Research, 40,* 159–170.

Olichney, J. M., Iragui, V. J., Kutas, M., Nowacki, R., & Jeste, D. V. (1997). N400 abnormalities in late life schizophrenia and related psychoses. *Biological Psychiatry, 42,* 13–23.

O'Reilly, R. C., Braver, T. S., & Cohen, J. D. (1999). A biologically based computational model of working memory. In A. Miyake & P. Shah (Eds.), *Models of working memory: Mechanisms of active maintenance and executive control* (pp. 375–411). New York: Cambridge University Press.

O'Reilly, R. C., Noelle, D. C., Braver, T. S., & Cohen, J. D. (2002). Prefrontal cortex and dynamic categorization tasks: Representational organization and neuromodulatory control. *Cerebral Cortex, 12,* 246–257.

Penades, R., Catalan, R., Salamero, M., Boget, T., Puig, O., Guarch, J., et al. (2006). Cognitive remediation therapy for outpatients with chronic schizophrenia: A controlled and randomized study. *Schizophrenia Research, 87,* 323–331.

Perlstein, W. M., Dixit, N. K., Carter, C. S., Noll, D. C., & Cohen, J. D. (2003). Prefrontal cortex dysfunction mediates deficits in working memory and prepotent responding in schizophrenia. *Biological Psychiatry, 53,* 25–38.

Pfammatter, M., Junghan, U. M., & Brenner, H. D. (2006). Efficacy of psychological therapy in schizophrenia: Conclusions from meta-analyses. *Schizophrenia Bulletin, 32*(Suppl. 1), S64–S80.

Phillips, W. A., & Silverstein, S. M. (2003). Convergence of biological and psychological perspectives on cognitive coordination in schizophrenia. *Behavioral and Brain Sciences, 26,* 65–82; discussion 82–137.

Ross, C. A., Margolis, R. L., Reading, S. A., Pletnikov, M., & Coyle, J. T. (2006). Neurobiology of schizophrenia. *Neuron, 52,* 139–153.

Rosvold, H. E., Mirsky, A. F., Sarason, I., Bransome, E. D., & Beck, L. H. (1956). A continuous performance test of brain damage. *Journal of Consulting Psychology, 20,* 343–350.

Rumelhart, D. E., & McClelland, J. L. (1986). *Parallel distributed processing: Explorations in the microstructure of cognition* (Vols. 1–2). Cambridge, MA: MIT Press.

Salisbury, D., O'Donnell, B. F., McCarley, R. W., Nestor, P. G., & Shenton, M. E. (2000). Event-related potentials elicited during a context-free homograph task in normal versus schizophrenic subjects. *Psychophysiology, 37,* 456–463.

Salzinger, K. (2006). Schizophrenia and the immediacy mechanism. *American Psychologist, 61,* 74–75.

Salzinger, K., Portnoy, S., & Feldman, R. S. (1966). Verbal behavior in schizophrenics and some comments toward a theory of schizophrenia. In P. Hoch & J. Zubin (Eds.), *Psychopathology of schizophrenia* (pp. 98–128). New York: Grune & Stratton.

Salzinger, K., Portnoy, S., Pisoni, D. B., & Feldman, R. S. (1970). The immediacy hypothesis and response-produced stimuli in schizophrenic speech. *Journal of Abnormal Psychology, 76*, 258–264.

Sawaguchi, T., & Goldman-Rakic, P. S. (1994). The role of D_1-dopamine receptor in working memory: Local injections of dopamine antagonists into the prefrontal cortex of rhesus monkeys performing an oculomotor delayed-response task. *Journal of Neurophysiology, 71*, 515–528.

Sawaguchi, T., Matsumura, M., & Kubota, K. (1990). Effects of dopamine antagonists on neuronal activity related to a delayed response task in monkey prefrontal cortex. *Journal of Neurophysiology, 63*, 1401–1410.

Seamans, J. K., & Yang, C. R. (2004). The principal features and mechanisms of dopamine modulation in the prefrontal cortex. *Progress in Neurobiology, 74*, 1–58.

Servan-Schreiber, D., Cohen, J. D., & Steingard, S. (1996). Schizophrenic deficits in the processing of context: A test of a theoretical model. *Archives of General Psychiatry, 53*, 1105–1113.

Shakow, D. (1962). Segmental set: A theory of the formal psychological deficit in schizophrenia. *Archives of General Psychiatry, 6*, 1–17.

Silverstein, S. M., Hatashita-Wong, M., Solak, B. A., Uhlhaas, P., Landa, Y., Wilkniss, S. M., et al. (2005). Effectiveness of a two-phase cognitive rehabilitation intervention for severely impaired schizophrenia patients. *Psychological Medicine, 35*, 829–837.

Silverstein, S. M., Kovacs, I., Corry, R., & Valone, C. (2000). Perceptual organization, the disorganization syndrome, and context processing in chronic schizophrenia. *Schizophrenia Research, 43*, 11–20.

Silverstein, S., Uhlhaas, P. J., Essex, B., Halpin, S., Schall, U., & Carr, V. (2006). Perceptual organization in first episode schizophrenia and ultra–high-risk states. *Schizophrenia Research, 83*, 41–52.

Sitnikova, T., Salisbury, D. F., Kuperberg, G., & Holcomb, P. J. (2002). Electrophysiological insights into language processing in schizophrenia. *Psychophysiology, 39*, 851–860.

Sitskoorn, M. M., Aleman, A., Ebisch, S. J., Appels, M. C., & Kahn, R. S. (2004). Cognitive deficits in relatives of patients with schizophrenia: A meta-analysis. *Schizophrenia Research, 71*, 285–295.

Snitz, B. E., MacDonald, A. W. III, & Carter, C. S. (2006). Cognitive deficits in unaffected first-degree relatives of schizophrenia patients: A meta-analytic review of putative endophenotypes. *Schizophrenia Bulletin, 32*, 179–194.

Snitz, B. E., MacDonald, A. III, Cohen, J. D., Cho, R. Y., Becker, T., & Carter, C. S. (2005). Lateral and medial hypofrontality in first-episode schizophrenia: Functional activity in a medication-naive state and effects of short-term atypical antipsychotic treatment. *American Journal of Psychiatry, 162*, 2322–2329.

Strandburgh, R. J., Marsh, J. T., Brown, W. S., Asarnow, R. F., Guthrie, D., Harper, R., et al. (1997). Event-related potential correlates of linguistic information processing in schizophrenics. *Biological Psychiatry, 42,* 596–608.

Stratta, P., Daneluzzo, E., Bustini, M., Casacchia, M., & Rossi, A. (1998). Schizophrenic deficits in the processing of context. *Archives of General Psychiatry, 55,* 186–187.

Stratta, P., Daneluzzo, E., Bustini, M., Prosperini, P., & Rossi, A. (2000). Processing of context information in schizophrenia: Relation to clinical symptoms and WCST performance. *Schizophrenia Research, 44,* 57–67.

Taylor, S. F., Kornblum, S., & Tandon, R. (1996). Facilitation and interference of selective attention in schizophrenia. *Journal of Psychiatric Research, 30,* 251–259.

Titone, D., Holzman, P. S., & Levy, D. L. (2002). Idiom processing in schizophrenia: Literal implausibility saves the day for idiom priming. *Journal of Abnormal Psychology, 11,* 313–320.

Titone, D., Levy, D. L., & Holzman, P. S. (2000). Contextual insensitivity in schizophrenic language processing: Evidence from lexical ambiguity. *Journal of Abnormal Psychology, 109,* 761–767.

Uhlhaas, P. J., Phillips, W. A., Mitchell, G., & Silverstein, S. M. (2006). Perceptual grouping in disorganized schizophrenia. *Psychiatry Research, 145,* 105–117.

Wager, T. D., & Smith, E. E. (2003). Neuroimaging studies of working memory: A meta-analysis. *Cognitive Affective and Behavioral Neuroscience, 3,* 255–274.

Williams, G. V., & Goldman-Rakic, P. S. (1995, August 17). Modulation of memory fields by dopamine D_1 receptors in prefrontal cortex. *Nature, 376,* 572–575.

Wykes, T., Newton, E., Landau, S., Rice, C., Thompson, N., & Frangou, S. (2007). Cognitive remediation therapy (CRT) for young early onset patients with schizophrenia: An exploratory randomized controlled trial. *Schizophrenia Research, 94,* 221–230.

Wykes, T., Reeder, C., Landau, S., Everitt, B., Knapp, M., Patel, A., et al. (2007). Cognitive remediation therapy in schizophrenia: Randomised controlled trial. *British Journal of Psychiatry, 190,* 421–427.

Wykes, T., Reeder, C., Williams, C., Corner, J., Rice, C., & Everitt, B. (2003). Are the effects of cognitive remediation therapy (CRT) durable? Results from an exploratory trial in schizophrenia. *Schizophrenia Research, 61,* 163–174.

3

PSYCHOSOCIAL MECHANISMS IN BIPOLAR DISORDER

SHERI L. JOHNSON, DANIEL FULFORD, AND LORI EISNER

Bipolar disorders are among the most severe of psychiatric disorders, with rates of suicide, hospitalization, and relapse that remain disturbingly high even with currently available treatment approaches (Goldberg, 2004). Although several milder forms of the disorder have been defined, we will focus on bipolar I disorder, which is defined by at least one lifetime episode of mania (or a *mixed episode*, defined as a manic episode that is accompanied by significant depressive symptoms). The *Diagnostic and Statistical Manual of Mental Disorders* (American Psychiatric Association, 2000) criteria for mania include extreme euphoria or irritability accompanied by a set of other symptoms, including racing thoughts, excessive talkativeness, unrealistically high self-esteem, increased goal activation, decreased need for sleep, and diminished awareness of danger. Symptoms must last for at least 1 week and cause severe impairment or necessitate hospitalization.

For decades, psychosocial researchers all but abandoned the study of bipolar disorder, assuming that the genetic roots of disorder implied the irrelevance of psychological mechanisms. In the past 15 years, there has been a shift in this perspective such that researchers have now begun to consider how the genetic vulnerability to this disorder might be expressed in psychological characteristics and how social and psychological variables might trigger episodes by increasing dysregulation of underlying biological pathways. This shift is consistent with a broader goal in psychopathology research of identifying endophenotypes of disorder; that is, rather than assuming that genes directly translate to symptoms, the expectation is that genes change key biological and psychological processes, which then might lead to symptom expression in the context of environmental and biological triggering events.

In this chapter, we provide an overview of some of the current models of how such processes might operate in bipolar disorder. It must be acknowledged, though, that bipolar disorder has received substantially less research funding and focus than other serious psychiatric illnesses (Clement, Singh, & Burns, 2003), leaving far too many questions unanswered. Hence, we present some of these ideas in the spirit of encouraging questions and research rather than on the basis of the assumption that these models are fully tested.

We focus on two psychological characteristics that have been theorized to relate to the underlying biological vulnerability to bipolar disorder: (a) *reward sensitivity* and (b) *negative emotional reactivity*. For both characteristics, we review the evidence that (a) these traits differentiate people with bipolar disorder from those without bipolar disorder and (b) these traits predict the course of disorder. It is worth noting that these are only two of the potential models of psychological vulnerability. For example, increasingly robust research documents that neuropsychological deficits can be found among people with bipolar disorder, even during periods of euthymia, as summarized within a recent meta-analysis (Martinez-Aran et al., 2000). Similarly, a host of articles have focused on the idea that mania is in part triggered by efforts to defend against depression (Bentall & Thompson, 1990; French, Richards, & Scholfield, 1996; Thomas & Bentall, 2002). Finally, it has long been noted that sleep loss can trigger episodes of mania (Barbini et al., 1998). Rather than cover each of these models, we provide an overview of two of the models that have been a growing focus of empirical research.

To begin, it is worth considering the genetic basis of bipolar disorder. Twin studies have firmly established that it has a strong heritability. Indeed, estimates suggest that heritability of bipolar disorder ranges from 66% to 85% (Shih, Belmonte, & Zandi, 2004). For some time, researchers searched for a single locus of disorder, and although many reported early promising results (e.g., Joffe, Horvath, & Tarvydas, 1986; Robertson, 1987), each finding has been met with a series of nonreplications (cf. Sklar, 2002). At this point, conventional wisdom is that bipolar disorder is likely to be polygenic, and a number of candidate gene loci have been identified. Given the polygenic nature of the disorder, it is likely that the disorder will eventually be found to relate to a set of psychological vulnerabilities rather than any single vulnerability. A recent review provided a comprehensive list of key candidate genes and potentially related biological and psychological mechanisms (Hasler, Drevets, Gould, Gottesman, & Manji, 2006). At this early stage, research is still underway to validate the different candidate genes as well as to identify the different psychological and biological mechanisms.

Before we discuss research on potential mechanisms, it makes sense to describe broad issues that complicate empirical studies of vulnerability in bipolar disorder. Perhaps one of the most difficult issues is the extremely high rates of comorbidity. In one epidemiological study, every single person who met criteria for lifetime bipolar disorder also met criteria for at least one comorbid psychiatric condition (Kessler, Chiu, Demler, & Walters, 2005). In other studies, levels of comorbidity have been as high as 65% (McElroy et al., 2001). Not only do people with bipolar disorder manifest high rates of a range of disorders, but family members of those with bipolar disorder also appear to be at high risk for myriad conditions.

Certain comorbid conditions appear particularly common among people with a history of mania. As captured by the name of the disorder, at least two thirds of people who experience an episode of mania will report an episode of major depression during their lifetime (Karkowski & Kendler, 1997; Kessler, Rubinow, Holmes, Abelson, & Zhao, 1997; Weissman & Myers, 1978), and family members are at increased risk for major depression as well. Similarly, more than half of people with bipolar disorder will meet diagnostic criteria for anxiety disorders (Simon et al., 2004). The high rates of depressive and anxiety disorders suggest the need to consider underlying models of vulnerability to emotion dysregulation. Beyond comorbid conditions involving extremes of emotion, as many as 60% of people with bipolar disorder will meet lifetime diagnostic criteria for alcohol and substance use disorders (Cassidy, Ahearn, & Carroll, 2001). Research on substance abuse has strongly implicated dysregulation in reward pathways, and we consider such models later in this chapter.

Researchers have found that monozygotic twins of persons with mania are at increased risk not only for mania (36.4%) but also for schizophrenia (13.6%; Cardno, Rijsdijk, Sham, Murray, & McGuffin, 2002). Indeed, 58% of people with bipolar disorder report at least one psychotic symptom during their lifetime (Goodwin & Jamison, 1990). Several studies have considered genetic loci that may increase susceptibility to both bipolar disorder and schizophrenia, including the regions 18p11 (Berrettini et al., 1997; Detera-Wadleigh et al., 1999), 8p22, 10p14 (Berrettini, 2003), 13q32, 22q11 (Badner & Gershon, 2002), and the catechol-O-methyltransferase gene (Badner & Gershon, 2002; Schwab et al., 1998; Shifman et al., 2004). Although bipolar disorder also has been related to a set of regions that have not been tied to schizophrenia, it is increasingly clear that it will be important to understand both shared and unique genetic vulnerability to these disorders.

The high rates of comorbidity may point toward key aspects of vulnerability in bipolar disorder. For example, recognition of the overlap with schizophrenia has led to interest in studying whether the neurocognitive deficits that accompany symptoms of schizophrenia can be observed within bipolar disorder (Cannon & Keller, 2006). Given the high levels of comorbidity, researchers face two major challenges: (a) validating the potential vulnerability characteristics involved in bipolar disorder and (b) determining which of these characteristics are uniquely tied to bipolar disorder. Research on these traits has operated with surprisingly little attention to comorbidity, a topic to which we will return.

Before we review research findings, it is important to note that many studies have relied on samples at risk for the development of disorder. Although analog studies have clear disadvantages, instruments such as the Hypomanic Personality Scale (Eckblad & Chapman, 1986) have been shown to have robust validity in predicting the onset of clinical diagnoses of bipolar spectrum disorder over a 10-year period (Kwapil et al., 2000). High-risk samples have the advantage of being free of medications, which might limit the very behavioral dysfunctions that researchers are attempting to assess. On the other hand, such studies may be limited because vulnerability characteristics might be less pronounced among such samples in our discussion. We include studies of high-risk samples, but we label them as such.

REWARD SENSITIVITY

Substantial research has accrued to support a brain-based system involved in reward responsivity that orchestrates behavior and cognition toward the pursuit of goals. More specifically, basic research suggests that dopaminergic pathways from the nucleus accumbens to the prefrontal cortex are activated when people anticipate reward (Knutson, Adams, Fong, & Hommer, 2001). Activation of this system is triggered by cues of incentive and, once activated, the system appears to facilitate energy, behavioral activation, and positive affect (Depue, Collins, & Luciana, 1996). For several decades, theoreticians have suggested that the outputs of this system show a remarkable correspondence with the symptoms of mania. Hence, bipolar disorder has been hypothesized to be the result of dysregulation in this pathway (Depue et al., 1996; Hestenes, 1992).

Certainly there is evidence that mania is related to dysregulations in dopaminergic function (as well as other neurobiological deficits). For example, drugs that increase levels of dopamine in the synaptic cleft, such as amphetamines and cocaine, have long been known to trigger episodes of mania among people vulnerable to the disorder (e.g., Jacobson & Silverstone, 1986). Other research has relied on the *behavioral sensitization paradigm*, which has been widely used to study biological processes through which neurobiological systems modulate high levels of dopamine. This research suggests that bipolar disorder is associated with differential responses to behavioral sensitization paradigms (Post, 1992; Strakowski, Sax, Setters, & Keck, 1996). Finally, sleep provides one mechanism to reregulate dopamine function (Ebert & Berger, 1998). It is intriguing that sleep deprivation has been shown to predict the onset of manic symptoms for as many as 75% of persons with a history of bipolar disorder (Wehr, Goodwin, Wirz-Justice, Breitmaier, & Craig, 1982), consistent with the idea of sensitivity to challenges to the dopamine system. Hence, biological research is consistent with the idea that bipolar disorder is related to deficits in the regulation of the dopamine system. Given these findings, one might expect that persons with bipolar disorder would demonstrate greater reactivity to psychosocial challenges to this system, such as cues of reward and incentive (Johnson, Ruggero, & Carver, 2005; B. Meyer, Johnson, & Carver, 1999).

A fair amount of research has focused on the idea that bipolar disorder involves excessive sensitivity of the behavioral activation system. Here, we discuss three general types of evidence: (a) overlap between symptoms of mania and signs of behavioral activation, (b) cross-sectional evidence for heightened reward responsivity within bipolar disorder, and (c) prospective evidence for heightened reward responsivity as a predictor of the course of symptoms within bipolar disorder.

Overlap Between Manic Symptoms and Behavioral Activation

Many of the symptoms of mania are consistent with signs of increased activation of the reward system, including increases in activity, pursuit of potentially reinforcing activities without attention to potential danger, and increased speed of thought. Robust evidence supports the idea that activation of the reward system produces increased positive affect (Knutson et al., 2001). Of interest is that factor analyses of mania symptoms have suggested that signs of activation—energy, elevated mood, increased activity, motor hyperactivity, and social engagement—are one of four core factors in manic symptoms (Swann et al., 2001).

Akiskal et al. (2001) argued that diagnostic sensitivity is enhanced by querying patients about activation before mood symptoms. That is, patients seem to be able to recall episodes of mood shifts, but they tie these mood changes specifically to increases in activation. Hence, there is some evidence that activation is not only an important component of the symptoms of mania but may even be a core component.

Despite the strong correspondence between the symptoms of mania and the expected outputs of a brain-based reward system, *Diagnostic and Statistical Manual of Mental Disorders* nomenclature lists either euphoria or irritability as being required for the diagnosis of mania. Many researchers have raised the question of whether irritability fits with models of reward sensitivity. We think that reward sensitivity could help explain the irritability seen during mania. On this front, consider a person who is highly engaged in pursuing a goal and then becomes thwarted. One would expect increases in goal pursuit to promote increased irritability in the context of such frustration. Consistent with this idea, Harmon-Jones et al. (2002) examined how risk for hypomania related to reactions to frustration among undergraduates. They provided false information to students that tuition at their school was likely to increase substantially (presumably information that would threaten the goal of graduation). Risk for hypomania was correlated with significantly higher midfrontal electroencephalogram (EEG) activation on the right compared with the left side (an index of approach motivation) after this frustrating information was presented. The findings, then, were consistent with the idea of greater goal engagement among persons at risk for hypomania. One could speculate that the irritability manifested during manic episodes might be related to goal frustration. Research is needed, though, to further test this aspect of the model.

Many of the core symptoms of mania mirror expected signs of increased goal engagement. Irritability is less intuitively related, but recent research suggests that goal frustration is related to risk for mania, which might help explain the presence of irritability during manic episodes.

Cross-Sectional Research on Measures of Reward Responsivity and Bipolar Disorder

Beyond the phenomenology of disorder, empirical studies support a role of the reward system in the etiology of bipolar disorder (for an overview of these studies, see Table 3.1). We begin by discussing data drawn from self-report assessments, and then we consider experimental evidence.

Early tests of the reward sensitivity model relied on the Behavioral Activation Scales (BAS; Carver & White, 1994) to measure self-reported sensitivity to incentive stimuli. The BAS Reward Responsiveness scale is designed to assess individual differences in the tendency to experience excitement and energy in contexts involving goals. Across three studies, persons with bipolar disorder endorsed significantly higher reward responsiveness than healthy control participants (Gruber & Johnson, in press; B. Meyer, Johnson, & Winters, 2001; Salavert et al., 2007), as did students with bipolar-spectrum disorder (Alloy et al., 2008), as well as students with high scores on measures of risk for bipolar disorder (Johnson & Carver, in press; B. Meyer et al., 1999; T. D. Meyer & Hofmann, 2005). Despite these positive findings, some studies have not documented group differences in BAS scores; for example, 16 students at high risk for mania as measured using the Hypomanic Checklist–32 (Angst et al., 2005) did not evince higher BAS scores than students at low risk (Holzwarth & Meyer, 2006). Similarly, in a study of 20 parents with bipolar disorder, neither the parents nor the offspring demonstrated

TABLE 3.1

Studies That Have Examined Reward Sensitivity in Bipolar Disorder

Study	Participants	Mood State Assessments	Stimuli Presented	Cognitive–Behavioral Outcome Measures
Chang et al. (2004)	12 young males with BP I (as diagnosed by the SADS) with at least 1 parent with BP I or II; 10 healthy young male controls	YMRS and CDI	fMRI while performing a visuospatial working memory task and an affective task using valenced images	Abnormalities in brain regions associated with reward sensitivity
Gruber et al. (2008)	34 high- and 83 low-risk participants defined by the HPS.	Current manic (ASRM) and depressive (BDI) symptoms	Film clips (3 positive, 2 negative, and 1 neutral)	Affect, facial expressions, and vagal tone at baseline and after each clip
Johnson & Carver (2006)	103 undiagnosed under-graduate students	ASRM and CES–D		Unrealistic ambitions as measured by the WASSUP
Johnson et al. (2005)	156 undiagnosed under-graduate students	ISS	The Go Task involving monetary reward	Reaction times in the Go Task
Lawrence et al. (2004)	12 adults with BP I and 9 adults with MDD	YRMS and BDI	fMRI while presented with facial identities	fMRI signal change; an emotion identification task and the Recogni-tion Memory Test or the Short Recognition Memory Test for Faces
Lozano & Johnson (2001)	39 adults with BP I as diagnosed by the SCID	MHRSD and BRMS		NEO Five-Factor Inventory and manic symptomatology
B. Meyer et al. (2004)	464 undiagnosed under-graduate students	ASRM and BDI		Goal relevance as mea-sured by the PPT
B. Meyer et al. (1999)	357 undiagnosed under-graduate students	ISS		Reward sensitivity as measured by BIS/BAS

(continues)

TABLE 3.1

Studies That Have Examined Reward Sensitivity in Bipolar Disorder   *(Continued)*

Study	Participants	Mood State Assessments	Stimuli Presented	Cognitive–Behavioral Outcome Measures
B. Meyer et al. (2001)	59 adults with BP I as diagnosed by the SCID	MHRSD and BRMS		Reward sensitivity as measured by BIS/BAS
T. D. Meyer & Krumm-Merabet (2003)	2,975 adolescents	CES–D		Relations between hypomanic symptoms and behavioral activation regulation as measured by performance-related questions
Stern & Berrenberg (1979)	156 undiagnosed undergraduate students	Mania scale	False success feedback in a coin flipping task	The illusion of control as measured by participant guesses after false success feedback
Sutton & Johnson (2002)	Undergraduates with high (> 30) and low (< 25) HPS scores		Positive, negative, and neutral pictures	Eyeblink reflex as measured by electromyogram responses to a loud acoustic probe
Swann et al. (2004)	45 adults with BP I as diagnosed by the SCID, 36 adults with substance abuse only, and 37 healthy adult controls	SADS–C	A computer task derived from the Continuous Performance Test	Impulsivity as assessed by the BIS
Yurgelun-Todd et al. (2000)	14 adult BP I as diagnosed by the SCID; 10 healthy adult controls	YMRS and Ham-D	fMRI while presented with facial identities	fMRI signal change; facial affect identification

Note. BP I and II = bipolar disorder I, bipolar disorder II; SADS = Schedule for Affective Disorders and Schizophrenia; YMRS = Young Mania Rating Scale; CDI = Children's Depression Inventory; CES–D = Center for Epidemiologic Studies Depression Scale; fMRI = functional magnetic resonance imaging; HPS = Hypomanic Personality Scale; ASRM = Altman Self-Rating Mania Scale; BDI = Beck Depression Inventory; ISS = Internal State Scale; MDD = major depressive disorder; SCID = Structured Clinical Interview for *DSM–IV*; MHRSD = Modified Hamilton Rating Scale for Depression; BRMS = Bech–Rafaelsen Mania Scale; WASSUP = Willingly Approached Set of Statistically Unrealistic Pursuits Scale; ASRM = Altman Self-Rating Mania Scale; PPT = Personal Projects Task; BIS/BAS = Behavioral Inhibition and Behavioral Activation Scales; SADS–C = Change version of the Schedule for Affective Disorders and Schizophrenia; BIS = Barratt Impulsivity Scale; Ham-D = Hamilton Rating Scale for Depression.

elevations of BAS scores (Jones, Tai, Evershed, Knowles, & Bentall, 2006). These studies were characterized by small sample sizes, though, and so larger sample sizes may be needed to detect the small group differences in BAS. Beyond these studies, Hayden et al. (2008) did not find elevated BAS self-report scores within a sample of people with bipolar disorder compared with a healthy control sample but did find that the sample with bipolar disorder evidenced greater behavioral responsivity to a reward task.

One might expect that persons who are more sensitive to reward would show different cognitive responses to reward and success. Several analog studies are consistent with this idea. In an early study, Stern and Berrenberg (1979) were interested in reactions to false success feedback, and they asked undergraduates to estimate the odds of their successfully guessing a coin toss after false success feedback. Of interest is the finding that undergraduates with a history of hypomanic symptoms were inappropriately confident about their ability to guess, but only after success feedback, whereas those without a history of hypomanic symptoms were not inappropriately confident after success.

In one analog study following from these findings (Johnson et al., 2005), undergraduates were given false success feedback on an eye–hand task and were paid a small amount of money ($3) as a reward for their excellent performance. Then, they were asked to choose the difficulty level of an eye–hand task to be performed next. Participants at high risk of mania chose more difficult tasks after false success feedback.

Congruent with the findings regarding confidence, differences in the appraisals of goals have been documented among people with current hypomanic symptoms. In one study, goal appraisals were assessed among college students endorsing hypomania using a modified version of Little's (1989) Personal Projects Analysis (B. Meyer, Beevers, & Johnson, 2004). Students with elevated hypomania construed their goals as more likely to be attained, more enjoyable, and more controllable.

As Johnson (2005) discussed in a previous review, people who experience rewards as more powerful and success as more obtainable might be expected to organize their life goals around the pursuit of those successes. Indeed, there is a fair amount of evidence that people with bipolar disorder do put more of an emphasis on the pursuit of goals during their lifetime. T. D. Meyer and Krumm-Merabet (2003) found that people at high risk for bipolar disorder endorsed extremely positive expectancies for academic and financial success, which were not accounted for by indexes of their ability. Johnson and Carver (2006) developed a scale to measure extreme life ambitions in a host of areas and found that people at risk for bipolar disorder endorsed extremely high expectations for success, but only in domains that were related to public recognition and admiration (e.g., fame, wealth). Their expectations for more intrinsic aspirations, such as love and interpersonal connectedness, were not elevated compared with others. Hence, people at risk for mania appear to set high expectations for materially rewarding life goals.

There thus is some evidence that people vulnerable to mania tend to perceive themselves as more emotionally reactive to cues of incentive, that they display greater shifts in confidence after an initial success–reward experience, and that they appraise their goals in a more positive manner. They also appear to set highly ambitious life goals.

Most of this research has used self-report scales. This is problematic because recent research suggests that different types of measures of BAS do not correlate well within bipolar disorder (Hayden et al., 2008). Several studies have begun to examine how bipolar disorder relates to psychophysiological and neurobiological responses to positive stimuli, with mixed results. In one study, students with high vulnerability to bipolar disorder as defined by the Hypomanic Personality Scale had greater psychophysiological reactivity to positive pictures than did those with low vulnerability to mania (Sutton & Johnson, 2002), but this finding was not replicated when positive film clips were used (Gruber, Johnson, Oveis, & Keltner, 2008). One EEG study found greater patterns of left frontal cortical activation among bipolar participants during a challenging goal-oriented task, which is suggestive of greater task engagement (Harmon-Jones et al., 2008). Similarly, another study found that EEG indices of left frontal laterality were increased among bipolar I participants after a mood induction task (Hayden et al., 2008). Two studies have found that persons with and without bipolar disorder differed in neural responses after viewing positive facial expressions (Chang et al., 2004; Lawrence et al., 2004), but one study failed to find such differences (Yurgelon-Todd et al., 2000).

It is unfortunate that the psychophysiological and neurobiological studies to date have relied on stimuli that were passively viewed rather than stimuli that were more engaging and personally relevant for participants, such as tasks involving reward or personal feedback. It is possible that more consistent results would be obtained with paradigms that were personally engaging because these tasks have been more powerful for studying psychophysiological responses to stressors (Kluger & DeNisi, 1996). The studies of behavioral and cognitive responses to reward-relevant stimuli, described earlier, have tended to find positive effects using more personally relevant feedback.

Evidence from many studies suggests that students at risk for mania and persons with diagnosable bipolar disorder demonstrate elevations in self-reported sensitivity to reward, although two studies have failed to replicate this finding. Other studies have found evidence for greater confidence after receipt of reward. Stated more broadly, diagnoses of bipolar disorder and risk of mania appear tied to a great focus on the pursuit of extrinsically reinforcing life goals. Each of these traits can be documented during asymptomatic periods. Studies of psychophysiological and neurobiological reactivity have yielded inconsistent findings, perhaps secondary to the reliance on passive rather than personally engaging stimuli. Hence, it will be important to continue to study whether the reward sensitivity model can be documented with laboratory paradigms that assess a broad range of response channels.

Given further support for the model, a key question is whether elevations in reward responsivity are unique to bipolar disorder. Given the substantial neurobiological research on reward pathways and substance abuse, it will be particularly important to study reward systems among individuals with bipolar disorder compared with individuals with substance abuse histories. Preliminary research suggests there may be subtle differences in the aspects of reward sensitivity associated with these two syndromes. In the research described earlier, bipolar disorder appears tied to elevations in BAS reward responsivity, or the tendency to be very excited and enthused in the context of reward. In contrast, results of an epidemiological study of more than 3,000 young adults suggest that lifetime diagnoses of substance abuse were related to elevations on the BAS Fun-Seeking scale rather than the Reward Responsivity scale (cf. Johnson, Turner, & Iwata, 2003). The Fun-Seeking scale was designed to capture the pursuit of rewards without attention to cues of danger (i.e., impulsivity). At baseline, people with bipolar disorder and those at risk for the disorder did not describe themselves as higher on measures of fun-seeking or impulsivity (B. Meyer et al., 1999, 2001). Two studies, though, suggest that fun-seeking and impulsivity increase as manic symptoms intensify (B. Meyer et al., 2001; Swann et al., 2001).

Swann, Dougherty, Pazzaglia, Pham, and Moeller (2004) studied impulsivity among people with bipolar disorder, carefully testing the role of current manic symptoms and substance abuse. They found that during remission, impulsivity was elevated only among people with comorbid substance abuse. Impulsivity levels become elevated during mania, though, for people with and without comorbid substance abuse. Their findings highlight the rigor that will be needed to understand the influence of subsyndromal and comorbid conditions on reward responsivity.

Prospective Studies of Reward Sensitivity in Bipolar Disorder

Given the cross-sectional evidence for greater reward sensitivity among people at risk for or diagnosed with bipolar disorder, a key question is whether this reward sensitivity helps predict the course of disorder. Several studies have suggested that among people with bipolar disorder, reward sensitivity and related characteristics predict higher risk for manic symptoms over time. That is, among people diagnosed with bipolar I disorder, BAS Reward Responsiveness predicted increases in manic symptoms over 6 months in one sample (B. Meyer et al., 2001) and greater risk of manic than depressive episodes over an 18-month period in another sample (Salavert et al., 2007).

Similar findings have emerged in samples with less severe forms of bipolar disorder. For example, BAS scores were found to predict increased risk of hypomanic episodes among college students with a bipolar-spectrum disorder over a 33-month period (Alloy et al., 2008) and increased hypomanic symptoms over a 1-week period in a nondiagnosed community sample (T. D. Meyer & Hofmann, 2005). In two prospective studies of life events, major life events involving goal attainment predicted increases on interview-based measures of manic symptoms among people diagnosed with bipolar I disorder (Johnson, Cuellar, et al., 2008; Johnson, Sandrow, Meyer, Winters, Miller, Keitner, & Solomon, 2000). Similarly, life events involving goal striving predicted increases in hypomanic symptoms among undergraduates diagnosed with bipolar-spectrum disorders (Nusslock, Abramson, Harmon-Jones, Alloy, & Hogan, 2007). Finally, people who endorse more engagement in goal pursuit have been found to be at increased risk of mania over the next 2 months (Lozano & Johnson, 2001). Hence, early evidence suggests that self-reported sensitivity to rewards, actual life events involving rewards, and increased goal pursuit are each related to greater risk for manic symptoms prospectively.

Summary of Reward Sensitivity Research in Bipolar Disorder

There is cross-sectional and prospective evidence to support the reward sensitivity model in bipolar disorder. There are several gaps in the research base, though. In particular, psychophysiological and biological aspects of reward sensitivity have not been consistently documented. Further research is needed that uses more personally engaging stimuli and more objective measures of responses to those stimuli.

NEGATIVE EMOTIONAL REACTIVITY

In considering the topic of emotional reactivity, it is important to distinguish between moods and emotions. *Moods* have been defined as prolonged states that are not tied to specific triggers (Ekman, 1994). In contrast, *emotions* have been defined as brief states triggered by specific stimuli, accompanied by distinct cognitive and psychophysiological profiles (Ekman, 1994). The episodes of mania and depression experienced by people with bipolar disorder are best characterized as extremes of mood.

Researchers have begun to examine whether high levels of emotion exist outside of mood episodes. People with bipolar disorder, even when euthymic, and people at high risk of bipolar disorder, have been found to report more frequent and intense emotions, both positive and negative, than do control participants (Bagby et al., 1996; Gruber & Johnson, in press; Hofmann & Meyer, 2006; Lovejoy & Steuerwald, 1995). In keeping with self-reported dispositions toward intense emotions, several biological reviews have described dysregulation in the brain pathways involved in emotion regulation. In nonclinical samples, research suggests that the amygdala is responsible for assigning emotional significance to negative and positive stimuli. Several studies have documented greater activity in this area during cognitive tasks among people with bipolar disorder compared with those with no mood disorder (Berns, Martin, & Proper, 2002; Kruger, Seminowicz, Goldapple, Kennedy, & Mayberg, 2003; Phillips, Drevets, Rauch, & Lane, 2003; Strakowski et al., 1999; see also Chen et al., 2004). Research also suggests diminished activation in regions responsible for planning and goal pursuit in the context of emotion, such as the prefrontal cortex and anterior cingulate (Phillips et al., 2003). The combination of heightened amygdala activity and diminished function of cortical regions among people with bipolar disorder would be expected to produce greater response to emotionally relevant stimuli and difficulty with emotion regulation.

There is also evidence that people with bipolar disorder are at high risk for depression in the context of negative social environments, which is consistent with the idea of emotional reactivity being involved with the disorder; that is, family criticism and hostility as well as negative life events both predict increases in bipolar depression (Johnson, 2005; Kim & Miklowitz, 2004; Yan, Hammen, Cohen, Daley, & Henry, 2004).

In sum, people with bipolar disorder describe frequent experiences of extreme emotions, and negative environments seem tied to the course of disorder. Moreover, current theory emphasizes neural circuits involved in emotion generation and regulation.

Given this evidence, it has been suggested that people with bipolar disorder are more emotionally reactive than people who do not have the disorder (Lovejoy & Steuerwald, 1995). To test this reactivity model, it is important to examine whether people with bipolar disorder experience intense emotional reactions to standardized threatening stimuli. That is, although a set of studies suggest that people with bipolar disorder frequently experience intense emotions, a more precise question relates to whether they experience more intense responses to a given situation than do other people. Laboratory paradigms involving standardized stimuli are needed because people with bipolar disorder might be experiencing negative emotions in response to lives that are fraught with financial, career, and social concerns (Ellicott, Hammen, Gitlin, & Brown, 1990). A set of studies have examined whether people with bipolar disorder experience a more powerful reaction to negatively valenced stimuli.

It is important to note some concerns about this literature. First, the valenced stimuli used vary substantially in whether they would be expected to elicit emotional reactions, from pictures of negative facial expressions, to negative film clips, to failure feedback on math or interpersonal tasks (for a summary of these studies, see Table 3.2). Emotion studies are further complicated

TABLE 3.2
Laboratory and Neuroimaging Studies That Have Examined Responses to Negative Stimuli

Study	Participants	Mood State Assessments	Stimulus Presented	Emotional Response Components Measured
Cuellar (2005)	35 people with BP I, 35 healthy control participants with no mood or psychotic disorder. Diagnosed by SCID.	BRMS < 7 and Modi-fied Ham-D < 10	A stooge listened to the participant describe a personally challenging issue and then expressed blame and criticism.	Affective reactivity and recovery
Ruggero & Johnson (2006)	28 people with BP I, 40 control participants with no mood or psychotic disorder. Diagnosed by SCID. Excluded: people in episodes, but not those with mild symptoms.	BRMS and Modified Ham-D < 15 (no current episodes) controlled for in analyses	Learned helplessness paradigm involving 0, 1, or 4 failures	Subjective affect and cognitive perform-ance on an anagram task after feedback
Gruber et al. (2008)	34 high- and 83 low-risk partici-pants defined by HPS.	Current manic (ASRM) and depressive (BDI) symptoms	Film clips (3 positive, 2 negative, 1 neutral)	Affect, facial expres-sions, and vagal tone at baseline and after each clip
Stern & Berrenberg (1979)	Undergraduates with high and low scores on a measure of hypomanic symptoms 6 weeks before testing		Participants were given false success feed-back or false failure feedback	Confidence ratings of likelihood of guessing a coin toss outcome
Sutton & Johnson (2002)	20 undergraduates with high (> 30) HPS scores, 20 undergraduates with low (< 25) HPS scores		Positive, negative, and neutral pictures	Eyeblink reflex as measured by electromyogram responses to a loud acoustic probe
Lawrence et al. (2004)	12 medicated patients with BP I with no episodes for 6 months, 9 patients with MDD, 11 healthy control participants.	All BRMS scores ≤ 7 BDI scores: MDD > BP > control	Viewed happy, sad, fearful, and neutral faces for 2 seconds each, with intensities	fMRI (1.5T)

90 JOHNSON, FULFORD, AND EISNER

Study	Sample	Measures	Task	Method
	Groups matched on age and gender. Excluded: individuals who were left handed or had a history of head injury, substance abuse, and comorbidity.		manipulated to 50% or 100% of a prototypical face; identified the gender of the face	
Yurgelun-Todd et al. (2000)	14 patients with BP affective disorder with no comorbid Axis I condition, 10 control participants with no Axis I condition. Diagnosed by SCID. Excluded: individuals who were left handed or had a history of organic brain disorder, head injury, or current substance abuse.	YMRS scores from 2 to 29 Ham-D scores from 4 to 24	Silently identify the facial expression shown in a set of happy and fearful faces	fMRI (1.5 T)
Chang et al. (2004)	12 children (ages 9–18) with BP I and one biological parent with BP I or BP II, 10 healthy control participants with no psychiatric diagnosis and no parent with a psychiatric diagnosis. Children diagnosed by St. Louis K-SADS and SADS–CPL; parents diagnosed by SCID.	YMRS and CDI	Negative and positive picture stimuli and a visuospatial working memory task	fMRI
Depue et al. (1985)	15 medicated students with cyclothymia, 7 control students with no history of psychiatric disorder. Diagnosed by SADS. Excluded: individuals with neurological diagnoses or drug abuse, individuals on medication related to cortisol	Varied; measured with the BDI	Challenging math test	Measured cortisol at baseline, after the challenge test, and 3 hours after challenge

(continues)

TABLE 3.2

Laboratory and Neuroimaging Studies That Have Examined Responses to Negative Stimuli   (Continued)

Study	Participants	Mood State Assessments	Stimulus Presented	Emotional Response Components Measured
Malhi, Lagopoulos, Sachdev, et al. (2004)	10 medicated outpatients with current hypomania and no comorbid Axis I or II condition, 10 control participants with no personal or family psychiatric history. Diagnosed by SCID. All right-handed females.	*M* YMRS BP = 24.3 *M* YMRS control = 0.9. No group differences on Fawcett–Clarke Pleasure Scale, MADRS, BDI, or State–Trait Anxiety Inventory	Patients viewed photos for 9 seconds that were relatively neutral (e.g., picture of woman opening letter) but with negative (e.g., "She failed her exams"), positive, and neutral captions; rated positivity and negativity of photos	fMRI (1.5T scanner)
Malhi, Lagopoulos, Ward, et al. (2004)	10 participants with BP, current major depression, and no comorbid Axis I or II disorder; 10 age-matched control participants with no personal or family psychiatric Axis I history. Diagnosed by SCID. All right-handed females.	Patients with BP higher than controls on the BDI, Ham-D, MADRS, YMRS, and lower on Fawcett–Clarke Pleasure Scale	Patients viewed photos for 9 seconds that were relatively neutral (e.g., picture of woman opening letter) but with negative (e.g., "She failed her exams"), positive, and neutral captions	fMRI (1.5T)
Lennox et al. (2004)	10 inpatients with current mania, 12 age-matched control participants with no personal or family history of mental illness. Diagnosed by standardized clinical interview. Matched on facial recognition Memory.		Pictures of faces in four intensities ranging from 0% to 125% of sadness and happiness; participants rated how happy or how sad faces were.	Event-related fMRI (3T)

Note. BP I = bipolar disorder I; SCID = Structured Clinical Interview for *DSM–IV*; BRMS = Bech-Rafaelsen Mania Scale; Ham-D = Hamilton Rating Scale for Depression; HPS = Hypomanic Personality Scale; ASRM = Altman Self-Rating Mania Scale; BDI = Beck Depression Inventory; MDD = major depressive disorder; fMRI = functional magnetic resonance imaging; YMRS = Young Mania Rating Scale; CDI = Children's Depression Inventory; St. Louis K-SADS = St. Louis Kiddie Schedule for Affective Disorders and Schizophrenia; SADS–CPL = Schedule for Affective Disorders and Schizophrenia for School-Age Children—Present and Lifetime Version); SADS = Schedule for Affective Disorders and Schizophrenia; MADRS = Montgomery Asberg Depression Rating Scale.

by the issue that emotions are defined as multichannel experiences, encompassing changes in subjective affect, psychophysiological responses, cognitive patterns, and corresponding brain regions. It is unfortunate that most researchers have not studied these channels within the same study; instead, they have examined each channel separately.

We begin by describing studies of emotional reactivity among asymptomatic participants at risk for bipolar disorder and those with bipolar disorder. We then describe findings for participants who were symptomatic at the time of testing.

Despite strong theoretical evidence, most psychological studies that have examined reactivity to negatively valenced stimuli have failed to obtain evidence for emotional reactivity within people diagnosed with bipolar disorder or those vulnerable to mania. That is, among studies of participants with bipolar disorder compared with control participants, groups did not differ in self-reported affect in response to interpersonal criticism (Cuellar et al., 2008) or in self-reported affect in response to failure feedback (Ruggero & Johnson, 2006). Among studies that have compared high-risk participants with low-risk participants, no group differences have been found in subjective affect responses to negative stimuli (Gruber et al., 2008; Stern & Berrenberg, 1979; Sutton & Johnson, 2002). Studies of other channels have not been particularly promising either: High- and low-risk participants have not differed in their behavioral (Gruber et al., 2008), physiological (Sutton & Johnson, 2002), or cognitive (Stern & Berrenberg, 1979) responses to negative stimuli.

Like the behavioral studies, neurobiological studies that have used standardized negative stimuli have not yielded consistent support for emotional reactivity as a facet of bipolar disorder. Although the studies described earlier that have examined brain activity outside of the context of standardized stimuli support the involvement of key brain pathways involved in emotion, findings regarding responses to specific stimuli have been inconsistent. Only one study found group differences in cortical or amygdala activation between people with and without bipolar disorder in response to negatively valenced stimuli, whereas another found a difference only among females with and without bipolar disorder (Lawrence et al., 2004; Yurgelon-Todd et al., 2000). This inconsistency extends to pediatric patients with bipolar disorder, a population for which findings suggest robust activation of emotion circuitry in response not only to negative pictures but also to cognitive (non-emotion-relevant) tasks (Chang et al., 2004). Hence, neuroimaging studies do not provide consistent findings of greater responses to negatively valenced stimuli among people with bipolar disorder as compared with the general population.

Given the lack of evidence for emotional reactivity as a generalized facet of bipolar disorder, one might wonder whether the phenomenon can be observed among only certain people with the disorder. For example, two studies have examined whether history of depression moderates responsivity to negative emotional stimuli. Neither study found support for this idea (Cuellar, 2005; Ruggero & Johnson, 2006).

Several studies, however, have suggested that current symptoms might moderate the extent of emotional reactivity observed among persons with bipolar disorder. Early self-report data suggested that reactivity to negative stimuli might increase during periods of depressive symptoms; that is, persons with bipolar disorder described themselves as overly responsive to cues of threat and punishment on the Behavioral Inhibition Scale (Carver & White, 1994) but only when they were experiencing depression (B. Meyer et al., 2001).

Although most studies have excluded participants with current symptoms, two laboratory studies of responses to standardized stimuli have included participants who were experiencing at least subsyndromal symptoms of depression (Depue, Kleiman, Davis, Hutchinson, & Krauss, 1985; Ruggero & Johnson, 2006). Both studies found evidence of greater reactivity; that is, one study found that persons with cyclothymia demonstrated prolonged elevation of cortisol 3 hours after a challenging math test (Depue et al., 1985). The other study found that persons with bipolar disorder demonstrated worse performance on a cognitive task after receiving failure feedback on a difficult anagram task than did those with no bipolar disorder. Both studies, then, found that people with bipolar spectrum disorder demonstrated elevated responses to failure.

Given that these studies differed from the studies with null results in that they recruited mildly symptomatic participants, it is possible that it will be easier to document reactivity to negative stimuli among a symptomatic sample. Consistent with this idea, people experiencing episodes of depression do show greater cortical activation compared with healthy control participants in response to negative stimuli (Lennox, Jacob, Calder, Lupson, & Bullmore, 2004; Malhi, Lagopoulos, Sachdev, et al., 2004; Malhi, Lagopoulos, Ward, et al., 2004). Although the evidence is congruent with state-dependent shifts in reactivity, we cannot identify a study that tracked changes in emotional reactivity as participants developed depressive symptoms. This would be a key goal for future research.

It is also important to consider the cross-study differences in tasks used. Almost all (for an exception, see Cuellar et al., 2008) of the emotional reactivity studies that have obtained null results asked participants only to passively view stimuli such as film clips or facial expressions, whereas studies that have documented emotional reactivity have used personal failure feedback. Hence, it will be important for future research to elucidate the role of symptoms and stimulus type on negative emotional reactivity within bipolar disorder. Given that research has documented excessive emotional reactivity in this population, a key goal would be to examine how this reactivity, when present, predicts the course of disorder.

OVERALL SUMMARY OF THE STATE OF THE SEARCH FOR AN ENDOPHENOTYPE

At the current time, it would be premature to state that an endophenotype for bipolar disorder has been discovered. Research on vulnerability characteristics is at a very early stage, and there are substantial gaps in each line of research. Very few studies have examined predictors of onset of the disorder, such that even the word *vulnerability* seems premature to use within psychological models of bipolar disorder. Even in studies of already-diagnosed participants there has been very little longitudinal research. For example, we can identify no published studies that have used emotion research paradigms to study the course of bipolar disorder, and only a few prospective studies relevant to reward responsivity. Furthermore, much of the research is reliant on self-report measures and, as is evidenced in studies of emotionality, some of the findings may not generalize once more rigorous experimental designs are used. There is a fundamental need for experimental laboratory research to provide more precise definitions of behavioral deficits that have begun to emerge from research that uses self-report scales.

Setting aside the methodological gaps, it is worth noting that findings are not entirely consistent at the current time, and even when findings are consistent, effect sizes tend to be small. One way of understanding such small effects is to bear in mind that many psychological characteristics may shift with mood state. Much of the research on bipolar disorder has also failed to control for subsyndromal symptoms of either depression or mania, and evidence suggests that even mild symptoms may shift the nature of cognitive processes, reward sensitivity, and emotionality (Johnson, Gruber, & Eisner, 2007). Studies are needed that examine how these potential vulnerability characteristics fluctuate with symptom state, and even with minor shifts in mood states. Similarly, treatments would be expected to influence emotionality and reward sensitivity but are rarely controlled for in analyses.

Beyond these potentially important confounds, the polygenic nature of bipolar disorder might be expected to result in a host of psychological characteristics involved in risk for the disorder, with each contributing only one small increment in vulnerability. Hence, there is a need for research that considers how different vulnerabilities interact to produce symptoms of disorder.

In considering the idea of multiple vulnerabilities, it may be helpful to consider the implications of comorbidity within bipolar disorder. To date, comorbid conditions have been largely ignored in studies of emotional reactivity and reward responsivity, with the exception of research on impulsivity (Swann et al., 2004). Without such research, it is difficult to determine whether traits such as emotional reactivity and reward sensitivity should be conceptualized as part of a shared vulnerability toward a range of syndromes or are better conceptualized as uniquely related to bipolar disorder.

Initial research suggests that emotional reactivity and reward responsivity are promising areas for study. With these early findings, we hope that researchers will begin to provide more well-controlled, longitudinal, and integrative studies of these processes.

CLINICAL IMPLICATIONS

The history of research on bipolar disorder has shaped the available psychosocial treatments in some unusual ways. As noted earlier, psychological research on bipolar disorder seemed to halt with the reliance on lithium and the recognition of the genetic basis of disorder. With this shift, few researchers focused on the development of psychosocial treatments (for an exception, see Cochran, 1984). In 1988, a National Institute of Mental Health consensus panel recognized the need for basic research on the psychosocial triggers of mania as well as the need for adjunctive psychosocial treatments to supplement pharmacotherapy (Prien & Potter, 1990). In response to this call for action, the National Institute of Mental Health began to fund psychosocial treatments. At the time these trials began, psychosocial studies had established only two factors—expressed emotion (Miklowitz, Goldstein, Nuechterlein, Snyder, & Mintz, 1988) and life events (see Johnson & Roberts, 1995, for a review)—as well-replicated predictors of the course of bipolar disorder. No prospective studies had been conducted to examine these variables as specific predictors of mania; thus, little was known about the triggers of mania. In the absence of much research on the psychosocial triggers of mania, clinical researchers began to test whether psychosocial treatments that were effective with other disorders could be applied to bipolar disorder. For example, cognitive therapy for depression was modified for bipolar disorder (Newman, Leahy, Beck, Reilly-Harrington, & Gyulai, 2002). Interpersonal psychotherapy for depression was modified to address schedule disruptions within bipolar disorder (Frank et al., 1994), family-focused therapy for schizophrenia was modified to address the expressed emotion difficulties associated with bipolar disorder (Miklowitz et al., 2004), and the McMaster family therapy model was adapted for concerns relevant to bipolar disorder (Miller, Solomon, Ryan, & Keitner, 2004). Hence, psychosocial treatments were borrowed from other disorders. It is fortunate that the clinical researchers involved in those trials had a keen understanding of the nature of bipolar disorder and developed many innovations to address its unique facets.

Overall, psychosocial treatments have been extremely helpful as adjuncts to pharmacological treatment of bipolar disorder. Psychosocial treatments clearly enhance treatment adherence and reduce hospitalization rates (Colom et al., 2004; Miklowitz, George, Richards, Simoneau, & Suddath, 2003; Rea et al., 2003). The importance of these targets notwithstanding, the first wave of trial results suggests that it may be easier to address depressive than manic symptoms within bipolar disorder (Scott, 2006). For example, cognitive therapy for bipolar disorder has not been found to be efficacious for persons with recurrent episodes of disorder (Scott et al., 2006), and it has been found to have limited effects over longer term follow-up periods (Lam, Hayward, Watkins, Wright, & Sham, 2005). Interpersonal psychotherapy for bipolar disorder has worked within acute periods but has not been found to improve outcomes when offered as a maintenance treatment (Frank et al., 2005). McMaster family therapy has not achieved significant success (Miller et al., 2004). whereas family-focused therapy has had large effects on depression and has been found to influence manic symptoms among adolescents (Miklowitz et al., 2004), but has had little influence on manic symptoms among adults (Miklowitz et al., 2003). Despite some positive and encouraging results regarding depression, treatment adherence, and hospitalization rates, the first wave of psychosocial treatment trials suggests there are major challenges in addressing manic symptoms.

It is our hope that the gains in basic research on psychosocial triggers over the past 15 years will enhance clinical research. For example, knowledge of the great vulnerability to sleep deprivation in people with bipolar disorder has led to some promising case reports focused on regulating sleep duration for people with bipolar disorder (Wehr et al., 1998). The ongoing support for family factors as critical risk factors for bipolar disorder has led to new ideas about how to address family concerns within this disorder (Fristad, Gavazzi, & Mackinaw-Koons, 2003; Miklowitz et al., 2004.

Our own work currently draws on a model of reward sensitivity and goal dysregulation (Johnson, 2005) to develop a mania prevention intervention (Johnson & Fulford, in press). In brief, the treatment uses intervention strategies based on motivational interviewing and cognitive–behavioral approaches to address several facets of goal dysregulation within bipolar disorder, including ambitious goal setting, reactivity to successes, shifts in cognition and confidence after successes, and goal pacing. Although our current findings are limited to open-trial data, clients to date report high levels of satisfaction with the intervention. Despite the preliminary nature of our research on this front, we believe it provides one example of how research elucidating risk variables for bipolar disorder could potentially inform clinical treatments.

CONCLUSIONS

Several models have been developed of psychological traits related to bipolar disorder. In this chapter, we have focused on evidence for reward sensitivity and negative emotional reactivity. Theories of excessive reward sensitivity in bipolar disorder are supported by evidence from self-report measures. Moreover, life events and reports of enhanced goal engagement predict increases in mania. Laboratory studies of responses to success have yielded less consistent findings; group differences in psychophysiological reactivity and cognitive shifts in confidence have been documented, but group differences in subjective affect and neurobiological responses to positive stimuli have not been consistently documented. Hence, further research is needed to clarify the processes involved in reward sensitivity.

Theory regarding negative emotional reactivity draws on the clear evidence that brain regions modulating emotion reactivity and regulation are involved in bipolar disorder. Despite strong theory, researchers studying persons who are asymptomatic have not documented deficits in these regions in response to standardized stimuli; neither have they identified differences in affective or behavioral responses to negative stimuli associated with bipolar disorder. Two studies that used failure feedback have found evidence of cognitive and cortisol reactivity among persons with mild bipolar depressive symptoms. Key goals will be to conduct research with more powerful emotion-relevant stimuli and with greater attention to state-dependent effects of mood.

Overall, there is a pressing need for more experimental psychopathology research on bipolar disorder. Identifying behavioral risk mechanisms is a key step in identifying endophenotypes of the disorder. In endophenotype research, one assumes not that genes directly translate to symptoms but that genes serve as diatheses to symptom expression in the context of environmental and biological triggering events. Much more research is needed to define the nature of triggering events as well as the unique responses to these triggering events. Such research provides the foundation for improved understanding of the connection between neurobiology and behavior in bipolar disorder.

REFERENCES

Akiskal, H. S., Hantouche, E. G., Bourgeois, M. L., Azorin, J. M., Sechter, D., Allilaire, J. F., et al. (2001). Toward a refined phenomenology of mania: Combining clinician-assessment and self-report in the French EPIMAN study. *Journal of Affective Disorders, 67*, 89–96.

Alloy, L. B., Abramson, L. Y., Walshaw, P. D., Cogswell, A., Grandin, L. D., Hughes, M. E., et al. (2008). Behavioral approach system and behavioral inhibition system sensitivities and bipolar spectrum disorders: Prospective prediction of bipolar mood episodes. *Bipolar Disorders, 10*, 310–322.

American Psychiatric Association. (2000). *Diagnostic and statistical manual of mental disorders* (4th ed., text revision). Washington, DC: Author.

Angst, J., Adolfsson, R., Benazzi, F., Gamma, A., Hantouche, E., Meyer, T., et al. (2005). The HCL-32: Towards a self-assessment took for hypomanic symptoms in outpatients. *Journal of Affective Disorders, 88*, 217–233.

Badner, J. A., & Gershon, E. S. (2002) Meta-analysis of whole-genome linkage scans of bipolar disorder and schizophrenia. *Molecular Psychiatry, 7*, 405–411.

Bagby, R. M., Young, L. T., Schuller, D. R., Bindseil, K. D., Cooke, R. G., Dickens, S. E., et al. (1996). Bipolar disorder, unipolar depression and the five-factor model of personality. *Journal of Affective Disorders, 41*, 25–32.

Barbini, B., Colombu, C., Benedetti, F., Camori, E., Bellodi, L., & Smeraldi, E. (1998). The unipolar–bipolar dichotomy and the response to sleep deprivation. *Psychiatry Research, 79*, 43–50.

Bentall, R. P., & Thompson, M. (1990). Emotional Stroop performance and the manic defence. *British Journal of Clinical Psychology, 29*, 235–237.

Berns, G. S., Martin, M., & Proper, S. M. (2002). Limbic hyperreactivity in bipolar II disorder. *American Journal of Psychiatry, 159*, 304–306.

Berrettini, W. H. (2003). Evidence for shared susceptibility in bipolar disorder and schizophrenia. *American Journal of Medical Genetics, 123C*, 59–64.

Berrettini, W. H., Ferraro, T. N., Goldin, L. R., Detera-Wadleigh, S. D., Choi, H., Muniec, D., et al. (1997). A linkage study of bipolar illness. *Archives of General Psychiatry, 54*, 27–35.

Cannon, T. D., & Keller, M. C. (2006). Endophenotypes in the genetic analyses of mental disorders. *Annual Review of Clinical Psychology, 2*, 267–290.

Cardno, A. G., Rijsdijk, F. V., Sham, P. C., Murray, R. M., & McGuffin, P. (2002). A twin study of genetic relationships between psychotic symptoms. *American Journal of Psychiatry, 159*, 539–545.

Carver, C. S., & Johnson, S. L. (in press). Tendencies toward mania and tendencies toward depression have distinct motivational, affective, and cognitive correlates. *Cognitive Therapy and Research*.

Carver, C. S., & White, T. L. (1994). Behavioral inhibition, behavioral activation, and affective responses to impending reward and punishment: The BIS/BAS scales. *Journal of Personality and Social Psychology, 67*, 319–333.

Cassidy, F., Ahearn, E. P., & Carroll, B. J. (2001). Substance abuse in bipolar disorder. *Bipolar Disorders, 3*, 181–188.

Chang, K., Adleman, N. E., Dienes, K., Simeonova, D. J., Menon, V., & Reiss, A. (2004). Anomalous prefrontal-subcortical activation in familial pediatric bipolar disorder: A functional magnetic resonance imaging investigation. *Archives of General Psychiatry, 61*, 781–792.

Chen, B. K., Sassi, R., Axelson, D., Hatch, J. P., Sanches, M., Nicoletti, M., et al. (2004). Cross-sectional study of abnormal amygdala development in adolescents and young adults with bipolar disorder. *Biological Psychiatry, 56*, 399–405.

Clement, S., Singh, S. P., & Burns, T. (2003). Status of bipolar disorder research: Bibliometric study. *British Journal of Psychiatry, 182*, 148–152.

Cochran, S. D. (1984). Preventing medical noncompliance in the outpatient treatment of bipolar affective disorders. *Journal of Consulting and Clinical Psychology, 52*, 873–878.

Colom, F., Vieta, E., Sanchez-Moreno, J., Martinez-Aran, A., Torrent, C., Reinares, M., et al. (2004). Psychoeducation in bipolar patients with comorbid personality disorders. *Bipolar Disorders, 6,* 294–298.

Cuellar, A. (2005). *Responses to interpersonal threat in bipolar disorder.* Unpublished doctoral dissertation, University of Miami.

Cuellar, A., Johnson, S. L., & Ruggero, C. (2008). *Affective dysregulation as a mediator of reactions to criticism in bipolar disorder.* Manuscript submitted for publication.

Depue, R. A., Collins, P. F., & Luciana, M. (1996). A model of neurobiology— environment interaction in developmental psychopathology. In M. F. Lenzenweger & J. J. Haugaard (Eds.), *Frontiers of developmental psychopathology* (pp. 44–77). New York: Oxford University Press.

Depue, R. A., Kleiman, R. M., Davis, P., Hutchinson, M., & Krauss, S. P. (1985). The behavioral high-risk paradigm and bipolar affective disorder: VIII. Serum free cortisol in nonpatient cyclothymic subjects selected by the General Behavior Inventory. *American Journal of Psychiatry, 142,* 175–181.

Detera-Wadleigh, S. D., Badner, J. A., Berrettini, W. H., Yoshikawa, T., Goldin, L. R., Turner, G., et al. (1999). A high-density genome scan detects evidence for a bipolar-disorder susceptibility locus on 13q32 and other potential loci on 1q32 and 18p11.2. *Genetics, 96,* 5604–5609.

Ebert, D., & Berger, M. (1998). Neurobiological similarities in antidepressant sleep deprivation and psychostimulant use: A psychostimulant theory of antidepressant sleep deprivation. *Psychopharmacology, 140,* 1–10.

Eckblad, M., & Chapman, L. J. (1986). Development and validation of a scale for hypomanic personality. *Journal of Abnormal Psychology, 95,* 214–222.

Ekman, P. (1994). Moods, emotions and traits. In P. Ekman & R. Davidson (Eds.), *The nature of basic emotions* (pp. 56–67). New York: Oxford University Press.

Ellicott, A., Hammen, C., Gitlin, M., & Brown, G. (1990). Life events and the course of bipolar disorder. *American Journal of Psychiatry, 147,* 1194–1198.

Frank, E., Kupfer, D. J., Ehlers, C. L., Monk, T. H., Corners, C., Carter, S., & Frankel, D. (1994). Interpersonal and social rhythm therapy for bipolar disorder: Integrating interpersonal and behavioral approaches. *Behavior Therapy, 17,* 143–149.

Frank, E., Kupfer, D. J., Thase, M. E., Mallinger, A. G., Swartz, H. A., Eagiolini, A. M., et al. (2005). Two-year outcomes for interpersonal and social rhythm therapy in individuals with bipolar I disorder. *Archives of General Psychiatry, 62,* 996–1004.

French, C. C., Richards, A., & Scholfield, E. J. (1996). Hypomania, anxiety and the emotional Stroop. *British Journal of Clinical Psychology, 35,* 617–626.

Fristad, M. A., Gavazzi, S. M., & Mackinaw-Koons, B. (2003). Family psychoeducation: An adjunctive intervention for children with bipolar disorder. *Biological Psychiatry, 53,* 1000–1008.

Goldberg, J. (2004). The changing landscape of psychopharmacology. In S. L. Johnson & R. L. Leahy (Eds.), *Psychological treatment of bipolar disorder* (pp. 109–138). New York: Guilford Press.

Goodwin, F. K., & Jamison, K. R. (1990). *Manic-depressive illness*. New York: Oxford University Press.

Gruber, J., & Johnson, S. L. (in press). Positive emotional traits and ambitious goals among people at risk for bipolar disorder: The need for specificity. *International Journal of Cognitive Therapy*.

Gruber, J. L., Johnson, S. L., Oveis, C., & Keltner, D. (2008). Risk for mania and positive emotional responding: Too much of a good thing? *Emotion, 8*(1), 23–33.

Harmon-Jones, E., Abramson, L. Y., Nusslock, R., Sigelman, J. D., Urosevic, S., Turonie, L. D., et al. (2008). Effect of bipolar disorder on left frontal cortical responses to goals differing in valence and task difficulty. *Biological Psychiatry, 63*, 693–698.

Harmon-Jones, E., Abramson, L. Y., Sigelman, J., Bohlig, A., Hogan, M. E., & Harmon-Jones, C. (2002). Proneness to hypomania/mania symptoms or depression symptoms and asymmetrical frontal cortical responses to an anger-evoking event. *Journal of Personality and Social Psychology, 82*, 610–618.

Hasler, G., Drevets, W. C., Gould, T. D., Gottesman, I. I., & Manji, H. K. (2006). Toward constructing an endophenotype strategy for bipolar disorders. *Biological Psychiatry, 60*, 93–105.

Hayden, E. P., Bodkins, M., Brenner, C., Shekhar, A., Nurnberger, J. I. Jr., O'Donnell, B., et al. (2008). A multimethod investigation of the behavioral activation system in bipolar disorder. *Journal of Abnormal Psychology, 117*, 164–170.

Hestenes, D. (1992). A neural network theory of manic-depressive illness. In D. S. Levine & S. J. Leven (Eds.), *Motivation, emotion, and goal direction in neural networks* (pp. 209–257). Hillsdale, NJ: Erlbaum.

Hofmann, B. U., & Meyer, T. D. (2006). Mood fluctuations in people putatively at risk for bipolar disorders. *British Journal of Clinical Psychology, 45*, 105–110.

Holzwarth, K., & Meyer, T. D. (2006). The dysregulation of the "Behavioral Activation System": An independent dimension. *Personality and Individual Differences, 41*, 319–328.

Jacobson, D., & Silverstone, T. (1986). Dextroamphetamine-induced arousal in human subjects as a model of mania. *Psychological Medicine, 16*, 323–329.

Joffe, R. T., Horvath, Z., & Tarvydas, I. (1986). Bipolar affective disorder and thalassemia minor. *American Journal of Psychiatry, 143*, 933.

Johnson, S. L. (2005). Life events in bipolar disorder: Towards more specific models. *Clinical Psychology Review, 25*, 1008–1027.

Johnson, S. L., & Carver, C. (2006). Extreme goal setting and vulnerability to mania among undiagnosed young adults. *Cognitive Therapy and Research, 30*, 377–395.

Johnson, S. L., Cuellar, A. K., Ruggero, C., Winett-Perlman, C., Goodnick, P., White, R., et al. (2008). Life events as predictors of mania and depression in bipolar I disorder. *Journal of Abnormal Psychology, 117*, 268–277.

Johnson, S. L., & Fulford, D. (in press). Preventing mania: A preliminary examination of the GOALS program. *Behavior Therapy*.

Johnson, S. L., Gruber, J. L., & Eisner, L. R. (2007). Emotion and bipolar disorder. In J. Rottenberg & S. L. Johnson (Eds.), *Emotion and psychopathology: Bridging affective and clinical science* (pp. 123–150). Washington, DC: American Psychological Association.

Johnson, S. L., & Roberts, J. E. (1995). Life events and bipolar disorder: Implications from biological theories. *Psychological Bulletin, 117,* 434–449.

Johnson, S. L., Ruggero, C. J., & Carver, C. S. (2005). Cognitive, behavioral, and affective responses to reward: Links with hypomanic symptoms. *Journal of Social and Clinical Psychology, 24,* 894–906.

Johnson, S. L., Sandrow, D., Meyer, B., Winters, R., Miller, I., Keitner, G., & Solomon, D. (2000). Increases in manic symptoms after life events involving goal-attainment. *Journal of Abnormal Psychology, 109,* 721–727.

Johnson, S. L., Turner, R. J., & Iwata, N. (2003). BIS/BAS levels and psychiatric disorder: An epidemiological study. *Journal of Psychopathology and Behavioral Assessment, 25,* 25–36.

Jones, S. H., Tai, S., Evershed, K., Knowles, R., & Bentall, R. (2006). Early detection of bipolar disorder: A pilot familial high-risk study of parents with bipolar disorder and their adolescent children. *Bipolar Disorders, 8,* 362–372.

Karkowski, L. M., & Kendler, K. S. (1997). An examination of the genetic relationship between bipolar and unipolar illness in an epidemiological sample. *Psychiatric Genetics, 7,* 159–163.

Kessler, R. C., Chiu, W. T., Demler, O., & Walters, E. E. (2005). Prevalence, severity, and comorbidity of 12-month *DSM–IV* disorders in the National Comorbidity Survey replication. *Archives of General Psychiatry, 62,* 617–627.

Kessler, R. C., Rubinow, D. R., Holmes, C., Abelson, J. M., & Zhao, S. (1997). The epidemiology of *DSM–III–R* bipolar I disorder in a general population survey. *Psychological Medicine, 27,* 1079–1089.

Kim, E. Y., & Miklowitz, D. J. (2004). Expressed emotion as a predictor of outcome among bipolar patients undergoing family therapy. *Journal of Affective Disorders, 82,* 343–352.

Kluger, A. N., & DeNisi, A. (1996). The effects of feedback interventions on performance: A historical review, a meta-analysis, and a preliminary feedback intervention theory. *Psychological Bulletin, 119,* 254–284.

Knutson, B., Adams, C. M., Fong, G. W., & Hommer, D. (2001). Anticipation of increasing monetary reward selectively recruits nucleus accumbens. *Journal of Neuroscience, 21,* 159.

Kruger, S., Seminowicz, S., Goldapple, K., Kennedy, S. H., & Mayberg, H. S. (2003). State and trait influences on mood regulation in bipolar disorder: Blood flow differences with an acute mood challenge. *Biological Psychiatry, 54,* 1274–1283.

Kwapil, T. R., Miller, M. B., Zinser, M. C., Chapman, L. C., Chapman, J., & Eckblad, M. (2000). A longitudinal study of high scorers on the Hypomanic Personality Scale. *Journal of Abnormal Psychology, 109,* 222–226.

Lam, D. H., Hayward, P., Watkins, E. R., Wright, K., & Sham, P. (2005). Relapse prevention in patients with bipolar disorder: Cognitive therapy outcome after two years. *American Journal of Psychiatry, 162,* 324–329.

Lawrence, N. S., Williams, A. M., Surguladze, S., Giampietro, V., Brammer, M. J., Andrew, C., et al. (2004). Subcortical and ventral prefrontal cortical neural responses to facial expressions distinguish patients with bipolar disorder and major depression. *Biological Psychiatry, 55,* 578–587.

Lennox, B. R., Jacob, R., Calder, A. J., Lupson, V., & Bullmore, E. T. (2004). Behavioural and neurocognitive responses to sad facial affect are attenuated in patients with mania. *Psychological Medicine, 34,* 795–802.

Little, B. R. (1989). Personal projects analysis: Trivial pursuits, magnificent obsessions and the search for coherence. In D. Buss & N. Cantor (Eds.), *Personality psychology: Recent trends and emerging directions* (pp. 15–31). New York: Springer-Verlag.

Lovejoy, M. C., & Steuerwald, B. L. (1995). Subsyndromal unipolar and bipolar disorders: Comparisons on positive and negative affect. *Journal of Abnormal Psychology, 104,* 381–384.

Lozano, B. E., & Johnson, S. L. (2001). Can personality traits predict increases in manic and depressive symptoms? *Journal of Affective Disorders, 63,* 103–111.

Malhi, G. S., Lagopoulos, J., Sachdev, P., Mitchell, P. B., Ivanovski, B., & Parker, G. B. (2004). Cognitive generation of affect in hypomania: An fMRI study. *Bipolar Disorders, 6,* 271–285.

Malhi, G. S., Lagopoulos, J., Ward, P. B., Kumari, V., Mitchell, P. B., Parker, G. B., et al. (2004). Cognitive generation of affect in bipolar depression: An fMRI study. *European Journal of Neuroscience, 19,* 741–745.

Martinez-Aran, A., Vieta, E., Colom, F., Reinares, M., Benabarre, A., Gasto, C., et al. (2000). Cognitive dysfunctions in bipolar disorder: Evidence of neuropsychological disturbances. *Psychotherapy and Psychosomatics, 69,* 2–18.

McElroy, S. L., Altshuler, L. L., Suppes, T., Keck, P. E. Jr., Frye, M. A., & Denicoff, K. D. (2001). Axis I psychiatric comorbidity and its relationship to historical illness variables in 288 patients with bipolar disorder. *American Journal of Psychiatry, 158,* 420–426.

Meyer, B., Beevers, C. G., & Johnson, S. L. (2004). Goal appraisals and vulnerability to bipolar disorder: A personal projects analysis. *Cognitive Therapy and Research, 28,* 173–182.

Meyer, B., Johnson, S. L., & Carver, C. S. (1999). Exploring behavioral activation and inhibition sensitivities among college students at risk for bipolar spectrum symptomatology. *Journal of Psychopathology and Behavioral Assessment, 21,* 275–292.

Meyer, B., Johnson, S. L., & Winters, R. (2001). Responsiveness to threat and incentive in bipolar disorder: Relations of the BIS/BAS scales with symptoms. *Journal of Psychopathology and Behavioral Assessment, 23,* 133–143.

Meyer, T. D., & Hofmann, B. U. (2005). Assessing the dysregulation of the behavioral activation system: The hypomanic personality scale and the BIS-BAS scales. *Journal of Personality Assessment, 85,* 318–324.

Meyer, T. D., & Krumm-Merabet, C. (2003). Academic performance and expectations for the future in relation to a vulnerability marker for bipolar disorders: The hypomanic temperament. *Personality and Individual Differences, 35,* 785–796.

Miklowitz, D. J., George, E. L., Axelson, D. A., Kim, E. Y., Birmaherm, B., Schneck, C., et al. (2004). Family-focused treatment for adolescents with bipolar disorder. *Journal of Affective Disorders, 82*(Suppl. 1), S113–S128.

Miklowitz, D. J., George, E. L., Richards, J. A., Simoneau, T. L., & Suddath, R. L. (2003). A randomized study of family-focused psychoeducation and pharmacotherapy in the outpatient management of bipolar disorder. *Archives of General Psychiatry, 60,* 904–912.

Miklowitz, D. J., Goldstein, M. J., Nuechterlein, K. H., Snyder, K. S., & Mintz, J. (1988). Family factors and the course of bipolar affective disorder. *Archives of General Psychiatry, 45,* 225–231.

Miller, I. W., Solomon, D. A., Ryan, C. E., & Keitner, G. I. (2004). Does adjunctive family therapy enhance recovery from bipolar I mood episodes? *Journal of Affective Disorders, 82,* 431–436.

Newman, C. F., Leahy, R. L., Beck, A. T., Reilly-Harrington, N. A., & Gyulai, L. (2002). *Bipolar disorder: A cognitive therapy approach.* Washington, DC: American Psychological Association.

Nusslock, R., Abramson, L. Y., Harmon-Jones, E., Alloy, L. B., & Hogan, M. E. (2007). A goal-striving life event and the onset of hypomanic and depressive episodes and symptoms: Perspective from the behavioral approach system (BAS) dysregulation theory. *Journal of Abnormal Psychology, 116,* 105–115.

Phillips, M. L., Drevets, W. C., Rauch, S. L., & Lane, R. (2003). Neurobiology of emotion perception II: Implications for major psychiatric disorders. *Biological Psychiatry, 54,* 515–528.

Post, R. M. (1992). Transduction of psychosocial stress into the neurobiology of recurrent affective disorder. *American Journal of Psychiatry, 149,* 999–1010.

Prien, R., & Potter, W. (1990). NIMH workshop report on the treatment of bipolar disorders. *Psychopharmacology Bulletin, 26,* 409–427

Rea, M. M., Tompson, M. C., Miklowitz, D. J., Goldstein, M. J., Hwang, S., & Mintz, J. (2003). Family-focused treatment versus individual treatment for bipolar disorder: Results of a randomized clinical trial. *Journal of Consulting and Clinical Psychology, 71,* 482–492.

Robertson, M. (1987, February 26). Molecular genetics of the mind. *Nature, 325,* 755.

Ruggero, C., & Johnson, S. L. (2006). Reactivity to a laboratory stressor among individuals with bipolar I disorder in full or partial remission. *Journal of Abnormal Psychology, 115,* 539–544.

Salavert, J., Caseras, X., Torrubia, R., Furest, S., Arranz, B., Duenas, R., et al. (2007). The functioning of the behavioral activation and inhibition systems in bipolar I euthymic patients and its influence in subsequent episodes over an eighteen-month period. *Personality and Individual Differences, 42,* 1323–1331.

Schwab, S. G., Hallmayer, J., Albus, M., Lerer, B., Hanses, C., Kanyas, K., et al. (1998). Further evidence for a susceptibility locus on chromosome 10p14-p11 in 72 families with schizophrenia by nonparametric linkage analysis. *American Journal of Medical Genetics, 81,* 302–307.

Scott, J. (2006). Psychotherapy for bipolar disorders—Efficacy and effectiveness. *Journal of Psychopharmacology, 20,* 46–50.

Scott, J., Paykel, E., Morriss, R., Bentall, R., Kinderman, P., Johnson, T., et al. (2006). Cognitive-behavioural therapy for severe and recurrent bipolar disorders: Randomised controlled trial. *British Journal of Psychiatry, 188,* 313–320.

Shifman, S., Bronstein, M., Sternfeld, M., Pisante, A., Weizman, A., Reznik, I., et al. (2004). COMT: A common susceptibility gene in bipolar disorder and schizophrenia. *American Journal of Medical Genetics, 128B,* 61–64.

Shih, R. A., Belmonte, P. L., & Zandi, P. P. (2004). A review of the evidence from family, twin and adoption studies for a genetic contribution to adult psychiatric disorders. *International Review of Psychiatry, 16,* 260–283.

Simon, N. M., Otto, M. W., Wisniewski, S. R., Fossey, M., Sagduyu, K., Frank, E., et al. (2004). Anxiety disorder comorbidity in bipolar disorder patients: Data from the first 500 participants in the Systematic Treatment Enhancement Program for Bipolar Disorder (STEP-BD). *American Journal of Psychiatry, 161,* 2222–2229.

Sklar, P. (2002). Linkage analysis in psychiatric disorders: The emerging picture. *Annual Review of Genomics and Human Genetics, 25,* 1–16.

Stern, G. S., & Berrenberg, J. L. (1979). Skill-set, success outcome, and mania as determinants of the illusion of control. *Journal of Research in Personality, 13,* 206–220.

Strakowski, S. M., Sax, K. W., Setters, M. J., & Keck, P. E. (1996). Enhanced response to repeated d-amphetamine challenge: Evidence for behavioral sensitization in humans. *Biological Psychiatry, 40,* 872–880.

Sutton, S. K., & Johnson, S. J. (2002). Hypomanic tendencies predict lower startle magnitudes during pleasant pictures. *Psychophysiology, 39*(Suppl.), S80.

Swann, A. C., Dougherty, D. M., Pazzaglia, P. J., Pham, M., & Moeller, F. G. (2004). Impulsivity: A link between bipolar disorder and substance abuse. *Bipolar Disorders, 6,* 204–212.

Swann, A. C., Janicak, P. L., Calabresec, J. R., Bowdend, C. L., Dilsaver, S. C., Morris, D. D., et al. (2001). Structure of mania: Depressive, irritable, and psychotic clusters with different retrospectively-assessed course patterns of illness in randomized clinical trial participants. *Journal of Affective Disorders, 67,* 123–132.

Thomas, J., & Bentall, R. P. (2002). Hypomanic traits and response styles to depression. *British Journal of Clinical Psychology, 41,* 309–313.

Wehr, T. A., Goodwin, F. K., Wirz-Justice, A., Breitmaier, J., & Craig, C. (1982). 48-hour sleep–wake cycles in manic-depressive illness: Naturalistic observations and sleep deprivation experiments. *Archives of General Psychiatry, 39,* 559–565.

Wehr, T. A., Turner, E. H., Shimada, J. M., Lowe, C. H., Barker, C., & Leibenluft, E. (1998). Treatment of a rapidly cycling bipolar patient by using extended bed rest and darkness to stabilize the timing and duration of sleep, *Biological Psychiatry*, *43*, 822–828.

Weissman, M. M., & Myers, J. K. (1978). Affective disorders in a US urban community: The use of Research Diagnostic Criteria in an epidemiological survey. *Archives of General Psychiatry, 35*, 1304–11.

Yan, L. J., Hammen, C., Cohen, A. N., Daley, S. E., & Henry, R. M. (2004). Expressed emotion versus relationship quality variables in the prediction of recurrence in bipolar patients. *Journal of Affective Disorders, 83*, 199–206.

Yurgelun-Todd, D. A., Gruber, S. A., Kanayama, G., Killgore, W. D., Baird, A. A., & Young, A. D. (2000). Functional magnetic resonance imaging during affect discrimination in bipolar affective disorder. *Bipolar Disorders, 2*, 237–248.

4

VULNERABILITY TO UNIPOLAR DEPRESSION: COGNITIVE–BEHAVIORAL MECHANISMS

LAUREN B. ALLOY, LYN Y. ABRAMSON, DAVID GRANT, AND RICHARD LIU

Depression is one of the most common forms of psychopathology in contemporary society (Kessler, 2002). It is often recurrent in nature (Judd, 1997); moreover, it is associated with significant impairment (Gotlib & Hammen, 2002; Greenberg, Kessler, Nells, Finkelstein, & Berndt, 1996; Roy, Mitchell, & Wilhelm, 2001; Sullivan, LaCroix, Russo, & Walker, 2001). Indeed, because of the confluence of several features associated with depression, including high lifetime prevalence, early age of onset, high chronicity, and great role impairment (Kessler, 2000), the World Health Organization Global Burden of Disease Study ranked it as the single most burdensome disease worldwide (Murray & Lopez, 1996).

A large body of research suggests that depression often occurs following stressful life events (for a review, see Monroe & Hadjiyannakis, 2002). However, individuals can vary widely in their responses to such events. Some individuals may develop severe or long-lasting depression, whereas others do not become depressed at all or may experience only mild dysphoria. Several factors have been proposed to explain such individual differences in response to life events. For example, the severity of a given negative life event, the amount of social support an individual receives in the face of a severe life event, and individual differences in one's biological constitution or psychological characteristics may all modulate reactivity to stressful events. From a cognitive perspective, the meaning or interpretation individuals give to the life events they experience influences whether they become depressed and whether they are vulnerable to recurrent, severe, or long-lasting episodes of depression. Two major cognitive theories of depression, *hopelessness theory* (Abramson, Metalsky, & Alloy, 1989; Alloy, Abramson, Metalsky, & Hartlage, 1988) and Beck's (1967, 1987) cognitive theory of depression reflect such *vulnerability–stress models*, in which variability in individual susceptibility to depression following stressful events is understood in terms of differences in cognitive patterns that affect how those events are interpreted. According to both theories, particular negative cognitive styles increase an individual's likelihood of developing episodes of depression after experiencing a negative life event—specifically, a cognitively mediated subtype of depression (Abramson & Alloy, 1990; Abramson et al., 1989). These theories propose that individuals who possess *depressogenic* cognitive styles are vulnerable to depression because they tend to generate interpretations of their experiences that have negative implications for themselves and their futures.

According to hopelessness theory (Abramson et al., 1989), people who exhibit a depressogenic inferential style are hypothesized to be vulnerable to developing episodes of depression, particularly a *hopelessness depression* (HD) subtype, when they are exposed to negative life events. This depressogenic inferential style is characterized by a tendency to attribute negative life events to stable (likely to persist over time) and global (likely to affect many areas of life) causes, to infer that negative consequences will follow from a current negative event, and to infer that the occurrence of a negative event in one's life means that one is fundamentally flawed or worthless. People who exhibit such an inferential style should be more likely to make negative inferences regarding the causes, consequences, and self-implications of any stressful event they experience, thereby increasing the likelihood that they will develop hopelessness, the proximal sufficient cause of the symptoms of hopelessness depression (for diagnostic criteria associated with HD, see Exhibit 4.1; for a graphical representation of the underlying theoretical model, see Figure 4.1).

In Beck's cognitive theory of depression (Beck, 1967, 1987; Beck, Rush, Shaw, & Emery, 1979), negative self-schemata involving themes of inadequacy, failure, loss, and worthlessness are hypothesized to contribute vulnerability to depression. These negative self-schemata are often represented as a set of dysfunctional attitudes, such as "If I fail partly, it is as bad as being a complete failure," or "I am nothing if a person I love doesn't love me." Researchers hypothesize that when people with such dysfunctional attitudes encounter negative life events, they develop negatively biased perceptions of their self (low self-esteem), world, and future (hopelessness), which then lead to depressive symptoms.

EXHIBIT 4.1
Diagnostic Criteria for Hopelessness Depression in the Temple–
Wisconsin Cognitive Vulnerability to Depression Project

A. Hopelessness must be present for at least 2 weeks for a definite diagnosis or at least 1 week for a probable diagnosis.
B. At least five of the following criteria symptoms must be present for at least 2 weeks, overlapping with each other on at least 12 of 14 days for a definite diagnosis, or at least four of the following symptoms must be present for at least 1 week, overlapping with each other on at least 6 out of 7 days for a probable diagnosis: sadness; retarded initiation of voluntary responses; suicidal ideation/acts; sleep disturbance—initial insomnia; lack of energy; self-blame, difficulty in concentration; psychomotor retardation; brooding/worrying; lowered self-esteem; dependency.
C. The onset of hopelessness must precede the onset of the criterial symptoms by at least 1 day and no more than 1 week.

Although hopelessness theory and Beck's theory differ in terms of some of their specifics, both hypothesize that cognitive vulnerability operates to increase risk for depression through its effects on processing or appraisals of personally relevant life experiences. Despite this similarity, however, studies have suggested that the negative attributional style component of cognitive vulnerability as defined by hopelessness theory and the dysfunctional attitude component of Beck's theory do represent distinct constructs (e.g., Gotlib, Lewinsohn, Seeley, Rohde, & Redner, 1993; Haeffel et al., 2003; Joiner & Rudd, 1996; Spangler, Simons, Monroe, & Thase, 1997).

A powerful strategy for testing these cognitive vulnerability hypotheses is the *behavioral high-risk design* (e.g., Alloy, Lipman, & Abramson, 1992; Depue et al., 1981). Like the genetic high-risk design, the behavioral high-risk design involves studying individuals hypothesized to be at high or low risk for developing a particular disorder but who do not currently have the disorder. In a behavioral high-risk design, however, individuals are selected on the basis of hypothesized psychological rather than genetic vulnerability or invulnerability to the disorder. For example, in testing the cognitive theories of depression, one would want to select nondepressed individuals who either have or do not have the hypothesized depressogenic cognitive styles. These groups of cognitively high- and low-risk individuals can then be compared with respect to their likelihood of having had past occurrences of depression (*retrospective design*) and their likelihood of experiencing depression in the future (*prospective design*). Recent studies that have used or approximated a behavioral high-risk design have provided substantial support for the cognitive theories of depression. For example, Alloy et al. (1992) used a retrospective behavioral high-risk design to test the attributional vulnerability hypothesis of the hopelessness theory. In this study, Alloy et al. examined the occurrence of major depressive disorder (MD) and HD during the previous

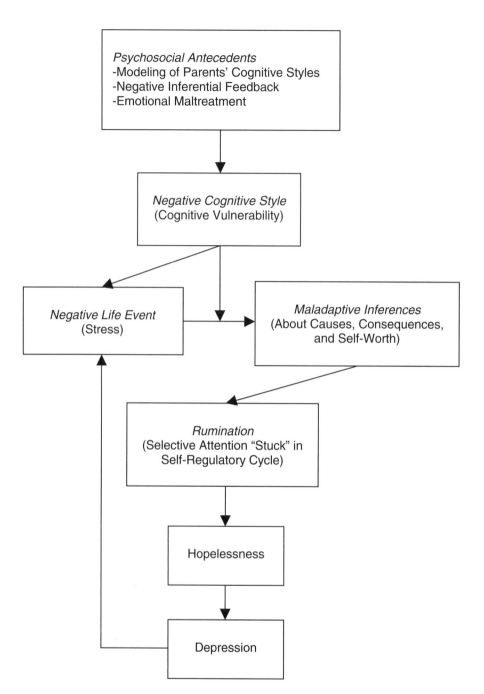

Figure 4.1. A cognitive vulnerability–stress model of hopelessness depression. Relations among the various components of the model are explained throughout the chapter.

2 years in currently nondepressed undergraduates who either did or did not exhibit attributional vulnerability for depression (indicated by an internal, stable, and global attributional style for negative events). Consistent with hopelessness theory, they found that attributionally vulnerable students were more likely to exhibit past MD and HD. In addition, vulnerable participants experienced more episodes, and experienced more severe episodes of these disorders, than attributionally invulnerable students. Furthermore, many prospective studies with children, adolescents, and adults have obtained considerable support for the cognitive vulnerability and vulnerability–stress hypotheses (for a review, see Alloy, Abramson, Whitehouse, et al., 2006).

These positive results stand in contrast to those found when typical *remitted depression designs*, which generally have found little support for the cognitive vulnerability hypotheses (e.g., Barnett & Gotlib, 1988; Persons & Miranda, 1992; Segal & Ingram, 1994), are used. In these studies, the cognitive styles of individuals who have recovered from depressive episodes are compared with the cognitive styles of individuals with no history of depression. However, there are several problems with using a remitted depression design to test cognitive vulnerability hypotheses (see Just, Abramson, & Alloy, 2001). For example, depressed individuals are a heterogeneous group, and the cognitive theories of depression seek to account for only a subgroup of depressed individuals (i.e., only those with a cognitively mediated subtype of depression). Given that only a subset of such previously depressed individuals are likely to have had a cognitively mediated depression, such heterogeneity can result in equivocal findings when one is comparing a group of remitted depressed individuals with nondepressed individuals, some of whom may also have a cognitive vulnerability but have not yet had a depressive episode.

Therefore, in keeping with the suggested methodology presented earlier, methods and important findings from the Temple–Wisconsin Cognitive Vulnerability to Depression (CVD) Project (Alloy & Abramson, 1999) are explained in detail in the sections that follow. The CVD Project uses a prospective behavioral high-risk design to test the cognitive vulnerability and other etiological hypotheses of both the hopelessness theory and Beck's theory of depression. The CVD Project is a collaborative, two-site study that assesses, among other factors, an individual's cognitive styles, the occurrence of negative life events, and the occurrence of both depressive symptoms and clinically significant depressive episodes.

DESIGN OF THE CVD PROJECT

Here, we describe the procedures for participant selection, the CVD Project sample, and the CVD Project assessments. The CVD Project employed state of the art assessments and multiple reliability and validity checks to insure the quality of the data collected.

Participant Selection

Participants were selected for inclusion in the CVD Project through a two-phase screening procedure. In the first phase, 5,378 freshmen (2,438 at Temple University [TU] and 2,940 at the University of Wisconsin—Madison [UW]) completed two measures of cognitive style: (a) the Cognitive Style Questionnaire (CSQ; Alloy et al., 2000), a modified version of the Attributional Style Questionnaire (Peterson et al., 1982), which assesses individuals' styles for inferring causes, consequences, and self-characteristics following the occurrence of positive and negative events, and (b) a modified version of the Dysfunctional Attitudes Scale (DAS; Weissman & Beck, 1978). The primary modifications made to the Attributional Style Questionnaire in designing the CSQ were that more hypothetical events were included (12 positive and 12 negative events), the hypothetical events were changed to more adequately reflect life events likely to be faced by college students, and the dimensions of consequences and self-characteristics are assessed in addition to the attributional dimensions of internality, stability, and globality. The DAS was modified by adding 24 items that specifically assess dysfunctional beliefs in the achievement and interpersonal domains. Individuals who scored in the highest (most negative) or lowest (most positive) quartile on both the DAS and the CSQ composite (stability + globality + consequences + self) for negative events were designated at high cognitive risk (HR) and low cognitive risk (LR) for depression, respectively (for more details, see Alloy & Abramson, 1999; Alloy et al., 2000). Thus, participants in the CVD Project were selected on the basis of the presence versus absence of vulnerability to depression as specified by both hopelessness theory (Abramson et al., 1989) and Beck's (1967, 1987) theory.

In the second phase of the screening process, a randomly selected sub-sample of HR and LR participants under age 30 were administered an expanded version of the Schedule for Affective Disorders and Schizophrenia—Lifetime (SADS–L) diagnostic interview (Endicott & Spitzer, 1978). The SADS–L was expanded to allow for diagnoses to be made according to the *Diagnostic and Statistical Manual of Mental Disorders* (3rd. ed., rev.; *DSM–III–R*; American Psychiatric Association, 1987) in addition to Research Diagnostic Criteria (RDC; Spitzer, Endicott, & Robins, 1978) diagnoses. Data were also recoded according to fourth edition of the *DSM* (*DSM–IV*; American Psychiatric Association, 1994). Individuals were excluded from participation in the study if they exhibited any current Axis I disorder, current psychotic symptoms, past history of any bipolar-spectrum disorder, or any serious medical illness that would preclude participation in a longitudinal study.

Participants who had a past unipolar mood disorder but had experienced a remission of the episode for a minimum of 2 months were retained so as not to result in an unrepresentative sample of HR participants. More specifically, inclusion of only the HR participants with no prior history of depressive episodes may have yielded an unrepresentative group of HR participants; for example, such a selection strategy would risk being overly inclusive of participants who exhibit protective factors, such as strong social support, that tend to buffer against the onset of depression. The final CVD Project sample included 173 HR (83 at TU, 90 at UW) and 176 LR (87 at TU, 89 at UW) participants. Demographic and cognitive style characteristics of the final sample are presented in Table 4.1 (for more details on the final sample's characteristics and representativeness, see Alloy & Abramson, 1999; Alloy et al., 2000).

Project Assessments

After agreeing to take part in the study, all participants completed a Time 1 assessment that included the Personality Disorders Examination (PDE; Loranger, 1988), an interview that assesses Axis II psychopathology and dimensions; a set of tasks designed to assess self-referent information processing (Self-Relevant Information Processing Task Battery; Alloy, Abramson,

TABLE 4.1
Characteristics of the Final Temple–Wisconsin Cognitive
Vulnerability to Depression Project Sample

Site	High-Risk Group	Low-Risk Group
Temple University		
No. participants	83	87
DAS mean item score	4.39 (0.55)	2.17 (0.29)
CSQ–Neg. Comp. mean item score	5.05 (0.47)	2.71 (0.43)
Age (years)	18.45 (1.40)	19.57 (2.98)
Average parental education (years)	13.76 (2.47)	13.45 (2.26)
Combined parental income (USD)	48,061 (36,013)	39,882 (25,906)
Sex (% women)	67.5	66.7
Ethnic group (% Caucasian)	68.3	57.7
University of Wisconsin		
No. participants	90	89
DAS mean item score	4.50 (0.44)	2.23 (0.33)
CSQ–Neg. Comp. mean item score	5.15 (0.40)	2.78 (0.37)
Age (years)	18.67 (0.37)	18.77 (1.14)
Average parental education (years)	15.20 (2.17)	15.03 (2.27)
Combined parental income (USD)	82,911 (100,473)	71,782 (53,219)
Sex (% women)	68.9	67.4
Ethnic group (% Caucasian)	95.6	92.1

Note. Unless otherwise noted, means are reported. Standard deviations are in parentheses. DAS = Dysfunctional Attitudes Scale; CSQ–Neg. Comp. = Cognitive Style Questionnaire—Composite for Negative Events; USD = U.S. dollars. Data from "The Temple–Wisconsin Cognitive Vulnerability to Depression Project: Lifetime History of Axis I Psychopathology in Individuals at High and Low Risk for Depression," by L. B. Alloy, L. Y. Abramson, M. E. Hogan, W. G. Whitehouse, D. T. Rose, M. S. Robinson, R. S. Kim, and J. B. Lapkin, 2000, *Journal of Abnormal Psychology, 109,* p. 407. Copyright 2000 by the American Psychological Association.

Murray, Whitehouse, & Hogan, 1997); as well as measures of cognitive style (CSQ, DAS, sociotropy–autonomy, self-consciousness), coping styles (rumination vs. distraction), social support, and hypothesized mediating cognitions (inferences for actual events and negative views of self, world, and future).

In addition, to assess the occurrence of negative life events, participants were given a combination self-report questionnaire and semistructured interview modeled after the Life Events and Difficulties Schedule (Brown & Harris, 1978). On completion of the Time 1 assessment, participants were followed longitudinally for 5.5 years. For the first 2.5 years of the follow-up, participants completed interview and questionnaire assessments every 6 weeks. For the remaining 3 years of the follow-up they were interviewed and completed questionnaires every 4 months. During each assessment, questionnaires and interviews were used to assess the occurrence of negative life events, inferences for these events, the components of Beck's (1967, 1987) negative cognitive triad (i.e., a negative view of self, world, and future), coping styles, social support, and the onset and offset of symptoms and *DSM–IV* and RDC episodes of depression and other psychopathology. Data from these assessments were also used to assess the onset and offset of symptoms and diagnoses of HD.

At the end of each year of follow-up, participants completed measures to reassess their inferential styles and dysfunctional attitudes as well as their coping styles and self-referent information processing. Furthermore, during the first 2.5 years of follow-up, participants and their parents completed a number of measures assessing parental history of psychopathology as well as parental cognitive styles, inferential feedback, and parenting styles. Participants' childhood life events and reports of childhood maltreatment were also assessed. Finally, at the end of the 5.5-year follow-up, participants completed a second PDE. For further details about the rationale, design, and methodology of the CVD Project, see Alloy and Abramson (1999). The results we present in this chapter focus primarily on findings from the first 2.5 years of follow-up.

FINDINGS FROM THE CVD PROJECT

In the following sections we review the findings from the CVD Project to date. Our findings provide strong support for hopelessness and Beck's theories of depression.

Negative Cognitive Styles and Vulnerability to Depression

A primary hypothesis of the cognitive theories of depression is that certain negative cognitive styles confer vulnerability to symptoms and diagnoses of depression. Although cognitive styles are not immutable (e.g., Just et al.,

2001) and are open to modification (e.g., through cognitive therapy; see DeRubeis & Hollon, 1995), these styles are typically viewed as relatively stable risk factors. Findings from the CVD Project have supported the relative stability of cognitive styles. Specifically, the participants' cognitive styles remained stable during and after episodes of major depression, relative to their cognitive styles preceding the intervening episode (Berrebbi, Alloy, & Abramson, 2008). In addition, cognitive vulnerability showed high relative stability, as evidenced by the moderate to high correlation ($r = .62$) between cognitive risk status at study onset and final assessment 7 years later (Romens, Abramson, & Alloy, in press). Finally, participants' attributions and inferences for particular negative life events remained stable over the 5-year follow-up (Raniere, 2000). Thus, cognitive styles appear to be a relatively trait-like vulnerability factor.

One method of testing the vulnerability hypotheses of the cognitive theories is to examine whether individuals who exhibit negative cognitive styles are more likely to have a history of depression than are individuals with positive cognitive styles. Thus, in the CVD Project HR participants were expected to have higher lifetime prevalence rates of episodic mood disorders, including MD, minor depression (MiD), and HD, than were LR participants. Controlling for current levels of depressive symptoms, HR participants did indeed exhibit higher lifetime rates of *DSM–III–R* and RDC MD and HD than did LR participants (Alloy et al., 2000) as well as marginally higher lifetime rates of RDC MiD (for more information, see Table 4.2). In fact, HR participants were approximately 3 times more likely to have experienced MD and almost 5 times more likely to have experienced HD relative to LR participants. The HR–LR differences in lifetime prevalence rates of MD and HD

TABLE 4.2
Lifetime Prevalence of Depressive Disorders as a Function
of Cognitive Risk Status

Diagnosis (criteria)	Low Risk (%, $n = 176$)	High Risk (%, $n = 173$)	Odds Ratio (95% CI)	p
Major depression (*DSM–III–R* or RDC)	17.0 ($n = 30$)	38.7 ($n = 67$)	3.01 (1.84, 4.94)	< .01
Minor depression (*DSM–III–R* or RDC)	11.9 ($n = 21$)	22.0 ($n = 38$)	2.11 (1.18, 3.77)	< .08
Hopelessness depression (project diagnosis)	11.9 ($n = 21$)	39.9 ($n = 69$)	4.87 (2.81, 8.44)	< .001

Note. CI = confidence interval; *DSM–III–R* = Diagnostic and Statistical Manual of Mental Disorders, third edition, revised; RDC = Research Diagnostic Criteria. Adapted from "The Temple–Wisconsin Cognitive Vulnerability to Depression Project: Lifetime History of Axis I Psychopathology in Individuals at High and Low Risk for Depression," by L. B. Alloy, L. Y. Abramson, M. E. Hogan, W. G. Whitehouse, D. T. Rose, M. S. Robinson, S. Matthew, R. S. Kim, and J. B. Lapkin, 2000, *Journal of Abnormal Psychology, 109,* p. 410. Copyright 2000 by the American Psychological Association.

were maintained when other hypothesized risk factors for depression, including inferential style for positive events, sociotropy, autonomy, self-consciousness, and stress-reactive rumination, were controlled statistically. It is interesting that the risk groups did not differ in lifetime rates of nonepisodic mood disorders, including *DSM–III–R* dysthymic disorder and RDC intermittent depressive disorder. In support of the specificity of cognitive vulnerability to the depressive disorders, there were also no risk group differences in participants' lifetime histories of anxiety disorders, substance use disorders, or other psychiatric disorders. Furthering these findings, Haeffel et al. (2003) used an unselected sample of undergraduates to examine more closely the role of the distinct manifestations of cognitive vulnerability (i.e., inferential styles and dysfunctional attitudes) included in the CVD Project. Haeffel et al. (2003) found that negative inferential styles, but not dysfunctional attitudes, uniquely predicted lifetime history of clinically significant depressive episodes and anxiety comorbid with depression.

Despite the strengths of these findings, they do not adequately address whether negative cognitive styles serve as a vulnerability factor for depression because the findings are equally supportive of the alternate hypothesis that negative cognitive styles are a consequence or "scar" left by the past experience of depression (cf. Lewinsohn, Steinmetz, Larson, & Franklin, 1981). Therefore, to adequately test the cognitive vulnerability hypothesis, truly prospective data are required. Results from the first 2.5 years of follow-up in the CVD Project indicate that risk group status predicted both first onsets and recurrences of depression during this time (Alloy, Abramson, Whitehouse, et al., 2006). Specifically, among individuals with no prior history of depression, HR participants were more likely than LR participants to experience a first onset of MD, MiD, and HD. These findings provide especially important support for the cognitive vulnerability hypothesis because they are based on a truly prospective test; that is, these results are uncontaminated by participants' prior history of depression. In addition, among individuals with a past history of depression, HR participants were more likely to experience recurrences of MD, MiD, and HD than were LR participants (for a summary of these results, see Table 4.3). Like the results of the retrospective analyses, there were no risk group differences in either first onsets or recurrences of anxiety disorders or other disorders. However, in the full sample, HR participants were more likely than LR participants to have an onset of an anxiety disorder comorbid with depression, but not an anxiety disorder alone. Furthermore, each of these results was maintained even after statistically controlling for participants' initial levels of depressive symptoms on entrance to the study, as assessed using the Beck Depression Inventory (Beck et al., 1979).

Thus, both retrospective and prospective results from the CVD Project have supported the vulnerability hypothesis of the cognitive theories of depression. Specifically, participants with negative cognitive styles were more

TABLE 4.3

Prospective Rates of Temple–Wisconsin Cognitive Vulnerability to Depression Project First Onsets and Recurrences of Depressive Disorders

Occurrence	Low Risk (%)	High Risk (%)	Odds Ratio (95% CI)	p
First onset (no prior depression)				
Any major depression	2.7	16.2	7.4 (1.6, 34.8)	.01
RDC minor depression	14.4	45.9	5.6 (2.2, 14.1)	.001
Hopelessness depression	3.6	35.1	11.6 (3.3, 41.3)	.001
Recurrences (prior depression)				
Any major depression	9.4	28.6	3.8 (1.3, 11.0)	.02
RDC minor depression	32.8	56.1	3.1 (1.4, 7.0)	.02
Hopelessness depression	18.8	50.0	4.1 (1.7, 10.0)	.002

Note. CI = confidence interval; RDC = Research Diagnostic Criteria. From "Prospective Incidence of First Onsets and Recurrences of Depression in Individuals at High and Low Cognitive Risk for Depression," by L. B. Alloy, L. Y. Abramson, W. G. Whitehouse, M. E. Hogan, C. Panzarella, and D. T. Rose, 2006, *Journal of Abnormal Psychology, 115,* p. 151. Copyright 2006 by the American Psychological Association.

likely to have had a past episode of MD and HD and were more likely to experience both first onsets and recurrences of MD, MiD, and HD during the 2.5-year follow-up than were participants with positive cognitive styles. Of importance, the risk group differences were not due to residual differences between the groups in levels of depressive symptoms. The CVD Project findings are important because they provide the first demonstration that, as predicted by the cognitive theories of depression, negative cognitive styles confer risk for full-blown, clinically significant depressive disorders. The results also provide support for the hypothesis that HD is a naturally occurring subtype of depression and that it conforms to theoretical description.

Negative Cognitive Styles: Specificity to Hopelessness Depression

Hopelessness theory (Abramson et al., 1989) proposes that negative cognitive styles confer vulnerability to HD specifically, rather than to other subtypes of depression. In support of this hypothesis, studies have found that negative cognitive styles, both alone and interacting with negative life events, are more strongly related to depressive symptoms hypothesized to be part of the HD symptom cluster (see Exhibit 4.1) than to symptoms not part of the HD symptom cluster (Alloy & Clements, 1998; Alloy, Just, & Panzarella, 1997; Hankin, Abramson, & Siler, 2001; Joiner et al., 2001; Metalsky & Joiner, 1997) or to symptoms of other forms of psychopathology (Alloy & Clements, 1998). In addition, preliminary analyses based on the first 2.5 years of prospective follow-up in the CVD Project indicate that cognitive risk predicts first onsets and recurrences of HD (as described earlier), but not of *DSM* melancholic depression.

Role of Hopelessness as a Mediator in Hopelessness Depression

Another tenet of the theory proposed by Abramson et al. (1989) is that in HD, hopelessness itself represents a proximal and sufficient cause of depressive symptomatology. Stated another way, the interaction between cognitive vulnerability and stress predicts symptoms of HD precisely because it increases the probability that an at-risk individual will become hopeless. To test this assertion empirically, Alloy and Clements (1998) sought to examine whether, as hypothesized, hopelessness plays a mediational role in the association between the vulnerability–stress interaction and manifestation of symptoms related to HD. Consistent with underlying theory; with previous research (e.g., Lynd-Stevenson, 1997; Metalsky & Joiner, 1992); and, more specifically, with hopelessness as the proximal cause of HD symptomatology, the results supported the role of hopelessness as a mediator in this association. Subsequent research has replicated these results (e.g., Abela, 2002), although not all studies have reported results consistent with the role of hopelessness as a mediator in the relationship between the vulnerability–stress interaction and depressive symptoms (e.g., Kapçi & Cramer, 2000). Of note, although hopelessness theory predicts only that this mediational relationship will hold in HD, much of the research conducted in this regard since Alloy and Clements's (1998) study has examined depressive symptomatology in a broad sense and has not focused strictly on HD.

Role of Rumination as a Mediator and Moderator

According to the *response styles theory of depression* (Nolen-Hoeksema, 1991), individuals who tend to ruminate in response to dysphoria will be at increased risk for experiencing more severe and prolonged depression than will individuals who tend to distract themselves from their dysphoria. *Rumination* refers to "behaviors and thoughts that focus one's attention on one's depressive symptoms and on the implications of these symptoms" (Nolen-Hoeksema, 1991, p. 569), whereas *distraction* refers to active attempts to ignore depressive symptoms by focusing on pleasant or neutral activities. Several studies have found support for this theory, demonstrating that rumination is associated with a greater likelihood of MD and longer and more severe episodes of depression (e.g., Just & Alloy, 1997; Morrow & Nolen-Hoeksema, 1990; Nolen-Hoeksema, 2000; Nolen-Hoeksema & Morrow, 1991; Nolen-Hoeksema, Morrow, & Fredrickson, 1993; Nolen-Hoeksema, Parker, & Larson, 1994; Spasojevic & Alloy, 2001). Abramson et al. (2002) described the expected relation between rumination and the cognitive vulnerabilities featured in hopelessness theory and Beck's theory. They hypothesized that rumination would mediate the effects of these cognitive vulnerabilities on the prospective development of depressive episodes. Consistent with this hypothesis, Spasojevic and Alloy (2001) found that a ruminative response style measured at Time 1 of the CVD Project mediated the association between cognitive risk status and the development of prospective episodes of MD. Rumination also mediated the effects of other risk factors (i.e., past history of depression, maladaptive dependency, and self-criticism) for the onset of MD during the follow-up period. Robinson and Alloy (2003), expanding on response styles theory, hypothesized that individuals who have negative inferential styles and who tend to ruminate about these negative cognitions in response to the occurrence of stressful life events (i.e., stress-reactive rumination) may be more likely to develop episodes of depression. Here, negative cognitive styles are thought to provide the negative content, but this negative content may be more likely to lead to depression when it is on one's mind than when it is not. Accordingly, Robinson and Alloy proposed that stress-reactive rumination would exacerbate the association between negative cognitive styles and the onset of a depressive episode. Consistent with this hypothesis, they found that stress-reactive rumination assessed at Time 1 of the CVD Project interacted with cognitive risk to predict prospective onsets of episodes of MD and HD. Among LR participants, there was no difference in the likelihood of future onset of depression on the basis of whether such individuals tended to engage in stress-reactive rumination. In contrast, among HR participants, individuals who were high in stress-reactive rumination evidenced a higher prospective incidence of MD and HD than HR individuals who did not tend to ruminate in response to stressors.

Cognitive Vulnerability and the Course of Depression

Recent research using the CVD sample demonstrates that, in addition to conferring vulnerability to both first episodes and to recurrences of depression, high cognitive risk is predictive of the course of depressive episodes. For example, Iacoviello, Alloy, Abramson, Whitehouse, and Hogan (2006) examined participants who had experienced at least one depressive episode in the first 2.5 years of the prospective phase of the CVD Project and found that, relative to LR participants, those at high risk experienced a greater number of depressive episodes. Furthermore, the HR participants experienced more severe episodes as reflected both by clinician ratings of symptom severity and by participant self-report. In addition, the HR participants experienced a more chronic depressive course, as represented by the proportion of total study days spent either in an episode of MD or MiD, experiencing prodromal depressive symptoms prior to a diagnosable episode, or in partial remission from a diagnosable episode. Contrary to the authors' hypotheses, however, HR participants did not experience a greater duration of episodes relative to LR participants (Iacoviello et al., 2006). These intriguing findings add to previous research suggesting that cognitive vulnerability plays a role in more than just the onset of a depressive episode; specifically, it is likely that vulnerability also helps determine the maintenance and severity of depressive symptoms, and thus, potentially also to the ease with which these symptoms are lessened over time.

Negative Cognitive Style and Suicidality

In addition to conferring vulnerability to depression, the cognitive theories hypothesize that negative cognitive styles should increase the risk of suicidality, ranging from suicidal ideation to completed suicides, and that levels of hopelessness should mediate this relation. Findings from the CVD project provide support for this hypothesis (Abramson et al., 1998). Specifically, HR participants were more likely than were LR participants to have a prior history of suicidality. HR participants also had higher levels of suicidality across the first 2.5 years of follow-up than did LR participants, and this relation was maintained even after statistically controlling for participants' prior history of suicidality and for other risk factors for suicidality, including prior history of *DSM–III–R* and/or RDC MD, RDC MiD, borderline personality traits, antisocial personality traits, and parental history of depression. Importantly, participants' mean levels of hopelessness mediated the association between cognitive vulnerability and suicidal ideation and attempts across the 2.5-year follow-up.

In another recent study of a subsample of CVD project participants, Smith, Alloy, and Abramson (2006) found that rumination and hopelessness prospectively predicted the presence and duration of suicidal ideation. In addition, hopelessness partially mediated the relationship between rumination and suicidal ideation, and fully mediated the association between rumination and duration of suicidality. Furthermore, rumination mediated the relationship between cognitive vulnerability and suicidal ideation. Thus, the available information suggests that as predicted by cognitive theories of depression, there is indeed a relationship between cognitive styles and suicidality. Smith, Alloy, and Abramson's findings speak to this relationship and tie together other findings from the CVD Project, helping to elucidate the nature of significant associations among cognitive styles, rumination, hopelessness, and suicidality.

Cognitive Vulnerability–Stress Interaction in Relation to Prospective Development of Depression

Because the cognitive theories of depression are vulnerability–stress models in which maladaptive cognitive styles are hypothesized to increase individuals' vulnerability to depression when met with negative life events, it is important to examine the interaction between cognitive style and the occurrence of negative life events in predicting onset/recurrence of depression. As indicated earlier, several studies have found that the cognitive vulnerability–stress combination predicts depressive symptoms (for a review, see Alloy, Abramson, Whitehouse, et al., 2006). However, some published studies have failed to find support for this hypothesis (Cole & Turner, 1993; Joiner & Wagner, 1995; Tiggemann, Winefield, Winefield, & Goldney, 1991).

To date, the vulnerability–stress hypothesis has received relatively little evaluation with data from the CVD Project. Preliminary investigation of this hypothesis using only the TU site data found that cognitive risk interacted with the number of negative events participants experienced in the prior 6-week interval to predict onsets of MD and MiD combined and of HD significantly. About 50% of HR participants who experienced high numbers of stressful events had an onset of MD or MiD, whereas fewer than 20% of participants in the other vulnerability–stress combinations had an onset of a depressive episode. In a second preliminary evaluation of the occurrence of depressive episodes across the first 2.5 years of follow-up in the CVD Project (Robinson, 1997), also using TU site data only, marginally significant to significant relationships were found between the Cognitive Style × Number of Negative Life Events interaction and number of episodes of any depressive disorder, including both major and minor episodes. As such, more definitive work remains to be done to evaluate the validity of the vulnerability–stress hypothesis in predicting depressive episodes in the CVD Project using data from both sites.

Cognitive Vulnerability and Stress Generation

Not only are negative life events hypothesized to interact with cognitive risk to increase an individual's vulnerability to the development of depression, but also depression may, in turn, lead to a greater likelihood of future negative life events (e.g., Daley et al., 1997; Davila, Hammen, Burge, Paley, & Daley, 1995; Hammen, 1991; Harkness, Monroe, Simons, & Thase, 1999). According to this *stress-generation model of depression* (Hammen, 1991), a reciprocal relation exists between depression and negative life events, with depressed individuals often experiencing an increase in the occurrence of negative life events that are interpersonal in nature or dependent on the individuals' behavior.

Although there is considerable support for the stress-generation effect, the specific personal factors in depressed individuals that increase risk for future stressful life events are unclear. Negative cognitive styles have been proposed as one such risk factor for stress generation (Hammen, 1991; Monroe & Simons, 1991). It is interesting that recent results from the CVD Project indicate that, compared with individuals with relatively positive cognitive styles, those with negative cognitive styles generated more negative life events (Safford, Alloy, Abramson, & Crossfield, 2007). Specifically, individuals with negative cognitive styles generated more "dependent" and interpersonal events over which they had some degree of control, in contrast to more independent or achievement-related events. Of importance, this relationship held only for women. Thus, underlying negative cognitive styles not only may increase risk for depression by influencing individuals' interpretations of stressful events they encounter but also lead to the generation of some negative life events that may help to trigger depression (i.e., a "two-hit" model; Safford et al., 2007).

Self-Referent Information Processing

According to the cognitive theories of depression, individuals who are cognitively vulnerable to depression tend to process information about themselves in a negatively biased manner. Specifically, hopelessness theory (Abramson et al., 1989) proposes that individuals with a negative cognitive style tend to form negative inferences about themselves when they experience a negative life event. Similarly, Beck (1967, 1987) has hypothesized that certain individuals possess negative self-schemata that negatively influence their perception, interpretation, and memories of personally relevant experiences.

Alloy, Abramson, Murray et al. (1997) tested these hypotheses using data from the Self-Referent Information Processing Task Battery, administered at the Time 1 assessment of the CVD Project. Given Beck's hypothesis that individuals with a negative self-schema should demonstrate biased information processing only for depression-relevant stimuli (i.e., stimuli related to themes of incompetence, worthlessness, and low motivation), Alloy et al. predicted that HR participants would exhibit information-processing biases for depression-relevant self-referent adjectives, but not depression-irrelevant adjectives. Partial support was obtained for this hypothesis. Specifically, as predicted, compared with LR participants, HR participants showed preferential self-referent processing for negative depression-relevant material (e.g., words such as *failure*, *passive*, and *useless*), as evidenced by relatively greater endorsement, faster processing, greater accessibility, better recall, and higher predictive certainty of this material. Also, HR participants were less likely than LR participants to process positive depression-relevant stimuli (e.g., words such as *resourceful*, *energetic*, and *important*). Finally, although contrary to prediction, there were risk group differences for the depression-irrelevant material on two of the tasks: LR participants were more likely than HR participants to perceive positive depression-irrelevant stimuli (e.g., words such as *thoughtful*) as self-descriptive and believed that they were more likely to engage in future positive depression-irrelevant behaviors (e.g., giving up a seat on a bus for an elderly lady); however, the group differences were larger for depression-relevant stimuli than for depression-irrelevant stimuli even on these tasks. It is important to note that all of the risk group differences were maintained even after statistically controlling for participants' levels of depressive symptoms. These findings are unique in demonstrating that the information-processing biases previously found in depressed individuals (see

Ingram, Miranda, & Segal, 1998; Segal, 1988) also extend to nondepressed individuals at high cognitive risk for depression.

Axis II Personality Functioning

In addition to the tendency to engage in negative information processing about themselves, individuals with cognitive vulnerability to depression may also be likely to exhibit Axis II personality dysfunction for several reasons. First, the comorbidity between depression and personality disorders is high (see Smith, Grandin, Alloy, & Abramson, 2006). Second, many Axis II personality disorders are associated with cognitive profiles that overlap with cognitive risk for depression (e.g., Cluster C, the "anxious/fearful cluster" is associated with feelings of weakness, incompetence, and helplessness). Consequently, using CVD Project data from both sites, Smith, Grandin, Alloy, and Abramson examined the associations between cognitive risk status and Axis II personality dimensions and diagnoses as assessed by the PDE given at Time 1. Controlling for past history of depression and current depressive symptoms, cognitive risk status was significantly associated with the presence versus absence of an Axis II diagnosis. Whereas only 1.8% of LR participants had an Axis II diagnosis, 6.6% of HR individuals had a personality disorder. In addition, controlling for past and current depression, HR status was significantly associated with higher scores on the paranoid, schizotypal, histrionic, narcissistic, avoidant, dependent, and obsessive–compulsive personality dimensions. These associations were maintained even when PDE items that conceptually overlapped with the measures of cognitive vulnerability to depression (CSQ and DAS) were removed from the dimensional scores. The significant association between cognitive vulnerability and Axis II personality characteristics independent of current and past depression points to the importance of interpersonal dysfunction among individuals who exhibit depressogenic cognitive styles.

Protective Role of Social Support

In an extension of the hopelessness theory of depression, Panzarella, Alloy, and Whitehouse (2006) proposed that a subtype of social support, *adaptive inferential feedback* (AIF), may have a salubrious effect on depression, reducing cognitive vulnerability for depression by decreasing negative cognitive styles and the likelihood of depressogenic inferences for future specific negative events. AIF involves being offered adaptive inferences for negative events (e.g., attributing stressful events to unstable and specific rather than stable and global causes; providing consequences and implications for self-worth for the stressful events that are more positive) by members of an individual's support network and, as such, is the converse of negative or depressogenic inferences. For example, after the breakup of a relationship, an individual might share the following with a friend: "I will never find a good partner. I must be unlovable." If the friend responds by offering an adaptive inferential alternative—for example—"Having problems in a relationship does not mean you are an unlovable person and does not mean you will not be able to have a successful relationship in the future. You are a warm, caring person"—then the affected individual may be more likely to reevaluate and modify the original maladaptive inference. AIF differs from other forms of social support (e.g., being treated to dinner by a friend) in that it directly challenges depressogenic cognitions by proposing an alternative, more adaptive inference.

Consistent with the expanded hopelessness theory of depression, Panzarella et al. (2006) found that, among individuals in the CVD Project (from the Temple site), the more AIF they reported at the start of the project, the less negative their inferential styles were at a 6-month follow-up, after partialing out general social support and stressful life events. Also as predicted, individuals who reported greater AIF tended to form inferences that were less negative for actual stressful life events. Finally, the interaction among AIF, cognitive risk, and stress was found to predict hopelessness, dysphoria, and the onset of HD. That is, social support appeared to moderate the cognitive vulnerability–stress interaction. HR participants with high stress and low levels of AIF were more likely than participants with zero, one, or two of the three risk factors to develop hopelessness, depressive symptoms, and HD. Thus, there is some evidence that a specific subtype of social support, AIF, can have an impact on cognitive styles, inferences for actual stressful events, and the development of depressive symptoms and disorders.

DEVELOPMENTAL ANTECEDENTS OF COGNITIVE VULNERABILITY TO DEPRESSION

Given the evidence that negative cognitive styles do indeed confer vulnerability to future episodes of both depression and suicidality, it is important to understand the factors that may contribute to the development of such negative cognitive styles. Data from the CVD Project allow an initial examination of several factors that may contribute to the development of these cognitive styles (for an in-depth review of the developmental findings from the CVD Project, see Alloy et al., 2004). As part of the CVD Project, we (Alloy & Abramson, 1999) assessed the cognitive styles and lifetime history of psychopathology of 335 of our participants' parents (217 mothers and 118 fathers). In addition, we asked participants and their parents to report the parents' inferential feedback styles and parenting styles. Finally, we assessed participants' reports of childhood maltreatment.

Parental Psychopathology

Because considerable past research has indicated that children of depressed parents are at increased risk for the development of negative attributional styles (e.g., Garber & Flynn, 2001; Hammen, 1992) and depressive episodes (e.g., Downey & Coyne, 1990), data from the CVD Project were used (Abramson et al., 2008) to examine the relation between participants' cognitive risk status and their parents' history of depression. Parental history of depression was assessed through participant reports (i.e., family history RDC method; Andreason, Endicott, Spitzer, & Winokur, 1977) and direct interviews of the parents themselves, using the expanded SADS–L.

Preliminary data from the CVD Project indicate that there was a relationship between the cognitive risk group status of participants and their parents' histories of depression (Abramson et al., 2008). This relationship, however, appears to be stronger for mothers' than for fathers' past histories of depression. Specifically, compared with LR participants, HR participants reported that their mothers were significantly more likely, and their fathers were marginally more likely, to have a history of depression. Also, in the direct interviews of the parents, mothers of HR participants were more likely than mothers of LR participants to have had a past history of depression. In the case of fathers' histories of depression, however, no group differences were found. These findings demonstrate a relation between parents' histories of depression and the cognitive styles of their nondepressed offspring and provide support for explorations of possible mediators of the association between parental depression and offspring's cognitive vulnerability to depression.

Modeling and Parental Inferential Feedback

Parents may influence the cognitive styles of their children through the modeling of their own cognitive style or by providing inferential feedback regarding the causes and consequences of negative events in their children's lives. However, studies have provided only limited support for a direct relation between parents' negative cognitive styles and those of their children. For example, in the CVD Project the mothers of HR participants had more dysfunctional attitudes than did mothers of LR participants, even after controlling for the mothers' levels of depressive symptoms (Alloy et al., 2001). In contrast, no risk group differences were observed in mothers' or fathers' inferential styles or in fathers' dysfunctional attitudes. In another study, however, the attributional styles of third-, fourth-, and fifth-graders were significantly related to those of their mothers but not their fathers (Seligman et al., 1984). Finally, in a third study, no relation was found between the attributional styles of sixth-graders and those of their mothers (Garber & Flynn, 2001). Thus, although there is some evidence that children may model their parents' cognitive styles, especially their mothers', future studies are required to further examine this relationship. Given the mixed results obtained thus far, future studies should examine possible moderating factors that may either strengthen or weaken the relationship (e.g., amount of time spent with the parent).

More consistent support has been found for the hypothesis that negative parental inferential feedback may contribute to the development of a negative cognitive style in their children. For example, according to both participants' and their parents' reports, and controlling for respondents' levels of depressive symptoms, both mothers and fathers of HR participants in the CVD Project provided more stable, global attributional feedback than did mothers and fathers of LR participants (Alloy et al., 2001). Similarly, controlling for respondents' levels of depressive symptoms, mothers of HR participants also provided more negative consequence feedback for negative events in their child's life than did mothers of LR participants, according to both respondents' reports, as did fathers of HR participants, according to the participants' reports. In addition, negative attributional and consequence feedback from mothers interacted with a history of high levels of childhood stressful life events to predict HR status (Crossfield, Alloy, Abramson, & Gibb, 2002). Moreover, the negative inferential feedback from parents predicted prospective onsets of depressive episodes in their children over the 2.5-year follow-up period, mediated, in part or totally, by the children's cognitive risk status (Alloy et al., 2001). These results have been supported in other studies. For example, sixth-graders' attributional styles for positive and negative life events were correlated with their mothers' attributional styles for the same child-relevant events (Garber & Flynn, 2001). Also, adolescents' attributional styles were significantly related to their fathers', but not mothers', attributional styles for the same child-relevant events (Turk & Bry, 1992). Thus, there is some evidence that parents may contribute to the development of negative cognitive styles in their children, not by the children modeling the attributions their parents make for negative events in the parents' lives but by the attributional and consequence feedback the children receive from their parents for negative events in the children's own lives.

Parenting Styles

Several studies have provided evidence that certain styles of parenting may also contribute to the development of a negative cognitive style in children (for a review, see Alloy, Abramson, Smith, Gibb, & Neeren, 2006). In particular, parenting characterized by lack of warmth and caring and by negative psychological control (criticism, intrusiveness, and guilt induction) is associated with depression and negative cognitive styles in offspring (Alloy, Abramson, Smith, et al., 2006). In the CVD Project, both HR participants and their fathers reported that the fathers exhibited less warmth and acceptance than did fathers of LR participants (Alloy et al., 2001). There were no group differences, however, for fathers' levels of either psychological control or firm control (discipline); neither were there any group differences in the mothers' parenting styles. Fathers' acceptance scores also predicted prospective onsets of MD, MiD, and HD episodes in their children, but only the prediction of HD episodes was mediated by the children's cognitive risk status (Alloy et al., 2001). It is interesting that although parental psychological control was not related to cognitive risk status based on negative inferential styles and dysfunctional attitudes in the CVD Project, such overcontrol by both parents was related to their offspring's greater tendency to ruminate (Spasojevic & Alloy, 2002). In a longitudinal study of sixth-graders and their mothers, higher levels of maternal psychological control were associated with increasing negativity of their children's attributional styles over a 1-year follow-up period, even after controlling for the mothers' histories of mood disorders (Garber & Flynn, 2001). In this study, neither parental acceptance versus rejection nor firm versus lax control was related to changes in the children's attributional styles. Finally, undergraduates with a negative cognitive style reported less maternal care when growing up than did undergraduates with a positive cognitive style (Whisman & Kwon, 1992). In this study, undergraduates' cognitive styles were not related to the degree of maternal overprotection reported during childhood.

Thus, although these studies suggest a relation between certain styles of parenting and children's cognitive styles, there is not yet an agreement as to which parenting styles are the most detrimental. In addition, few studies other than the CVD Project (Alloy et al., 2001; Spasojevic & Alloy, 2002) have examined the parenting practices of fathers. Future studies, therefore, should seek to clarify the relation between parenting practices and children's negative cognitive styles and include fathers in this evaluation.

Childhood Maltreatment

In extending the etiological chain of hopelessness theory, Rose and Abramson (1992) proposed a developmental pathway by which negative life events, especially childhood maltreatment, may lead to the development of a negative cognitive style. Specifically, they suggested that when maltreatment occurs, individuals attempt to understand the causes, consequences, and meanings of the abuse so that future negative events may be avoided and hopefulness may be maintained. Thus, after the occurrence of maltreatment, children may initially make hopefulness-inducing attributions about the event. For example, a child may initially explain being beaten or verbally abused by his or her father by saying "He was just in a bad mood today"—an external, unstable, and specific explanation. With the repeated occurrence of maltreatment, however, these hopefulness-inducing attributions may be disconfirmed, leading the child to begin making more hopelessness-inducing attributions about its occurrence. For example, a child may explain the maltreatment by thinking "I'm a terrible person who deserves all the bad things that happen to me," which is an internal, stable, and global explanation that entails negative consequences and negative self-characteristics. Over time, the child's hopelessness-inducing attributions may generalize to initially unrelated negative events. In this way, a relatively stable and global negative cognitive style may develop.

Researchers have recently begun to examine the relation between childhood maltreatment and cognitive styles. These initial evaluations have supported Rose and Abramson's hypotheses (for a review, see Alloy, Abramson, Smith, et al., 2006). For example, after controlling for their levels of depressive symptoms, HR participants in the CVD Project reported significantly higher levels of childhood emotional, but not physical or sexual, maltreatment than did LR participants (Gibb, Alloy, Abramson, Rose, Whitehouse, Donovan, et al., 2001). In addition, participants' cognitive risk status fully mediated the relation between reported levels of childhood emotional maltreatment and the occurrence of *DSM–III–R* and RDC nonendogenous MD during the first 2.5 years of follow-up. Furthermore, participants' cognitive risk status fully mediated, and their average levels of hopelessness partially mediated, the relation between reported levels of childhood emotional maltreatment and the occurrence of HD during the first 2.5 years of follow-up. In addressing the possibility that the association of childhood emotional maltreatment with negative cognitive styles is actually due to genetic influences or a negative family environment in general, Gibb, Abramson, and Alloy (2004) also examined the relation between emotional maltreatment by nonrelatives (i.e., peer victimization) during development and negative cognitive styles. Gibb et al. found that even when parental maltreatment and parental history of psychopathology were controlled, there was still a significant relationship between peer victimization and cognitive HR status. These findings cannot be easily explained by third-variable accounts such as genetic influence or a general negative family context.

Similarly, in a study of the CVD Project participants' average levels of suicidality (assessed by both questionnaire and interview) across the first 2.5 years of follow-up, participants' cognitive risk status and average levels of hopelessness partially mediated the relation between reported levels of childhood emotional maltreatment and average levels of suicidality (Gibb, Alloy, Abramson, Rose, Whitehouse, & Hogan, 2001). Rose and Abramson's (1992) developmental model is also supported by the results of a recent cross-sectional study; specifically, the results were consistent with the hypothesis that high levels of childhood emotional maltreatment lead to more negative inferences about that maltreatment, which then lead to the development of a negative inferential style and that this inferential style then leaves one vulnerable to hopelessness and the symptoms of HD (Gibb, Alloy, Abramson, & Marx, 2003).

In addition to supporting Rose and Abramson's (1992) developmental model, these results provide support for their hypothesis that childhood emotional maltreatment may be more likely than either childhood physical or sexual maltreatment to contribute to the development of a negative cognitive style. Specifically, Rose and Abramson hypothesized that with childhood emotional maltreatment, the depressogenic cognitions are directly supplied to the child by the abuser. In contrast, with childhood physical and sexual maltreatment the child must generate his or her own negative cognitions. Childhood physical and sexual maltreatment consequently may allow greater opportunity for the child to make depressogenic attributions and inferences regarding the occurrence of maltreatment that are less depressogenic.

Although these studies provide some evidence for a relation between childhood emotional maltreatment and negative cognitive styles, prospective, longitudinal research is needed to assess the degree to which emotional maltreatment contributes to increased negativity in cognitive styles and risk to depression over time. Along these lines, Gibb et al. (2006) examined the role of emotional maltreatment in predicting change in attributional style over a 6-month period in fourth- and fifth-grade children. Greater emotional maltreatment occurring both during the 6-month follow-up and in the 6 months before Time 1 predicted a worsening of children's attributional styles (the styles became more negative) over the 6-month follow-up. Moreover, using data from the TU site of the CVD Project, Liu, Alloy, and Abramson (in press) found that emotional maltreatment from adults and peers, assessed prospectively, predicted time to onset of MD and MiD; specifically, greater levels of emotional abuse predicted a shorter time to onset of depressive episodes. In sum, there is growing evidence that emotional maltreatment may contribute to risk for depression in part by contributing to the development of negative cognitive styles.

CLINICAL AND TREATMENT IMPLICATIONS

The prevalence and sheer scope of depression, as well as the enormous negative impact that it ultimately imposes on society as a whole, necessitate a thorough and empirically guided understanding of the disorder. The foregoing discussion has, to a large extent, focused on important advances in the theoretical formulation of depression. Furthermore, a large complement of research findings speaks both to the validity of the underlying theory and to factors that may play a key role in the amelioration of depression. Nevertheless, a vital step in addressing these issues lies in translating sound theory and empirical research into effective clinical practice. Fortunately, in the present case, great strides have already been made in this direction. Effective, empirically supported treatment for depression is currently at the disposal of clinicians;

in addition, ongoing research will surely inform and ultimately improve on existing treatment approaches.

One such approach that derives from the cognitive vulnerability–stress theories of depression and has received considerable attention and empirical support is *cognitive–behavioral therapy* (CBT). Although a comprehensive description of CBT is beyond the scope of this chapter, a main tenet of this treatment approach is that there exist intimate interconnections among an individual's thoughts/cognitions, behaviors, and feelings—the last of which include symptoms of depression (e.g., Beck, 1983; Beck et al., 1979). Thus, to achieve symptom reduction and remission, a CBT approach addresses a given client's maladaptive cognitions as well as his or her maladaptive behaviors.

With respect to cognitions, clients are taught a set of tools that have as their focus a more objective and adaptive—and therefore less depressogenic—interpretation of reality (Beck, 1983; Beck et al., 1979). Techniques for achieving this include identifying and modifying maladaptive inferences and automatic thoughts (e.g., "I don't know what I'm doing"; "People will find out that I am a fraud"), as well as schema modification and cognitive restructuring, which ultimately alter a client's deeper maladaptive core beliefs, which underlie negative automatic thoughts (e.g., "I am incompetent"; "I am unlovable"). In implementing these cognitive strategies clients often gain a better appreciation of the maladaptive ways in which they interpret environmental events and they are, therefore, better able to process events in a more nondepressogenic manner. This work also often allows the client to reduce the degree to which he or she engages in a negative attributional style. In the end, this increasingly adaptive interpretation and attribution reduce the symptoms of depression. In addition to achieving symptom reduction through cognitive restructuring and other strategies aimed at addressing cognitive factors in depression, these techniques may also reduce the likelihood that a client will generate certain types of negative life events that may serve as precursors to the development of depressive symptoms (Safford et al., 2007).

Given that the cognitive theories of depression are vulnerability–stress models, another way to treat depression from this perspective is to reduce the stressfulness of depressed individuals' environments. The behavioral components of CBT attempt to accomplish this by increasing positive reinforcement and reducing punishment in a client's environment (e.g., Addis & Martell, 2004; Beck et al., 1979; Martell, Addis, & Jacobson, 2001). For example, a client is encouraged to engage in activities he or she finds pleasurable, starting with goals that are, for most individuals, relatively uncomplicated and easily attainable (e.g., getting outside on a sunny day, completing a minor task that one has been putting off) and building from there both in the frequency and complexity of reinforcing activities. In addition, clients are often encouraged to adopt a problem-solving approach to adversity in their lives, to reduce the degree to which they experience punishment from their environment.

The beauty of the behavioral underpinnings of CBT lies in their relative simplicity. Furthermore, they are often self-propagating in a sense; that is, increasing positive reinforcement begets larger scale activities that also increase positive reinforcement, and the same type of relationship holds for reduction of punishment. These processes are also aided by increases in energy that often accompany the implementation of these behavioral strategies. Behaviorally oriented components of CBT have also been packaged as a stand-alone treatment for depression, termed *behavioral activation* (e.g., Addis & Martell, 2004; Martell et al., 2001).

Together, the cognitive and behavioral components of CBT as a treatment for depression represent a powerful combination, and they often build on one another in a client's achievement of symptom reduction. CBT has been demonstrably effective in treating even severe depression (e.g., DeRubeis & Crits-Christoph, 1998; DeRubeis, Gelfand, Tang, & Simons, 1999) and has thus earned the status of an empirically supported treatment for depression as ascribed by the American Psychological Association (Chambless & Ollendick, 2001).

To further traditional CBT approaches to the treatment of depression, other aspects and correlates of the disorder assessed in the CVD Project should be addressed in future studies. One of these is the role played by positive events. That is, do positive events provide a buffering effect, protecting against the occurrence of depression? Given the CVD Project findings thus far, which suggest a significant prospective relationship between cognitive vulnerability and future depression, researchers should continue to examine the therapeutic impact of modifying individuals' cognitive styles. For example, results from one study suggest that therapists providing CBT may reduce clients' depressive symptoms by reducing the negativity of clients' attributional styles (DeRubeis & Hollon, 1995). In addition, there is evidence that training children to make less negative attributions about the negative events in their lives can help protect against future depression (Gillham, Reivich, Jaycox, & Seligman, 1995; Jaycox, Reivich, Gillham, & Seligman, 1994). Given that negative cognitive styles may be especially likely to confer vulnerability to depression when exacerbated by rumination, training individuals in more effective methods of coping with stressful events—rather than directly trying to alter their cognitive style—may also alter vulnerability to depression.

Furthermore, building positive cognitive styles in children through parental education in modeling and providing feedback about more benign inferences for stressful events, as well as direct training in generating positive interpretations of stressful events in schools, might help reduce the development of negative cognitive style and therefore might also reduce the occurrence of depression. Finally, parenting classes that teach parents less abusive ways of raising their children may also aid in the prevention of cognitive vulnerability to depression.

Other environmental and individual-difference variables that may serve as protective factors against the development of hopelessness and depression will also need to be explored in future studies. For example, there is substantial evidence that social support can help buffer against the occurrence of depression when people experience stressful events (e.g., Cohen & Wills, 1985; Panzarella et al., 2006). Future analyses of the CVD Project data will allow an investigation of these potential protective factors.

Thus, it is heartening that there exist effective and empirically supported treatments for depression in present-day clinical practice. These treatment approaches address both underlying cognitive factors and behavioral correlates of the disorder, often with positive results. Future research, including that afforded by the CVD Project and similar studies, will inform the treatment and prevention literatures and, in the foreseeable future, will also allow professionals engaged in intervention efforts with depressed individuals to expand their repertoires of effective tools with which to ameliorate depressive symptomatology and, in so doing, to also ease the burden of depression in a broader societal context.

CONCLUSIONS

In this chapter, we have reviewed the findings to date from the CVD Project that indicate negative inferential styles and dysfunctional attitudes as conceptualized in the hopelessness theory of depression and Beck's (1967, 1987) theory of depression, alone and in combination with rumination, confer vulnerability to stressful life events, suicidality, and clinically significant depressive disorders, especially hopelessness depression. We have also discussed preliminary results regarding developmental factors associated with depressogenic cognitive styles, specifically, a history of childhood emotional maltreatment, negative parenting styles, and negative parental inferential feedback regarding the causes and consequences of negative events in the child's life.

There are, however, many important theoretical issues that remain to be addressed with the CVD Project data. Although analyses to date have indicated that individuals with negative cognitive styles are at higher risk for experiencing clinically significant depression, future analyses will be needed to evaluate whether nondepressed individuals at high cognitive risk are more likely than low-risk individuals to develop depression only when they experience stressful life events or whether cognitive risk may confer vulnerability to depression even in the absence of negative life events. In the CVD Project, negative life events were assessed repeatedly (every 6 weeks for the first 2.5 years of follow-up) and dated to the day they occurred, making prospective evaluation of this cognitive vulnerability–stress hypothesis possible. Although preliminary investigations of the vulnerability–stress hypothesis have been conducted, a more thorough evaluation is necessary. In addition, it will be important to test whether any predictive effect of the Cognitive Risk × Stress interaction for future depressive episodes is mediated by the occurrence of hopelessness, as predicted by hopelessness theory, and whether it is specific to HD as opposed to other possible subtypes of depression.

Finally, there is still much room for future research on cognitive vulnerabilities to depression outside of the CVD Project. Most important, the CVD Project combined both inferential styles and dysfunctional attitudes in defining negative cognitive style. Although this method of selecting participants provides the strongest possible test of the cognitive theories of depression, it does not allow for an examination of the unique contribution of inferential styles and dysfunctional attitudes in the prediction of depression. As such, the CVD Project represents an important step in research examining cognitive vulnerability to depression. Future studies are needed, however, to more specifically and separately test the predictions of Beck's (1967, 1987) theory and the hopelessness theory of depression (e.g., Haeffel et al., 2003).

REFERENCES

Abela, J. R. Z. (2002). Depressive mood reactions to failure in the achievement domain: A test of the integration of the hopelessness and self-esteem theories of depression. *Cognitive Therapy and Research, 26,* 531–552.

Abramson, L. Y., & Alloy, L. B. (1990). Search for the "negative cognition" subtype of depression. In D. C. McCann & N. Endler (Eds.), *Depression: New directions in theory, research and practice* (pp. 77–109). Toronto, Ontario, Canada: Wall & Thompson.

Abramson, L. Y., Alloy, L. B., Chiara, A., Tashman, N., Whitehouse, W. G., & Hogan, M. E. (2008). *The Temple–Wisconsin Cognitive Vulnerability to Depression Project: Axis I psychopathology in the parents of individuals at high and low cognitive risk for depression.* Manuscript in preparation.

Abramson, L. Y., Alloy, L. B., Hankin, B. L., Haeffel, G. J., MacCoon, D. G., & Gibb, B. E. (2002). Cognitive vulnerability–stress models of depression in a self-regulatory and psychobiological context. In I. H. Gotlib & C. L. Hammen (Eds.), *Handbook of depression* (3rd ed., pp. 268–294). New York: Guilford Press.

Abramson, L. Y., Alloy, L. B., Hogan, M. E., Whitehouse, W. G., Cornette, M., Akhavan, S., & Chiara, A. (1998). Suicidality and cognitive vulnerability to depression among college students. *Journal of Adolescence, 21,* 473–487.

Abramson, L. Y., Metalsky, G. I., & Alloy, L. B. (1989). Hopelessness depression: A theory-based subtype of depression. *Psychological Review, 96,* 358–372.

Addis, M. E., & Martell, C. R. (2004). Overcoming depression one step at a time: *The new behavioral activation approach to getting your life back*. Oakland, CA: New Harbinger Publications.

Alloy, L. B., & Abramson, L. Y. (1999). The Temple–Wisconsin Cognitive Vulnerability to Depression (CVD) Project: Conceptual background, design and methods. *Journal of Cognitive Psychotherapy, 13*, 227–262.

Alloy, L. B., Abramson, L. Y., Gibb, B. E., Crossfield, A. G., Pieracci, A. M., Spasojevic, J., & Steinberg, J. A. (2004). Developmental antecedents of cognitive vulnerability to depression: Review of findings from the Cognitive Vulnerability to Depression Project. *Journal of Cognitive Psychotherapy, 18*, 115–133.

Alloy, L. B., Abramson, L. Y., Hogan, M. E., Whitehouse, W. G., Rose, D. T., Robinson, M. S., et al. (2000). The Temple–Wisconsin Cognitive Vulnerability to Depression Project: Lifetime history of Axis I psychopathology in individuals at high and low cognitive risk for depression. *Journal of Abnormal Psychology, 109*, 403–418.

Alloy, L. B., Abramson, L. Y., Metalsky, G. I., & Hartlage, S. (1988). The hopelessness theory of depression: Attributional aspects. *British Journal of Clinical Psychology, 27*, 5–21.

Alloy, L. B., Abramson, L. Y., Murray, L. A., Whitehouse, W. G., & Hogan, M. E. (1997). Self-referent information processing in individuals at high and low cognitive risk for depression. *Cognition & Emotion, 11*, 539–568.

Alloy, L. B., Abramson, L. Y., Smith, J. M., Gibb, B. E., & Neeren, A. M. (2006). Role of parenting and maltreatment histories in unipolar and bipolar mood disorders: Mediation by cognitive vulnerability to depression. *Clinical Child and Family Psychology Review, 9*, 23–64.

Alloy, L. B., Abramson, L. Y., Tashman, N. A., Steinberg, D. L., Hogan, M. E., Whitehouse, W. G., et al. (2001). Developmental origins of cognitive vulnerability to depression: Parenting, cognitive, and inferential feedback styles of the parents of individuals at high and low cognitive risk for depression. *Cognitive Therapy and Research, 25*, 397–423.

Alloy, L. B., Abramson, L. Y., Whitehouse, W. G., Hogan, M. E., Panzarella, C., & Rose, D. T. (2006). Prospective incidence of first onsets and recurrences of depression in individuals at high and low cognitive risk for depression. *Journal of Abnormal Psychology, 115*, 145–156.

Alloy, L. B., & Clements, C. M. (1998). Hopelessness theory of depression: Tests of the symptom component. *Cognitive Therapy and Research, 22*, 303–335.

Alloy, L. B., Just, N., & Panzarella, C. (1997). Attributional style, daily life events, and hopelessness depression: Subtype validation by prospective variability and specificity of symptoms. *Cognitive Therapy and Research, 21*, 321–344.

Alloy, L. B., Lipman, A., & Abramson, L. Y. (1992). Attributional style as a vulnerability factor for depression: Validation by past history of mood disorders. *Cognitive Therapy and Research, 16*, 391–407.

American Psychiatric Association. (1987). *Diagnostic and statistical manual of mental disorders* (3rd ed., revised). Washington, DC: Author.

American Psychiatric Association. (1994). *Diagnostic and statistical manual of mental disorders* (4th ed.). Washington, DC: Author.

Andreason, N., Endicott, J., Spitzer, R. L., & Winokur, G. (1977). The family history method using diagnostic criteria: Reliability and validity. *Archives of General Psychiatry, 34,* 1229–1235.

Barnett, P. A., & Gotlib, I. H. (1988). Psychosocial functioning and depression: Distinguishing among antecedents, concomitants and consequences. *Psychological Bulletin, 104,* 97–126.

Beck, A. T. (1967). *Depression: Clinical, experimental, and theoretical aspects.* New York: Harper & Row.

Beck, A. T. (1983). Cognitive therapy of depression: New perspectives. In P. J. Clayton & J. E. Barrett (Eds.), *Treatment of depression: Old controversies and new approaches* (pp. 265–284). New York: Raven Press.

Beck, A. T. (1987). Cognitive models of depression. *Journal of Cognitive Psychotherapy, 1,* 5–37.

Beck, A. T., Rush, A. J., Shaw, B. F., & Emery, G. (1979). *Cognitive therapy of depression.* New York: Guilford Press.

Berrebbi, D. S., Alloy, L. B., & Abramson, L. Y. (2008). *Stability in negative cognitive styles despite intervening episodes of depression.* Manuscript in preparation.

Brown, G. W., & Harris, T. O. (1978). *Social origins of depression: A study of psychiatric disorder in women.* New York: Free Press.

Chambless, D. L., & Ollendick, T. H. (2001). Empirically supported psychological interventions: Controversies and evidence. *Annual Review of Psychology, 52,* 685–716.

Cohen, S., & Wills, T. A. (1985). Stress, social support and the buffering hypothesis. *Psychological Bulletin, 98,* 310–357.

Cole, D. A., & Turner, J. E. (1993). Models of cognitive mediation and moderation in child depression. *Journal of Abnormal Psychology, 102,* 271–281.

Crossfield, A. G., Alloy, L. B., Abramson, L. Y., & Gibb, B. E. (2002). The development of depressogenic cognitive styles: The role of negative childhood life events and parental inferential feedback. *Journal of Cognitive Psychotherapy, 16,* 487–502.

Daley, S. E., Hammen, C., Burge, D., Davila, J., Paley, B., Lindberg, N., & Herzberg, D. S. (1997). Predictors of the generation lf episodic stress: A longitudinal study of late adolescent women. *Journal of Abnormal Psychology, 106,* 251–259.

Davila, J., Hammen, C., Burge, D., Paley, B., & Daley, S. E. (1995). Poor interpersonal problem solving as a mechanism of stress generation in depression among adolescent women. *Journal of Abnormal Psychology, 104,* 592–600.

Depue, R. A., Slater, J., Wolfstetter-Kausch, H., Klein, D., Goplerud, E., & Farr, D. (1981). A behavioral paradigm for identifying persons at risk for bipolar spectrum disorder: A conceptual framework and five validation studies. *Journal of Abnormal Psychology, 90,* 381–437.

DeRubeis, R. J., & Crits-Christoph, P. (1998). Empirically supported individual and group psychological treatments for adult mental disorders. *Journal of Consulting and Clinical Psychology, 66*, 37–52.

DeRubeis, R. J., Gelfand, L. A., Tang, T. Z., & Simons, A. D. (1999). Medications versus cognitive behavior therapy for severely depressed outpatients: Mega-analysis of four randomized comparisons. *American Journal of Psychiatry, 156*, 1007–1013.

DeRubeis, R. J., & Hollon, S. D. (1995). Explanatory style in the treatment of depression. In G. M. Buchanan & M. E. P. Seligman (Eds.), *Explanatory style* (pp. 99–111). Hillsdale, NJ: Erlbaum.

Downey, G., & Coyne, J. C. (1990). Children of depressed parents: An integrative review. *Psychological Bulletin, 108*, 50–76.

Endicott, J., & Spitzer, R. A. (1978). A diagnostic interview: The Schedule for Affective Disorders and Schizophrenia. *Archives of General Psychiatry, 35*, 837–844.

Garber, J., & Flynn, C. (2001). Predictors of depressive cognitions in young adolescents. *Cognitive Therapy and Research, 25*, 353–376.

Gibb, B. E., Abramson, L. Y., & Alloy, L. B. (2004). Emotional maltreatment from parents, verbal peer victimization, and cognitive vulnerability to depression. *Cognitive Therapy and Research, 28*, 1–21.

Gibb, B. E., Alloy, L. B., Abramson, L. Y., & Marx, B. P. (2003). Childhood maltreatment and maltreatment-specific inferences: A test of Rose and Abramson's (1992) extension of the hopelessness theory. *Cognition & Emotion, 17*, 917–931.

Gibb, B. E., Alloy, L. B., Abramson, L. Y., Rose, D. T., Whitehouse, W. G., Donovan, P., et al. (2001). History of childhood maltreatment, depressogenic cognitive style, and episodes of depression in adulthood. *Cognitive Therapy and Research, 25*, 425–446.

Gibb, B. E., Alloy, L. B., Abramson, L. Y., Rose, D. T., Whitehouse, W. G., & Hogan, M. E. (2001). Childhood maltreatment and college students' current suicidal ideation: A test of the hopelessness theory. *Suicide and Life Threatening Behavior, 31*, 405–415.

Gibb, B. E., Alloy, L. B., Walshaw, P. D., Comer, J. S., Shen, G. H. C., & Villari, A. G. (2006). Predictors of attributional style change in children. *Journal of Abnormal Child Psychology, 34*, 425–439.

Gillham, J. E., Reivich, K. J., Jaycox, L. H., & Seligman, M. E. P. (1995). Prevention of depressive symptoms in schoolchildren: Two-year follow-up. *Psychological Science, 6*, 343–351.

Gotlib, I. H., & Hammen, C. L. (2002). Introduction. In I. H. Gotlib & C. L. Hammen (Eds.), *Handbook of depression* (3rd ed., pp. 1–20). New York: Guilford Press.

Gotlib, I. H., Lewinsohn, P. M., Seeley, J. R., Rohde, P., & Redner, J. E. (1993). Negative cognitions and attributional style in depressed adolescents: An examination of stability and specificity. *Journal of Abnormal Psychology, 102*, 607–615.

Greenberg, P., Kessler, R., Nells, T., Finkelstein, S., & Berndt, E. R. (1996). Depression in the workplace: An economic perspective. In J. P. Feighner & W. F. Boyer

(Eds.), *Selective serotonin reuptake inhibitors: Advances in basic research and clinical practice* (pp. 327–363). New York: Wiley.

Haeffel, G. J., Abramson, L. Y., Voelz, Z. R., Metalsky, G. I., Halberstadt, L., Dykman, B. M., et al. (2003). Cognitive vulnerability to depression and lifetime history of Axis I psychopathology: A comparison of negative cognitive styles (CSQ) and dysfunctional attitudes (DAS). *Journal of Cognitive Psychotherapy, 17*, 3–22.

Hammen, C. (1991). Generation of stress in the course of unipolar depression. *Journal of Abnormal Psychology, 100*, 555–561.

Hammen, C. (1992). The family-environment context of depression: A perspective on children's risk. In D. Cicchetti & S. Toth (Eds.), *Rochester Symposium on Developmental Psychopathology* (Vol. IV, pp. 145–153). Rochester, NY: University of Rochester Press.

Hankin, B. L., Abramson, L. Y., & Siler, M. (2001). A prospective test of the hopelessness theory of depression in adolescence. *Cognitive Therapy and Research, 25*, 607–632.

Harkness, K. L., Monroe, S. M., Simons, A. D., & Thase, M. (1999). The generation of life events in recurrent and non-recurrent depression. *Psychological Medicine, 29*, 135–144.

Iacoviello, B. M., Alloy, L. B., Abramson, L. Y., Whitehouse, W. G., & Hogan, M. E. (2006). The course of depression in individuals at high and low cognitive risk for depression: A prospective study. *Journal of Affective Disorders, 93*, 61–69.

Ingram, R. E., Miranda, J., & Segal, Z. V. (1998). *Cognitive vulnerability to depression.* New York: Guilford Press.

Jaycox, L. H., Reivich, K. J., Gillham, J., & Seligman, M. E. P. (1994). Prevention of depressive symptoms in school children. *Behaviour Research and Therapy, 32*, 801–816.

Joiner, T. E., Jr., & Rudd, M. D. (1996). Toward a categorization of depression-related psychological constructs. *Cognitive Therapy and Research, 20*, 51–68.

Joiner, T. E., Steer, R. A., Abramson, L. Y., Alloy, L. B., Metalsky, G. I., & Schmidt, N. B. (2001). Hopelessness depression as a distinct dimension of depressive symptoms among clinical and non-clinical samples. *Behaviour Research and Therapy, 39*, 523–536.

Joiner, T. E., & Wagner, K. D. (1995). Attribution style and depression in children and adolescents: A meta-analytic review. *Clinical Psychology Review, 15*, 777–798.

Judd, L. L. (1997). The clinical course of unipolar major depressive disorders. *Archives of General Psychiatry, 54*, 898–991.

Just, N., Abramson, L. Y., & Alloy, L. B. (2001). Remitted depression studies as tests of the cognitive vulnerability hypotheses of depression onset: A critique and conceptual analysis. *Clinical Psychology Review, 21*, 63–83.

Just, N., & Alloy, L. B. (1997). The response styles theory of depression: Tests and an extension of the theory. *Journal of Abnormal Psychology, 106*, 221 229.

Kapçi, E. G., & Cramer, D. (2000). The mediation component of the hopelessness depression in relation to negative life events. *Counseling Psychology Quarterly, 13*, 413–423.

Kessler, R. C. (2000). Burden of depression. In S. Kasper & A. Carlsson (Eds.), *Selective serotonin reuptake inhibitors 1990–2000: A decade of developments* (pp. 1–14). Copenhagen, Denmark: H. Lundbeck A/S.

Kessler, R. C. (2002). Epidemiology of depression. In I. H. Gotlib & C. L. Hammen (Eds.), *Handbook of depression* (3rd ed., pp. 23–42). New York: Guilford Press.

Lewinsohn, P. M., Steinmertz, J., Larson, D., & Franklin, J. (1981). Depression related cognitions: Antecedents or consequences? *Journal of Abnormal Psychology, 90*, 213–219.

Liu, R., Alloy, L. B., & Abramson, L. Y. (in press). Emotional maltreatment and depression: Prospective prediction of depressive episodes. *Depression & Anxiety.*

Loranger, A. W. (1988). *Personality Disorder Examination (PDE) manual.* Yonkers, NY: DV Communications.

Lynd-Stevenson, R. M. (1997). Generalized and event-specific hopelessness: Salvaging the mediation hypothesis of the hopelessness theory. *British Journal of Clinical Psychology, 36*, 73–83.

Martell, C. R., Addis, M. E., & Jacobson, N. S. (2001). *Depression in context: Strategies for guided action.* New York: Norton.

Metalsky, G. I., & Joiner, T. E. (1992). Vulnerability to depressive symptomatology: A prospective test of the diathesis–stress and causal mediation components of the hopelessness theory of depression. *Journal of Personality and Social Psychology, 63*, 667–675.

Metalsky, G. I., & Joiner, T. E., Jr. (1997). The Hopelessness Depression Symptom Questionnaire. *Cognitive Therapy and Research, 21*, 359–384.

Monroe, S. M., & Hadjiyannakis, K. (2002). The social environment and depression: Focusing on severe life stress. In I. H. Gotlib & C. L. Hammen (Eds.), *Handbook of depression* (3rd ed., pp. 314–340). New York: Guilford Press.

Monroe, S. M., & Simons, A. D. (1991). Diathesis–stress theories in the context of life stress research: Implications for the depressive disorders. *Psychological Bulletin, 110*, 406–425.

Morrow, J., & Nolen-Hoeksema, S. (1990). Effects of responses to depression on the remediation of depressive affect. *Journal of Personality and Social Psychology, 58*, 519–527.

Murray, C. J. L., & Lopez, A. D. (Eds.). (1996). *The global burden of disease: A comprehensive assessment of mortality and disability from diseases, injuries, and risk factors in 1990 and projected to 2020.* Cambridge, MA: Harvard University Press.

Nolen-Hoeksema, S. (1991). Responses to depression and their effects on the duration of the depressive episode. *Journal of Abnormal Psychology, 100*, 20–28.

Nolen-Hoeksema, S. (2000). Ruminative responses predict depressive disorders. *Journal of Abnormal Psychology, 109*, 504–511.

Nolen-Hoeksema, S., & Morrow, J. (1991). A prospective study of depression and posttraumatic stress symptoms after a natural disaster: The 1989 Loma Prieta earthquake. *Journal of Personality and Social Psychology, 61*, 115–121.

Nolen-Hoeksema, S., Morrow, J., & Fredrickson, B. L. (1993). Response styles and the duration of episodes of depressed mood. *Journal of Abnormal Psychology, 102*, 20–28.

Nolen-Hoeksema, S., Parker, L. E., & Larson, J. (1994). Ruminative coping with depressed mood following loss. *Journal of Personality and Social Psychology, 67*, 92–104.

Panzarella, C., Alloy, L. B., & Whitehouse, W. G. (2006). Expanded hopelessness theory of depression: On the mechanisms by which social support protects against depression. *Cognitive Therapy and Research, 30*, 307–333.

Persons, J. B., & Miranda, J. (1992). Cognitive theories of vulnerability to depression: Reconciling negative evidence. *Cognitive Therapy and Research, 16*, 485–502.

Peterson, C. R., Semmel, A., von Baeyer, C., Abramson, L. Y., Metalsky, G. I., & Seligman, M. E. P. (1982). The Attributional Style Questionnaire. *Cognitive Therapy and Research, 6*, 287–300.

Raniere, D. F. (2000). *Long-term stability of inferences about major stressful life-events: Comparing retrospective reports among individuals at high versus low cognitive risk for depression.* Unpublished doctoral dissertation, Temple University, Philadelphia.

Robinson, M. S. (1997). *The role of negative inferential style and stress-reactive rumination on negative inferences in the etiology of depression: Empirical investigation and clinical implications.* Unpublished doctoral dissertation, Temple University, Philadelphia.

Robinson, M. S., & Alloy, L. B. (2003). Negative cognitive styles and stress-reactive rumination interact to predict depression: A prospective study. *Cognitive Therapy and Research, 27*, 275–291.

Romens, S. E., Abramson, L. Y., & Alloy, L. B. (in press). High and low cognitive risk for depression: Stability from late adolescence to early adulthood. *Cognitive Therapy and Research.*

Rose, D. T., & Abramson, L. Y. (1992). Developmental predictors of depressive cognitive style: Research and theory. In D. Cicchetti & S. L. Toth (Eds.), *Rochester Symposium on Developmental Psychopathology* (Vol. IV, pp. 323–349). Hillsdale, NJ: Erlbaum.

Roy, K., Mitchell, P., & Wilhelm, K. (2001). Depression and smoking: Examining correlates in a subset of depressed patients. *Australian and New Zealand Journal of Psychiatry, 35*, 329–335.

Safford, S. M., Alloy, L. B., Abramson, L. Y., & Crossfield, A. G. (2007). Negative cognitive style as a predictor of negative life events in depression-prone individuals: A test of the stress generation hypothesis. *Journal of Affective Disorders, 99*, 147–154.

Segal, Z. V. (1988). Appraisal of the self-schema construct in cognitive models of depression. *Psychological Bulletin, 103*, 147–162.

Segal, Z. V., & Ingram, R. E. (1994). Mood priming and construct activation in tests of cognitive vulnerability to unipolar depression. *Clinical Psychology Review, 14,* 663–695.

Seligman, M. E. P., Peterson, C., Kaslow, N. J., Tannenbaum, R. L., Alloy, L. B., & Abramson, L. Y. (1984). Attributional style and depressive symptoms among children. *Journal of Abnormal Psychology, 93,* 235–238.

Smith, J. M., Alloy, L. B., & Abramson, L. Y. (2006). Cognitive vulnerability to depression, rumination, hopelessness, and suicidal ideation: Multiple pathways to self-injurious thinking. *Suicide and Life-Threatening Behavior, 36,* 443–454.

Smith, J. M., Grandin, L. D., Alloy, L. B., & Abramson, L. Y. (2006). Cognitive vulnerability to depression and Axis II personality dysfunction. *Cognitive Therapy and Research, 30,* 609–621.

Spangler, D. L., Simons, A. D., Monroe, S. M., & Thase, M. E. (1997). Comparison of cognitive models of depression: Relationships between cognitive constructs and cognitive diathesis–stress match. *Journal of Abnormal Psychology, 106,* 395–403.

Spasojevic, J., & Alloy, L. B. (2001). Rumination as a common mechanism relating depressive risk factors to depression. *Emotion, 1,* 25–37.

Spasojevic, J., & Alloy, L. B. (2002). Who becomes a depressive ruminator? Developmental antecedents of ruminative response style. *Journal of Cognitive Psychotherapy, 16,* 405–419.

Spitzer, R. L., Endicott, J., & Robins, E. (1978). Research diagnostic criteria: Rationale and reliability. *Archives of General Psychiatry, 35,* 773–782.

Sullivan, M. D., LaCroix, A. Z., Russo, J. E., & Walker, E. A. (2001). Depression and self-reported physical health in patients with coronary disease: Mediating and moderating factors. *Psychosomatic Medicine, 63,* 248–256.

Tiggemann, M., Winefield, A. H., Winefield, H. R., & Goldney, R. D. (1991). The prediction of psychological distress from attributional style: A test of the hopelessness model of depression. *Australian Journal of Psychology, 43,* 125–127.

Turk, E., & Bry, B. H. (1992). Adolescents' and parents' explanatory styles and parents' causal explanations about their adolescents. *Cognitive Therapy and Research, 16,* 349–357.

Weissman, A., & Beck, A. T. (1978, April). *Development and validation of the Dysfunctional Attitudes Scale: A preliminary investigation.* Paper presented at the Annual Meeting of the American Educational Research Association, Toronto, Ontario, Canada.

Whisman, M. A., & Kwon, P. (1992). Parental representations, cognitive distortions, and mild depression. *Cognitive Therapy and Research, 16,* 557–568.

5

PSYCHOPATHOLOGICAL MECHANISMS ACROSS ANXIETY DISORDERS

SIMON A. REGO, KATHERINE L. MULLER,
AND WILLIAM C. SANDERSON

We have come a long way in understanding anxiety disorders since the first edition of the *Diagnostic and Statistical Manual of Mental Disorders* (*DSM–I*; American Psychiatric Association, 1952). For example, epidemiological studies have shown that anxiety disorders are more prevalent than any other class of disorder, accounting for approximately one third of all costs of mental illnesses and representing the single largest mental health problem in the United States today. In addition, conservative estimates indicate that 25% to 30% of the U.S. population will meet criteria for an anxiety disorder at some point in their lives (Gauthier, 1999; Kessler, Berglund, Demler, Jin, & Walters, 2005), and preliminary data suggest that this risk is increasing (Kessler, Berglund, et al., 2005).

Anxiety disorders have an early onset (evident in children as young as 3 months), occur more often in females, tend to be chronic, and often remain present (though in a somewhat less severe form) even if treated successfully (Barlow, 2002). They are particularly prevalent in primary care settings; result in substantial costs to both individuals and health care systems (in terms of financial costs, decreased productivity, decreased quality of living); and increase the risk of suicide (Kessler, Chiu, Demler, & Walters, 2005), mortality, and substance abuse.

Most experts in the field attribute increased understanding of anxiety disorders to a boom in research that was spurred by the publication of the third revision of the *DSM* (*DSM–III*; American Psychiatric Association, 1980). Unlike *DSM–I*, which lumped all of the anxiety disorders together into one broad category ("anxiety neurosis"), *DSM–III* established distinct sets of diagnostic criteria dividing anxiety into a range of specific disorders, which for the most part, except for minor revisions in the diagnostic criteria, remain today (e.g., panic disorder [PD], obsessive–compulsive disorder [OCD], social phobia). Armed with a more reliable and valid classification system, researchers were able to determine the epidemiology of anxiety disorders, formulate conceptual models positing the etiology and maintenance of anxiety disorders, and design effective evidence-based interventions for the anxiety disorders.

Along the way, however, there have been questions and concerns raised about classification of the anxiety disorders. For example, some critics have questioned whether all of the disorders currently listed in the Anxiety Disorders section of the text revision of the fourth *DSM* (*DSM–IV–TR*; American Psychiatric Association, 2000) are in the appropriate category. For example, factor analytic findings by Cox, Clara, and Enns (2002) revealed that posttraumatic stress disorder (PTSD) showed no affinity with a factor defined by panic and phobic disorders but instead loaded on a factor defined primarily by mood disorders. Other critics have questioned the validity of using a purely categorical approach in general and have suggested that incorporating a dimensional diagnostic system would be more appropriate (Brown & Barlow, 2005; Krueger, Watson, & Barlow, 2005; Widiger & Coker, 2003). As an example, Krueger et al. (2005) pointed out that for several of the Axis II (personality) disorders, individuals need to meet criteria for only five of nine symptoms to be formally diagnosed; thus, it is possible that individuals meeting criteria for one of these disorders may share only one common feature. This highlights the fact that persons who meet diagnostic criteria for a specific mental disorder can still vary greatly in terms of their symptom presentations.

It appears that research and treatment of the anxiety disorders have followed a similar trend. For example, researchers initially studied each of the anxiety disorders in isolation, then moved to examining comorbidity, and most recently have begun to look for common/shared characteristics or underlying syndromes (e.g., Barlow, 2002). Likewise, treatment protocols were initially developed and tested on each of the disorders separately, then adapted to account for comorbidity, and finally have moved toward more unified approaches (e.g., Barlow, Allen, & Choate, 2004).

It is with this history in mind that we address in this chapter the behavioral mechanisms underlying specific anxiety disorders. In particular, we focus on three common factors that cut across each of the anxiety disorders: (a) anxiety, (b) fear, and (c) avoidance. We believe that these common factors represent the basic evolved psychological mechanisms underlying humans' identification of, and response to, danger—what we commonly refer to as the emotions of anxiety and fear. Thus, we begin with a discussion of the nature and adaptive function of these mechanisms. This is followed by a discussion of the phenomenology of each of the specific anxiety disorders in light of these basic dimensions. From this vantage point, anxiety disorders are conceptualized as psychopathological expressions of these core adaptive mechanisms. Finally, we review the basic psychotherapeutic treatment components used to treat anxiety disorders and discuss how they are used to target the proposed behavioral mechanisms.

THE NATURE OF ANXIETY AND FEAR

Anxiety

Despite the tremendous progress in understanding the nature and treatment of anxiety disorders, researchers have not yet arrived at a unified definition of *anxiety*. What most definitions of anxiety have in common, however, is that they involve a future-oriented, apprehensive anticipation of some danger or misfortune. In addition, most definitions of anxiety include a set of accompanying somatic symptoms (i.e., physiological arousal). When "appropriately" triggered (e.g., in the face of true danger), anxiety is believed to be an adaptive or protective function that motivates the individual to behave in a way to manage the danger. For example, the anticipation of danger and the accompanying negative emotional state may motivate the individual to take action to minimize the threat (e.g., if one is worried about passing a test, then the anxiety may serve as a motivation to study because studying may decrease the anxiety) or to avoid the threat (e.g., if one is fearful of flying, then the anxiety may be relieved by avoiding the "threat.").

The anxiety response consists of several components, including the subjective experience of affect, a set of expressive behaviors, an integrated neurobiological response, and a cognitive perception/appraisal (Barlow, 2002). Complicating matters is the fact that affect and cognitions appear to be under the control of separate and partially independent neurological systems (Zajonc, 1984) that allow for emotional activation both with and without the intermediation of higher cognitive processes (LeDoux, 1996). Why would this be the case?

Evolutionary models of anxiety typically propose that to survive and ultimately be successful in reproducing, organisms must be able to respond quickly and efficiently to life-threatening situations. Those that were able to do so in the past survived and thus were more likely to reproduce and pass on their genes. As a result, this characteristic is represented in the population. And although anxiety (or something resembling it) can be found in almost all animals, it is in humans that we see several unique applications—

and complications—that are associated with our higher cognitive processes. For example, some researchers believe that although our ability to anticipate the future is unique, it also gives rise to the hypervigilance that is thought to maintain pathological anxiety (Barlow, 2002). In addition, research has shown that our physical and intellectual performance are actually driven and enhanced by anxiety (up to a certain point), after which they both deteriorate (Broadhurst, 1957; Yerkes & Dodson, 1908).

The main problem emphasized by evolutionary models, however, is that although our environment has changed tremendously within a very short period of time (at least in the context of millions of years of evolution), the nature of our anxiety reaction has not caught up. It appears that the brain may not have been designed to receive so many danger inputs, and this may lead to pathological anxiety. For example, in the evolutionary environment, for millions of years humans were aware of threats that occurred only within their small group, and thus the "inputs" were minimal. In the current environment, the media explosion within the past 50 years has caused humans to be bombarded with information about dangers that may, in fact, represent only a small risk. This information overload is one example of how rapid changes in the environment that are not mirrored by changes in the brain may lead to pathological anxiety in vulnerable individuals.

Thus, anxiety can be thought of as a historically adaptive, automated, multicomponent response to future stimuli or situations that are perceived as dangerous. *Pathological anxiety*, by definition, is anxiety that is out of proportion to the actual threat. This is believed to be the function of an archaic evolutionary response system that may overrespond to dangers (i.e., a "better safe than sorry" system) because human evolution was guided by reaction to "real" threats, not minimal, irrelevant threats passed on by the media. Anxiety is not be confused with the experience of fear, however, a topic to which we now turn.

Fear

Whereas anxiety is thought of as the apprehensive anticipation of some future danger, *fear* is generally considered to be an emotional response and/or behavioral reaction to a specific, imminent danger. Many researchers refer to the experience of fear as an alarm reaction that fires when we are directly and imminently threatened. Most of us know this as the *fight-or-flight* emergency response. For example, a student with a fear of public speaking may feel anxious after hearing an announcement in class that the students will be required to do a presentation at some point during the semester. The anxiety would be linked to that student's anticipation of giving the presentation and would likely intensify as the date of the presentation approaches. The fear response, on the other hand, would emerge when that student actually is called on in class to give the presentation.

Thus, the experience of fear is characterized by a more focused response that matches the perceived demands of the situation. In other words, the emotional response generated by the knowledge that a mugger could be present in a parking lot would be much different than the emotional response generated if one were actually confronted by the mugger. Under the appropriate circumstances, this alarm serves its purpose and mobilizes the organism to defend itself or escape from the dangerous situation. On occasion, however, this ancient alarm system can misfire (i.e., produce a false alarm, becoming activated when no real danger is present) and cause what is defined in the *DSM* as a *panic attack* (Barlow, 2002).

The subjective experience of a panic attack was first described in *DSM–III* and, for the most part, the definition remains unchanged. According to *DSM–IV–TR*, a *panic attack* is defined as a discrete period of intense fear or discomfort, in which 4 (or more) of 13 physiological, behavioral, and cognitive symptoms develop abruptly and reach a peak within 10 minutes. The physiological and cognitive symptoms include the following: palpitations; pounding heart or accelerated heart rate; sweating, trembling, or shaking; sensations of shortness of breath or smothering; a feeling of choking; chest pain or chest pressure or discomfort; nausea or abdominal distress; feeling dizzy, unsteady, light-headed, or faint; feelings of unreality or being detached from oneself; numbness or tingling sensations; and chills or hot flushes. Cognitive symptoms include a fear of losing control or going crazy or a fear of dying. The behavioral features of panic consist of an urge to avoid or escape from the situation.

Although it is obvious that panic attacks constitute the central feature of PD, in fact, they invariably occur in each of the major anxiety disorders. Therefore, we assert that each of the anxiety disorders can be conceptualized in terms of panic attacks, or false alarms, that are triggered by stimuli perceived to pose some sort of threat to the individual. What differentiates the major anxiety disorders is the trigger for the panic attack. For example, in social anxiety disorder (SAD) the trigger is likely to be a social interaction, in PTSD the trigger may be a situation or stimulus that resembles the initial trauma, in OCD (contamination subtype) the trigger may be a doorknob that is perceived as dirty, and in specific phobia (SP, animal subtype) the triggering stimulus may be a dog.

In addition, we propose that subsequent to these false alarms, perhaps as a way to manage the highly uncomfortable alarm reactions themselves, individuals begin to experience increasing anxious apprehension and involuntary urges (e.g., breathe more rapidly) that together instinctively lead them to monitor their environment for any signs of danger and to engage in activities that will keep them out of danger, thereby reducing the likelihood of a panic attack being triggered.

In sum, we propose two broad aspects of the response to danger: (a) anxiety and (b) fear (i.e., panic). Anxiety is primarily concerned with preparing to manage a future threat, whereas fear involves an acute response to a specific and imminent danger. It is essential to add here that although these response systems clearly have adaptive functions, not only in our evolutionary history but also in the contemporary environment, they can be triggered whenever danger is perceived by the individual—whether realistic or not. This latter point is relevant to the existence of anxiety disorders, which by definition consist of anxiety/fear reactions that are out of proportion to the actual threat.

In the next section, we detail the three major psychopathological behavioral mechanisms believed to underlie the development and maintenance of each of the anxiety disorders. The terms *psychopathological mechanism* and *psychopathological behavioral mechanism* are meant to be used interchangeably and are typically assumed to include both behavioral and cognitive mechanisms.

PSYCHOPATHOLOGICAL BEHAVIORAL MECHANISMS IN ANXIETY DISORDERS

The previous discussion emphasized the fundamental role that the perception of danger plays in triggering functional anxiety. As would be expected, the core psychopathological mechanisms in anxiety disorders are related to the perception and response to danger; specifically, *anxiety* is the mechanism related to the perception of future danger, *fear/panic* is the mechanism related to the perception of imminent danger, and *behavioral escape* and/or *avoidance* are responses related to coping with the perceived danger. What distinguishes functional (appropriate) anxiety from pathological anxiety is the validity of the perception of danger. In the following paragraphs, we discuss in detail these three core psychopathological behavioral mechanisms (see Table 5.1). This is followed by a discussion of the specific manifestations of these mechanisms across the anxiety disorders.

TABLE 5.1
Behavioral Mechanisms in the Anxiety Disorders

Mechanism	Definition	References
Anxiety	A future-oriented mood state, containing both cognitive and physiological components, in which one is ready or prepared to attempt to cope with upcoming negative events.	Barlow (2002), Beck et al. (1985), Clark (1999), Craske & Pontillo (2001)
Fear/Panic	An automated response (alarm reaction) that fires in the presence of actual specific and imminent danger.	Barlow (2002), Stein (2006), Klein (1993), Anderson & Insel (2006)
Avoidance	An internal or external response performed to avoid or escape from dangerous situations.	Barlow (2002) Clark (1999), Borkovec (1994), Craske (1999)

Barlow (2002) suggested that a better and more precise term for anxiety is *anxious apprehension* because it "conveys the notion that anxiety is a future-oriented mood state in which one is ready or prepared to attempt to cope with upcoming negative events" (p. 64). He asserted that this anxious apprehension contains both a cognitive component (vigilance) and physiological/somatic component (readiness), to allow the individual to be prepared to deal with the potential negative event. Thus, under the right conditions (e.g., if entering into a potentially dangerous area), anxious apprehension is considered an adaptive response because it prepares the individual to fight or flee.

In essence, it is the job of the cognitive component to scan the environment for sources of threat or danger. This increased vigilance (hypervigilance) requires the organism to narrow its attention in order to sift quickly through a large amount of information so it can make quick decisions. However, what if errors (i.e., cognitive biases) were to exist in the functioning of this cognitive component? Several researchers (e.g., Beck, Emery, & Greenberg, 1985; Clark, 1999; Craske & Pontillo, 2001) have argued that errors in the cognitive component of anxious apprehension play a major role in the development and maintenance of anxiety disorders. These researchers assert that in pathological cases of anxiety there exist three main cognitive biases or disturbances in information processing: (a) attentional biases, (b) judgment/interpretative biases, and (c) memory biases.

Attentional biases involve the selective processing of threatening information, making one more likely to detect any potential source of danger in their environment. For example, an individual with a specific phobia of dogs who goes for a walk outside would be vigilant for, and likely to detect, the presence of nearby dogs (e.g., barking, dog tags clanging, nails scratching on the sidewalk, etc.) much more quickly than someone without the phobia (and thus without this attentional bias). According to Craske and Pontillo (2001), the research has consistently demonstrated that an attentional bias for threat-related information exists in anxious populations. They discussed several processes that may account for these attentional biases, including strategic or controlled attention in favor of threat-related stimuli (e.g., focusing attention on the dog chained to the tree), interference effects (e.g., being unable to play catch if a dog is outside), and automatic (noneffortful) and nonstrategic processing biases toward threat-related information (e.g., hearing a dog bark in the distance). As Clark (1999) noted, however, these attentional biases can also direct attention away from threat cues. For example, a patient with social phobia may avoid looking at other people in feared situations to avoid detecting negative evaluation.

Craske and Pontillo (2001) noted that attentional biases tend to be content specific and tied to personal relevance (e.g., dogs for persons who have a dog phobia, social situations for persons with social phobia). Therefore, they asserted that these biases, rather than being viewed as global deficits (i.e., a personality trait such as general overanxiousness), tend to be seen as emotion, context, and task specific and as differing between the anxiety disorders. Thus, an individual with PTSD due to a physical assault that occurred when returning home on a deserted street one night would not necessarily show attentional biases when at work during the day but clearly would show an attentional bias when in a circumstance that resembled the initial traumatic situation. The greater the match between the environmental stimuli and individual (i.e., high personal relevance), the more likely it is that a "fear network" will be activated (cf. Foa & Kozak, 1986).

Although different theories have been proposed to explain the origin of these biases, some (e.g., Beck et al., 1985) attribute the biases to core belief systems (or schemata) that contain a danger-laden focus. Beck and Clark (1997) asserted that once these schemas are activated, they distort information such that individuals overestimate the magnitude and severity of threat (e.g., "If I have a panic attack, I will die!"), underestimate the extent of their coping resources (e.g., "I was lucky to get out alive last time!"), and lead to the overuse of compensatory self-protective strategies (e.g., "I must always sit in the aisle seat, carry my cell phone, and know how to get out fast!"). This in turn is hypothesized to lead to distorted information processing about the world, self, and future via negative automatic thoughts and images of danger.

Judgment/interpretative biases involve the interpretation of ambiguous stimuli as threatening. According to Craske and Pontillo (2001), judgment/interpretative biases are involved in pathological cases of anxiety and include either the heightened estimation of personal risk or the overestimation of the danger of the fear response (i.e., the physiological component of anxious apprehension). Butler and Mathews (1983) found that anxious individuals exhibited biased estimates of the probability of future threat (increased probability of danger) and an increased tendency to interpret ambiguous stimuli as threatening. For example, an individual with a social phobia who is forced to give a speech may be more likely to attend to and interpret a neutral face in the audience as being negative/critical or to view a momentary lapse in his memory as being seen by audience members as evidence that he is stupid. In addition, Butler and Mathews cited the work of Taylor and Rachman (1994), who found that an overestimation of the fear response (e.g., "If I panic, I will lose it!") characterizes phobic individuals, which they assert may be derived from a more general tendency to overpredict danger.

Finally, researchers (e.g., Barlow, 2002; Craske & Pontillo, 2001) suggest that *memory biases* (e.g., the tendency to report continual preoccupation with anxiety- and danger-related themes, even in the absence of objective triggers of some type) may also play a role in pathological cases of anxiety. However, they warn that the empirical findings in support of memory biases have been inconsistent and may occur only under specific conditions, such as when mood at encoding and retrieval are similar in valence (i.e., positive vs. negative) as well as arousal (i.e., high vs. low; cf. Eich, 1995).

Thus, in patients with anxiety disorders, disturbances in information processing or biases (attentional, judgment/interpretative, memory) found in the cognitive component of anxious apprehension can cause an individual to pay selective attention (implicitly or explicitly) to personally relevant stimuli. When this occurs in the appropriate context and/or mood, it can lead to or enhance the perception of threat and/or distort judgments of risk. This in turn can intensify the physiologic/somatic component of anxious apprehension, leading to a state of persistent hypervigilance and hyperarousal (i.e., persistent readiness) that can then be further misinterpreted as evidence heightened personal risk or danger in the fear response and maintain anxiety over time (e.g., "If I feel so anxious, I must be in a dangerous situation").

The classic example of this would be in the case of patients with PD, who, on entering a place where they previously experienced an attack (memory bias), turn their attention toward their body (attentional bias) and, in so doing, notice benign bodily sensations and use this as evidence that something is wrong (judgment/interpretative bias). If this pattern continues to escalate, these individuals can end up experiencing a recurrence of panic attacks, a topic we discuss in the next section.

FEAR AND PANIC ATTACKS: RESPONSE TO IMMINENT DANGER

If anxious apprehension evolved to prepare the individual to deal with a potentially dangerous or life-threatening event, then how would the individual respond if the event were to actually occur? Many researchers link the presence of a specific threat to the emotion of fear and describe an "alarm reaction" (panic attack) that occurs in the face of actual imminent danger. During these true alarms, a series of physiological (and cognitive) events take place that allow the individual to either defend him or herself or escape (i.e., the fight-or-flight reaction). When they are working adaptively, these automated reactions go largely unnoticed. For example, individuals who narrowly miss being in serious car accidents often report not noticing their fear reaction (e.g., heart pounding, sweaty, tense) until they are safely out of harm's way—because their attention was initially focused on the external situation. However, what would happen if the alarm reaction were to fire in the absence of true, imminent danger?

This maladaptive firing of the fear response (i.e., firing in the absence of danger) has been labeled by some researchers a *false alarm* and, just as disturbances in information processing can have a deleterious impact on anxious apprehension, the inability to extinguish or inhibit false alarms is considered to be a hallmark of most anxiety disorders (Anderson & Insel, 2006). Researchers have endeavored to conceptualize each of the anxiety disorders in terms of different false alarms that can be linked to a specific context that is perceived by the individual as threatening. In addition, some researchers have proposed that these false alarms are mediated by specific neurocircuitry with a particular evolutionary origin (Stein, 2006); that is, perhaps the nature of pathological anxiety experienced by humans today has been shaped by actual threats in our evolutionary environment.

In SAD, for example, an individual with an exaggerated opinion of his or her low status (e.g., "People find me boring") or who overestimates threat ("People will notice I am blushing and think I am weird") will likely experience anxious apprehension when entering a social situation and may become hypervigilant for signs of danger (e.g., looks of disapproval or boredom from others, evidence that his or her anxiety is visible to others, etc.). However, it is only when the individual (via a dysfunctional information-processing system) selectively attends to certain threat-related stimuli (facial expressions of others, body temperature) and misinterprets them as threatening ("They look bored—it's happening!") that an escalation of anxiety occurs culminating in a false alarm.

With regard to PD, some researchers (e.g., Klein, 1993) have proposed that the false alarm is due to a false "suffocation" alarm, whereas others (e.g., Barlow, 2002) have proposed that it is simply due to a random misfiring of the fight-or-flight alarm in biologically and psychologically vulnerable individuals who find themselves in stressful circumstances. In either case, individuals experiencing recurrent false alarms (panic attacks) are likely doing so because of a misperception (that is often implicit) of imminent danger, which in this case takes the form of bodily sensations (e.g., palpitations, increased heart rate, etc.). It is important to note that these misinterpreted sensations are basically the same as those found in normal anxious apprehension (as we discussed in the previous section) but that a false alarm occurs only when these sensations are catastrophically misinterpreted as being much more dangerous than they really are. In particular, researchers believe that it is the interpretation of the sensations as indicative of an immediately impending physical or mental disaster that leads to the exacerbation of the fear response.

Finally, in PTSD, although the current circumstances may be safe, cues that serve as reminders of the past trauma (e.g., sounds, smells, memories, dreams, etc.) may be selectively attended to, implicitly recalled, and misinterpreted as dangerous and thus lead to a state of heightened anxiety and increased hypervigilance that can quickly trigger a false alarm. Thus, an individual who was mugged and now has PTSD may feel an increase in anxious apprehension when entering the neighborhood in which the mugging occurred but may experience a fear response (panic, false alarm) only if he encounters a person who looks like the mugger. Of course, conditioned fear may also play an important role, along with avoidance behaviors of the cues that trigger anxiety. We address these avoidance behaviors in the next section.

AVOIDANCE BEHAVIOR: RESPONSE TO ELIMINATE DANGER

As mentioned earlier, avoidance of stimuli that trigger anxiety is one of the most common ways individuals manage their anxiety. It should be noted that although avoidance behaviors are typically thought of as observable behaviors (e.g., moving away from a spider), they can also take the form of internal mental processes (e.g., distraction, pushing thoughts away, mental rituals, etc.). Avoidance behaviors include both the avoidance of encountering an observed stimulus as well as the escape from a situation perceived as threatening.

As in the case of accurate information processing and true alarm reactions (e.g., facing a truly life-threatening danger), avoidance behaviors are evolutionarily adaptive because they help steer the individual out of harm's way. For example, it would be totally appropriate to avoid entering into a dark alley at night in a neighborhood known for its high crime rate or to run from a building in which one detects smoke.

In individuals with anxiety disorders, however, the excessive use of avoidance behaviors is considered to be reflective of a maladaptive coping style that occurs in response to triggers of anxious apprehension (Barlow, 2002). It is also considered by many researchers to be a central mechanism in the maintenance of anxiety disorders. In particular, behavioral models of anxiety disorders, derived from conditioning theory, explain the repeated use of avoidance behaviors in terms of negative reinforcement. In other words, the avoidance response terminates the uncomfortable anxiety symptoms in response to the stimulus, and the removal of the negative state of anxiety/fear (relief) increases the likelihood that one will engage in the same behavior (avoidance) the next time he or she is in a similar situation or experiencing a similar affective state.

Cognitive models of anxiety disorders, on the other hand, propose that individuals repeatedly use avoidance behaviors as a way of managing their tendency to overpredict danger and/or the likelihood of dangerous outcomes. They assert that the true mechanism behind avoidance behavior is that it keeps the individual out of the dangerous situation. As a result, this mechanism prevents the individual from engaging in "reality testing"—or discovering that there is no real reason to be afraid of the situation or trigger. In other words, by avoiding the feared situation, the individual never discovers if his or her fears would have been realized and, as a consequence, fear is maintained. Of interest is that more recent work (e.g., Borkovec, 1994; Craske, 1999) has led researchers to conceptualize the process of worry as an additional (and similarly maladaptive) attempt to cope with chronic anxiety that functions by enabling individuals to avoid full access to the threatening mental material that is tied to their emotional core of anxiety. Thus, worry is thought to function in a manner similar to other, more observable avoidance behaviors in that it serves as a negative reinforcer (e.g., worrying helps the individual avoid negative affect).

Note, however, that it is difficult for individuals whose anxious apprehension has become generalized to many different contexts to engage in avoidance behaviors (Barlow, 2002). Instead, these individuals develop more subtle behaviors that some (e.g., Clark, 1999) have termed *safety behaviors* (coping behaviors used to manage their immediate reactions [e.g., fainting or falling] in feared situations). In these cases the individual may enter the feared situation and may not appear to be engaging in any avoidance behaviors. However, on closer inspection, one may find that the individual is engaging in some form of safety behavior to prevent or minimize the feared danger. For example, a person with PD who fears he or she will faint may enter a crowded room but lean on a wall to prevent falling down and injuring him- or herself. Similarly, when caught up in a cycle of worry, a person with generalized anxiety disorder (GAD) may engage in distraction as a form of emotional avoidance or psychological escape.

In sum, disturbances in anxious apprehension (via biases in information processing), fear and panic (via false alarms), and avoidance behaviors constitute three primary psychopathological mechanisms found across all anxiety disorders. These mechanisms appear to be involved in the etiology and maintenance of the respective disorders. As mentioned earlier, however, the specifics of these dimensions tend to be tied to personal relevance and are often context specific; thus, they can differ widely between the range of anxiety disorders and even between individuals with a particular diagnosis. We explore these differences in the following section.

PHENOMENOLOGY OF ANXIETY DISORDERS

In this section, we review how the psychopathological mechanisms detailed thus far play out in each anxiety disorders. Although, as suggested previously, the basic nature of the mechanisms is similar across the various disorders, the specific triggers and presentation of the anxiety are distinct for each of the respective disorders.

Panic Disorder

According to *DSM–IV–TR*, individuals with PD experience recurrent, unexpected panic attacks (see first part of chapter for definition), which must be followed by at least 1 month of persistent concern about having additional attacks, worry about the implications of the attacks or their consequences (e.g., losing control, having a heart attack), or the making of a significant change in behavior because of the attacks (e.g., decreased physical activity, carrying cell phone more often in case of emergency).

Panic attacks occur spontaneously in the general population and, in fact, have been estimated to occur in as much as 10% to 14% of the population (Barlow, 2002), yet only a small percentage of individuals who experience a panic attack go on to develop PD. Therefore, it is important to understand both how panic attacks originate and the psychopathological mechanisms that maintain them.

Panic attacks can occur spontaneously for a variety of reasons. For example, Barlow (2002) suggested that individuals who experience a panic attack may have an inherited biological vulnerability that is expressed through an increase in anxiety sensitivity or a more intense stress response. Although for many individuals this vulnerability can lay dormant, in those who experience panic attacks the vulnerability is thought to be "activated" by early negative psychological experiences that lead to low perceptions of self-control (Barlow, 2002). Thus, panic attacks are thought to emerge within the context of stressful life events, in individuals with a high sensitivity to anxiety and a sense of learned uncontrollability.

Triggers for panic attacks can include any unexplained arousal or somatic sensations (including those found in anxious apprehension) as well as any other stimuli associated with the first attack. In addition, certain activities (e.g., exercise, sex), substances (e.g., alcohol, caffeine), or mood states (e.g., anger, excitement) that generate sensations similar to those experienced during a previous attack can become triggers for future attacks.

Thus, panic attacks can be viewed as being generated by a fear and catastrophic misinterpretation of the sensations associated with anxious apprehension. According to Smits, Powers, Cho, and Telch (2004), this *fear of fear,* or the tendency to respond fearfully to benign bodily sensations, figures prominently in several theoretical accounts of PD. Smits et al. described several lines of research that have provided evidence consistent with a fear-of-fear hypothesis, including descriptive studies, laboratory challenge studies, and prospective studies. In addition, Clark's (1986) cognitive theory of panic posits that for patients who panic, the somatic sensations accompanying a state of apprehension are catastrophically misinterpreted, which results in a further increase in apprehension, followed by elevated somatic sensations, and so on, until a full-blown panic attack occurs.

In keeping with the psychopathological mechanisms described earlier in this chapter, the fear of fear in PD can be explained as occurring because of a maladaptive interaction between biases in information processing during states of anxious apprehension, the misfiring of the fear response (false alarms), and behavioral avoidance. For example, individuals who are concerned about having additional attacks or worried about the implications of the attacks become apprehensive about future attacks and hypervigilant for signs of danger (Barlow, 2002). Because the "danger" in the case of PD can be either internal or external, individuals increase their focus on internal body sensations and constantly monitor their internal environment for signs of abnormality while also checking their external environment for safety cues or methods for escape in the event of danger.

Recall, however, that these individuals are already likely to possess a diminished sense of perceived self-control (judgment bias) that makes them more sensitive to the experience of anxious apprehension and thus more likely to detect its physiological component (i.e., somatic sensations). Accordingly, these individuals begin to detect (attentional bias) the signs of a future attack (e.g., a heart palpitation) with increasing frequency and misinterpret these symptoms as further evidence of imminent catastrophe (memory bias), making them increasingly apprehensive and escalating further the somatic response. This rise in apprehension makes the possibility of a false alarm more and more likely ("The danger is here!"), which further strengthens beliefs about low control (judgment bias) and increases apprehension about future attacks.

In addition to anxious apprehension and hypervigilance, individuals with PD engage in avoidance behaviors that are aimed at avoiding the internal sensations and/or external situations associated with attacks (Barlow, 2002). For example, they may avoid certain activities (e.g., exercise, sex) and foods and beverages (e.g., spicy, caffeine containing) associated with the feared sensations. In many cases, this can also lead to the development of agoraphobia or to the avoidance (or endurance with great distress) of situations in which it might be difficult to escape or in which help might not be available in the event of panic attack or panic-like symptoms (e.g., being alone at home, riding in elevators, going through tunnels, crowded places).

Individuals experiencing panic may also engage in more subtle avoidance behaviors ("safety behaviors") to manage their fears of the sensations (e.g., carrying a water bottle for dry mouth, standing near walls for feeling faint, walking slowly for racing heart) and situations (carrying a cell phone at all times, sitting only in an aisle seat at theaters, distracting themselves using crossword puzzles). Although these avoidant behaviors all "work" by decreasing anxious apprehension in the short term (i.e., negative reinforcement) and thus are likely to be held onto as coping mechanisms, the end result is that the catastrophic thoughts about the sensations and/or situations are never fully confronted or examined, and therefore faulty cognitions remain uncorrected.

Generalized Anxiety Disorder

According to DSM–IV–TR, individuals with GAD experience excessive worry that is distressing and difficult to control, more days than not for a period of at least 6 months. They worry about a number of events or activities, find it difficult to control the worry, and endorse at least three physiological symptoms that are associated with the worry (e.g., restlessness, being easily fatigued, difficulty concentrating, irritability, muscle tension, disturbed sleep). Of importance, the focus of the anxiety and worry must not be confined to features of another *DSM–IV–TR* Axis I disorder (e.g., having a panic attack).

In most cognitive–behavioral models of GAD worry is considered to be primarily a verbal/linguistic (as opposed to imaginal) activity (Borkovec, 1994) that involves the generation of multiple potential future threats or catastrophes. In an evolutionary sense, the function of worry can clearly be adaptive in that it would allow individuals to anticipate future threats and prepare them to cope. Craske (1999) suggested that worry may be seen as an initial stage in the anticipation of threat, during which anxious arousal is reduced and conceptual planning can take place (Barlow, 2002). In GAD, however, the process of worry is viewed as maladaptive because it has become excessive (out of proportion to the threat) and uncontrollable.

Triggers in GAD can include nearly any situation in which the outcome of a potentially threatening future event is uncertain (Barlow, 2002). For example, individuals with GAD tend to worry about their relationships, work, finances, physical health, and their future. They may also worry about minor matters, such as being on time, what outfit to wear, or what to eat for dinner. Other triggers may include current/immediate problems to which a solution is not readily available, or even the process of worrying itself (i.e., *meta-worry*, or worry about worrying).

In keeping with the psychopathological dimensions described earlier in this chapter, individuals with GAD appear to display an attentional bias toward threatening stimuli, an interpretative bias of perceiving ambiguous situations as threatening, and a judgment bias of seeing negative outcomes as more likely. Some researchers (e.g., Mathews, 1990) propose that in combination, these biases function by maintaining hypervigilance toward personally relevant threat cues, which leads to an increased detection of threat. With increased detection of threat, fear levels rise, which in turn often leads to cognitive avoidance of these threat cues—a move that prevents elaboration (i.e., processing) of the threatening material (Barlow, 2002).

Thus, as in the case of individuals with PD, a vicious cycle can be said to exist in individuals with GAD, in which worry leads to hypervigilance for threatening cues, which are detected more frequently and in turn intensify the worry process. In addition, some researchers (e.g., Wells, 1999) have proposed that fears that worry itself is dangerous may further exacerbate the worry cycle.

As noted earlier, in many instances worry functions as a facilitator of cognitive avoidance. Researchers (e.g., Borkovec, 1994) have proposed that this avoidant function works as a negative reinforcer from two separate channels: (a) the nonoccurrence of predicted negative outcomes and (b) real reductions in somatic arousal that are associated with the initial worry process (Barlow, 2002). In other words, individuals with GAD believe that their feared predictions are prevented by worrying when in fact they were worrying about low-base-rate events that rarely happen anyway. At the same time, they also experience a reduction in anxiety in the short term by worrying ("relief"). Some researchers (e.g., Borkovec, 1994), however, believe that this artificial reduction in anxiety prevents full access to the individual's fear network and thus interferes with successful emotional processing and, as a result, ultimately maintains the threatening meaning found in the threat cues (Barlow, 2002).

Although the avoidance in GAD is notably more cognitive (internal) than behavioral (external), individuals with GAD may also avoid situations in which their feared cues are present and will also engage in preventative behaviors associated with their worry—such as seeking reassurance from loved ones to confirm that they made it to their destination to stop their anxiety about the individual getting into a car accident. In addition, individuals with GAD may avoid pursuing their desired goals out of a fear of failure or other negative outcome (Roemer & Orsillo, 2002).

Therefore, GAD may be viewed as being maintained by a rigid habit of making inaccurate predictions about future events that interferes with adaptive responding to current circumstances and helps the individual to avoid emotional, experiential, and cognitive processing (Barlow, 2002). This avoidance reduces the physiological component of anxious apprehension in the short term but prevents elaboration (emotional processing, disconfirmation of catastrophic predictions) and responsiveness to current environmental contingencies (behavioral inaction), which in turn allows for the continuation of threatening associations, situations, and predictions. This process of worry (chronic apprehension about potential future threats) in turn can escalate into repeated false alarms (fight-or-flight responses)—but without any fighting or fleeing behaviors available (Borkovec, Hazlett-Stevens, & Diaz, 1999).

Obsessive–Compulsive Disorder

According to *DSM–IV–TR*, individuals with OCD experience recurrent obsessions (i.e., persistent thoughts, images, impulses, or ideas that are experienced as unwanted, intrusive, or inappropriate and that cause marked anxiety or distress) and/or compulsions (i.e., repetitive behaviors or mental acts performed with the goal of reducing anxiety or distress) that are time consuming (e.g., take up more than 1 hour per day) or cause marked distress or significant impairment. At some point during the course of the disorder, the individual must recognize that the obsessions and/or compulsions are excessive or unreasonable.

Most models of OCD acknowledge the commonality of occasional intrusive thoughts in the general population. Yet, given the high frequency of intrusive thoughts in the general population (Rachman & de Silva, 1978), only a relatively small percentage of individuals develop obsessions and compulsions at a level severe enough to warrant a diagnosis of OCD (Barlow, 2002).

Researchers have focused on both how intrusive thoughts arise and, more important, how they transition into obsessions.

With regard to the origin of intrusive thoughts, data suggest that they often arise when an individual is under stress or in a state of anxious apprehension (Barlow, 2002). This is consistent with data that demonstrate an increased availability of negatively valenced cognitions exists while one is in a negative mood state. Some researchers (e.g., Barlow, 2002) have proposed that as with the other anxiety disorders, individuals with OCD have a biological and/or psychological vulnerability increasing their susceptibility to experiencing a strong stress response, which in turn serves as a nonspecific generator of intrusive thoughts.

Yet recall that although intrusive thoughts are common, not all intrusive thoughts become obsessions. Therefore, given the commonality of intrusive thoughts, some other psychopathological mechanisms must be in place to help transform an intrusive thought into an obsession. As with the other disorders, we will examine how OCD is caused and maintained across three dimensions: (a) anxiety, (b) fear/panic (false alarms), and (c) avoidance behaviors.

Cognitive models of OCD (e.g., Rachman, 1997, 1998; Salkovskis, 1985) propose that the intrusive thoughts per se do not matter as much as the way in which the individual appraises or interprets the thoughts because it is the response to the thoughts that enables those thoughts to become obsessions. In particular, researchers believe that in individuals with OCD anxiety is generated by cognitive biases, such as beliefs that certain thoughts are important, dangerous, and/or indicators of a bad or abnormal character. Some researchers believe that these cognitive biases may be derived from a sense of excessive responsibility, as well as a rigid code of conduct and perfectionism that may date back as far as early childhood (Barlow, 2002). In addition, it appears that the rigidity of one's belief system can be associated with the severity of OCD and that the sense of excessive responsibility may encourage a phenomenon called *thought–action fusion* (Rachman, 1993), a specific bias in which the individual believes that thinking something is as bad as doing it or that thinking something makes a bad event more likely to occur (Barlow, 2002).

Perhaps because of their heightened sense of responsibility, individuals with OCD appear to be hypervigilant for signs of danger and less able to tolerate any uncertainty and ambiguity that could possibly signal a threat (Barlow, 2002). Thus, they are more vulnerable to experience doubts about the veracity of their experience (attentional and judgment biases), to have trouble making decisions, and to require excessive information in their decision making. In essence, they appear to have a cognitive bias for assuming danger exists unless they can assure themselves of safety (Barlow, 2002).

Therefore, the false alarm in OCD could be viewed as a response to intrusive thoughts that are interpreted as being unacceptable because they signal potential danger for which the individual feels responsible (cognitive bias). Once the individual experiences fear in reaction to the intrusive thoughts, he or she will become hypervigilant for other thoughts that are similar in theme, in order to prevent or suppress them in an attempt to gain control. This often backfires: Evidence (e.g., Wegner, Schneider, Carter, & White, 1987) suggests that suppression of thoughts leads to an increase in the salience of thoughts, making them even increasingly more challenging to suppress, and then often leads to neutralizing rituals or avoidance behaviors, in an effort to control an unpredictable and therefore stressful environment (Barlow, 2002).

Individuals with OCD most closely resemble those with GAD, and differ from those with other anxiety disorders, in that they are most often anxious over internal cognitive stimuli versus somatic events (as in the case of PD) or external objects or situations (as in the case of persons with specific or social phobias). Because obsessive thoughts are more difficult to control by means of avoidance behaviors, individuals strongly resist these experiences and/or develop mental or behavioral strategies to neutralize them (i.e., compulsions). The increasing anxious apprehension about future intrusive thoughts sets the stage for false alarms, which then also become associated with the obsessive thoughts (Barlow, 2002).

In sum, in individuals who develop OCD, intense negative affect from stressful life events causes intrusive thoughts that are judged to be unacceptable, and attempts are made to avoid or suppress the thoughts (Barlow, 2002). The recurrence of the intrusive thoughts causes an intensification of the anxious apprehension along with a belief that the thoughts are unpredictable and uncontrollable. This in turn causes a narrowing of attention onto the content of the thoughts that are deemed unacceptable. At this point, each of the intrusive thoughts can then act as discrete triggers in their ability to elicit separate alarm reactions (Barlow, 2002). For example, in an individual diagnosed with OCD, the content of the intrusive thoughts and related information-processing biases may center on the theme of contamination. This would trigger anxious apprehension whenever the person confronts a doorknob and may escalate into a false alarm if he or she accidentally comes into contact with a doorknob. Thus, the individual may then engage in avoidance behaviors around doors.

Social Anxiety Disorder

According to *DSM–IV–TR*, individuals with social anxiety disorder (SAD) experience a marked and persistent fear of social or performance situations in which they may be judged negatively or embarrassment may occur. The fear can be limited to one situation or may be so broad that the person experiences anxiety around almost anyone, at any time. Exposure to the social or performance situation almost invariably provokes an immediate anxiety response. Most often, the social or performance situations are avoided, although they are sometimes endured with extreme discomfort, and the desire for social interaction remains.

Although as many as 90% of adults report that they have been shy at one time in their lives, not all shy people develop SAD. This has led some researchers to propose that temperamental and personality factors such as shyness and behavioral inhibition play a role in the development of SAD but do not fully explain its development (Barlow, 2002). More recent models (e.g., Barlow, 2002; Clark & Wells, 1995; Rapee & Heimberg, 1997) have proposed that, as with the other anxiety disorders, individuals who develop SAD have a biological and psychological vulnerability to anxious apprehension, which, under stressful situations, results in a false alarm that then becomes associated with social-evaluative situations.

Still other researchers (e.g., Stein, 2006) emphasize the fact that sensitivity to anger, criticism, or other means of social disapproval was adaptive in certain situations throughout evolution and may indeed be adaptive today. This sensitivity becomes exaggerated and/or distorted in individuals who develop social phobia. Increasingly, however, researchers (e.g., Stein, 2006) are integrating these ideas into comprehensive models of social phobia. For example, Stein (2006) described the false alarms in social phobia as "appeasement displays" and noted the existence of data that support the notion that displays of embarrassment mitigate negative reactions of others. Stein proposed that persons with social phobia misperceive the need for social appeasement by means of distortions in their view of their status (low) and/or overestimates of threat from social surroundings—which would then theoretically trigger repetitive false alarms.

Therefore, the triggers in SAD would include any situations in which the individual believes that he or she may be judged negatively or in which embarrassment may occur. Examples would include attending a social event, having to speak or write in front of others, or using public bathrooms.

In keeping with the psychopathological mechanisms described earlier in this chapter, a substantial amount of data suggests that individuals with social phobia display cognitive biases (attentional, memory, and judgmental) toward socially threatening information. For example, persons with social phobia have been found to (a) have a memory bias for critical faces, (b) experience negative images of themselves performing poorly in social situations, and (c) interpret external social information in a less positive way than those without social anxiety (Hirsch, Clark, & Mathews, 2006). In addition, persons with social phobia have been found to engage in self-focused attention when in socially threatening situations. This self-focused attention is thought to be part of a maladaptive attempt to prevent an embarrassing and humiliating situation but ends up distracting attentional resources that are necessary for optimal task performance and interfere with information processing that could provide disconfirming evidence against negative beliefs (Barlow, 2002).

In terms of judgment biases, research suggests that both probability and cost biases contribute to the maintenance of social phobia. *Probability biases* involve associating feared stimuli or fearful responses with an unrealistically high probability of harm, and *cost biases* involve exaggerating the negative consequences of the anticipated harmful event. Foa, Huppert, and Cahill (2006) proposed that probability biases may be more important in anxiety disorders that are characterized by concerns about severe negative outcomes, whereas cost biases may be more important in anxiety disorders that are characterized by concerns about mild negative events. They suggested that cost biases may be more prominent in SAD relative to the other anxiety disorders because individuals with SAD are concerned about mild negative events in addition to severe negative events (in Smits et al., 2006).

These cognitive biases are thought to account for the persistence of fear despite the fact that the individuals realize that their fears are excessive or unreasonable. In addition, even if they manage to confront their fears and be around others, these individuals are usually very anxious beforehand, are intensely uncomfortable throughout the encounter, and worry for hours afterward about how they were judged. These biases also are believed to form the platform for future false alarms in that relatively minor negative life events involving performance or social interactions begin to generate anxious apprehension, particularly if an alarm is associated with these events (Barlow, 2002).

Thus, individuals with social phobia may be predisposed to experience false alarms in social situations because of a combination of biological and psychological factors. Once experienced, the repeated false alarms may lead to a perceived lack of internal control and to the development of the belief that events are controllable only by others. In response to these false alarms, persons with social phobia begin to avoid situations or engage in numerous safety behaviors while in situations that prevent learning or observing of corrective information.

Specific Phobias

According to *DSM–IV–TR*, individuals with SPs experience a marked, persistent, and excessive or unreasonable fear when in the presence of, or when anticipating an encounter with, a specific object or situation. The focus of the fear may be anticipated harm from some aspect of the object or situation (e.g., an individual may fear dogs because of concerns about being bitten) or concerns about losing control, panicking, and fainting that might occur on exposure to the feared object. Exposure to the phobic stimulus almost invariably provokes an immediate anxiety response, which may take the form of a situationally bound or situationally predisposed panic attack. Because marked anticipatory anxiety occurs in the presence of the phobic situation, such situations are usually avoided. Less commonly, the person forces him- or herself to endure the phobic situation, but it is experienced with intense anxiety. Adults with this disorder must recognize that the phobia is excessive or unreasonable.

There are several subtypes of SP, and each has its own specific triggers. For example, in the animal subtype, the fear may be cued by various animals or insects; in the natural environment subtype, the fear may be cued by storms, heights, or water; in the blood–injection-injury subtype, the fear may be cued by seeing blood or an injury, or by receiving an injection or seeing an invasive medical procedure; in the situational subtype, the fear may be cued by public transportation, tunnels, bridges, elevators, flying, driving or enclosed places; and in the "other" subtype, the fear may be cued by situations that might lead to choking, vomiting, or contracting an illness, "space" phobias (i.e., the individual is afraid of falling down if away from walls or other means of physical support) and, in children, by loud sounds or costumed characters.

Studies on information processing for individuals with SPs have found mixed results for two of the three main biases discussed in this chapter: (a) biases in attention and (b) biases in memory. With regard to biases in attention, research studies have frequently found a fragile and not-always-replicated effect (Barlow, 2002). In addition, little is known about the evolutionary significance of the function of a bias, although some have proposed that it may facilitate escape from danger. With regard to memory biases, one reason for the inconsistencies in findings may be due to the fact that studies have examined different aspects of memory. Nevertheless, the research suggests that there exists at least limited evidence of deficits in recognition for phobia-related stimuli, as well as enhanced implicit memory for fear-related characteristics of phobic situations (Barlow, 2002).

Ample evidence suggests, however, that judgment biases (e.g., distorted thinking) play a role in the maintenance of SPs. These distortions have been found across a broad range of SPs and include both feared objects and situations. Further evidence comes from the fact that individuals with SPs are frequently inaccurate when reporting their expected fear level prior to encountering a feared stimulus and are more likely to assume high correlations between their feared stimulus and negative consequences (Barlow, 2002). Finally, some evidence suggests that individuals with SP of insects report distorted perceptions about degree of activity in animals and insects, as well as the direction of movement, and that they can respond to triggers even when outside of their awareness (Barlow, 2002).

Given the existence of distorted information processing, it seems logical to assume that feared objects and situations would increase anxious apprehension that could ultimately trigger a false alarm reaction in response to an encounter with the phobia stimulus, yet not all objects are the same in their ability to condition a fear response. Researchers have found that the association of the false alarm needs to be with an object or situation that has a high probability of acquiring phobic properties—objects or situations with some have real danger or pain associated with them (i.e., prepared learning; Barlow, 2002). This type of emotional learning/conditioning in general, and fear conditioning specifically, does not seem to depend on conscious awareness.

Although researchers have proposed that genetics plays a role in the origins of SPs, they also have argued that these prepared reactions need to interact with environmental influences, by means of early experiences, to create an SP. These early experiences are thought to consist of direct conditioning, vicarious acquisition, or information/instruction. Note, however, that whereas direct experiences are frequently cited by individuals with SPs, a significant proportion of phobic persons do not identify any of these three early experiences, so clearly they cannot account for the creation of all phobias (Barlow, 2002).

Researchers have argued that regardless of how the conditioning occurs, once false alarms become strongly associated with the object or situation the anxiety then occurs in the presence of the object or situation primarily because the fear of experiencing another (unpredictable) false alarm is triggered by being in the context of cues signaling the possibility of alarm. In addition, blocking an individual's urge ("action tendency") to escape is thought to intensify the fear reaction (Barlow, 2002).

Therefore, individuals with SPs are likely to have a nonspecific genetic predisposition to experience reactions along with a psychological vulnerability to experience anxiety (Barlow, 2002). These vulnerabilities interact with specific stressful life experiences, which can generate a false alarm. If the false alarms are associated with a specific predisposition or "prepared" situations to which the individual has been sensitized (e.g., through early learning experiences), then anxiety develops in response to the possibility of having additional alarm responses. The false alarms then become the focus of anxious apprehension leading to the phobia. In addition, vicarious experience and misinformation lead to false alarms that become conditioned with object or situation (Barlow, 2002).

This process has been found to be similar across phobia types. Note, however, that there is mixed evidence suggesting that individuals with SPs have some fear of experiencing the symptoms of arousal, but this fear is not experienced to the same degree as in individuals with other anxiety disorders, and it may vary according to different types of SP. Also note that blood–injury-injection phobias appear to display a unique pattern of responding that includes a *diphasic response*, in which heart rate and blood pressure initially increase, followed by a sudden decrease in arousal, often accompanied by fainting. However, a substantial minority of blood–injury-injection phobias are not associated with a history of fainting, and some persons faint without fear (Barlow, 2002). It is thought that individuals who faint develop a phobia in response to this and thus that fainting may actually be an anxiety trigger rather than a phobic response.

Posttraumatic Stress Disorder

According to *DSM–IV–TR*, individuals with PTSD develop a set of characteristic symptoms following the direct experience, witnessing, or learning of an event that involves actual or threatened death or serious injury, to the individual or another person. In adults, the individual's response to the event must involve intense fear, helplessness, or horror. Whereas most people who experience such events recover from them, people with PTSD continue to experience anxiety for months or even years after the event. They report reliving the trauma through intrusive thoughts, flashbacks, and nightmares; avoiding stimuli associated with the trauma; feeling detached or estranged from loved ones; and having trouble concentrating and sleeping. Thus, PTSD can be thought of as an abnormal response to a traumatic event (Stein, 2006).

In terms of triggers for false alarms, many researchers believe that the intense basic emotions (true alarms) experienced during a traumatic event lead to false (learned) alarms that occur during exposure to situations that symbolize or resemble an aspect of the traumatic event (e.g., anniversaries of the trauma; sights, smells, or feelings associated with the trauma). However, given the work done on information-processing biases, it is clear that one must also develop the *belief* that these events, including one's own emotional reactions to them, are proceeding in an unpredictable uncontrollable manner (judgment bias), which in turn elevates anxious apprehension and increases the odds of experiencing a panic attack. In fact, Stein (2006) considered the reexperiencing and hyperarousal symptoms in PTSD as similar to the "positive" (e.g., panicky) symptoms in other anxiety disorders, only with a focus on the traumatic event.

More recent cognitive models of the trauma response have suggested that the development and maintenance of acute and chronic PTSD are strongly mediated by cognitive responses to the traumatic event (Bryant, 2003). For example, some researchers have proposed that PTSD can be explained in terms of excessively negative (catastrophic) appraisals of the trauma and a disturbance of autobiographical memory. In terms of catastrophic appraisals, Bryant (2003) stated there is evidence that people who are at high risk for developing PTSD exaggerate both the probability of future negative events occurring and the adverse effects of these events (cf. Warda & Bryant, 1998). He also noted that they display cognitive biases for events related to external harm, somatic sensations, and social concerns (cf. Smith & Bryant, 2000). Finally, Bryant stated that there is also evidence that individuals at risk for PTSD respond to a hyperventilation task with more dysfunctional interpretations about their somatic sensations—and that there is initial evidence that catastrophic appraisals about oneself predict subsequent PTSD.

According to Bryant (2003), there is also initial support for the proposition that management of autobiographical memories in the acute phase influences adjustment. He cited evidence from a study that showed poor retrieval of specific memories in an acute phase of trauma accounted for 25% of the variance in severity of subsequent PTSD symptoms.

Of interest is the fact that Bryant (2003) suggested that it is also possible that appraisals may help explain many of the discrepant findings about the predictive power of different symptoms. For example, he noted that the mixed findings concerning the predictive utility of dissociative symptoms may be explained by the role of appraisals. He asserted that one person may experience depersonalization and attribute this to the normative response that one has after trauma, whereas another person experiencing depersonalization may catastrophically believe that this reaction is a sign of madness. He concluded, therefore, that the appraisals of the symptom, rather than the symptom itself, may be critical in determining the influence it will have on subsequent adaptation.

Finally, several studies have found that individuals who develop PTSD display a cognitive and behavioral style that leads toward the avoidance of aversive information in order to manage their traumatic memories. In a pattern consistent with classical conditioning models, avoidance of the experience of negative affect results in the numbing of general responsiveness. In other words, the experiencing of fear by means of several false/learned alarms in response to memories or other aspects of the trauma results in a persistent avoidance of stimuli associated with the trauma (e.g., thoughts, feelings, memories, reminders) and/or the interoceptive cues that signal the possibility of another false/learned alarm. This accounts for the avoidance/numbing cluster of symptoms in PTSD (i.e., it represents avoidance of aversive emotional reactions or alarms). Stein (2006) considered this similar to the negative or avoidance symptoms found in other anxiety disorders.

CLINICAL IMPLICATIONS: TREATMENT AND ITS RELATION TO THE PSYCHOPATHOLOGICAL MECHANISMS

We have described three primary psychopathological mechanisms involved in the development and maintenance of anxiety disorders. We followed that with a discussion of how these influence the development and maintenance of each of the major anxiety disorders. We now turn our attention to the clinical implications of these mechanisms.

Cognitive–behavioral therapy (CBT) is the most evidence-based psychological treatment for the various anxiety disorders (Nathan & Gorman, 2007). Thus, we focus our attention on the clinical implications of the identified mechanisms as they relate to CBT. Most CBT treatment packages for anxiety disorders contain the following four elements, each of which we describe in the following paragraphs: (a) psychoeducation, (b) techniques to lower physical arousal, (c) cognitive restructuring, and (d) exposure. Together, these strategies are believed to target the cognitive and behavioral dysfunctions (i.e., psychopathological mechanisms) associated with anxiety disorders.

Note that although we may emphasize the use of a particular treatment strategy to address a particular mechanism (e.g., cognitive restructuring to correct cognitive biases), the relationships are in fact not quite so direct. Psychological variables mediating change in behavioral and cognitive treatment strategies for anxiety disorders are thought to be similar (Gauthier, 1999), but although a particular intervention may be best described as cognitive or behavioral this does not necessarily mean that it does not have impact on the other modality (e.g., exposure, primarily seen as a behavioral strategy, can ultimately provide information that will correct cognitive biases).

Psychoeducation

Psychoeducation is a therapeutic strategy with two principal aims: (a) to provide corrective information to the individual about his or her fears and (b) to provide the individual with an understanding of his or her disorder. Thus, this strategy is believed to facilitate correction of the individual's faulty beliefs and, as a result, lead to more accurate information processing.

Individuals with anxiety disorders often have erroneous beliefs about the origins and/or contributors to their anxiety symptoms, and they may have consulted with several different health care providers and received different diagnoses and/or explanations about their condition. Without a clear explanation and model of their diagnosis, patients will often develop their own theories, frequently imagining the worst-case scenario, and devise their own strategies for handling their symptoms (see our discussion of avoidance in the "Exposure" section). Psychoeducation is aimed at teaching patients a new model for interpreting their ongoing anxiety. According to Beck and Clark (1997), "One of the most effective ways of deactivating the primal threat mode is to counter it with more elaborative, strategic processing of information resulting from the activation of the constructive, reflective modes of thinking" (p. 55).

The psychoeducation phase of treatment typically begins at the first session and continues throughout the treatment. During the initial sessions, explanations and definitions of the origin and development of anxiety and panic may be provided. In addition, each of the symptoms associated with the patient's disorder may be identified and explained via the creation of an idiosyncratic model. As treatment progresses, psychoeducation may include handouts and books targeting common myths or errors found in patients with the same diagnosis, as well as the maladaptive coping strategies they have been using. Throughout treatment, psychoeducation strategies are also used to explicitly address the errors in logic that patients make—ideally *in vivo*, when the biases are activated and most amenable to correction.

Techniques to Lower Physical Arousal

Physical hyperarousal is a cardinal symptom of anxiety disorders. Although it is clear that the hyperarousal occurs in the context of the individual's threatening stimulus, for many persons, the hyperarousal is chronic as a result of persistent anxious apprehension.

Patients with anxiety disorders may have a biological predisposition to experience greater amounts of anxiety and/or be more sensitive or reactive to it. In addition, they display biases in their information processing that cause them to selectively attend to their symptoms and judge them as threatening. Thus, they frequently feel helpless in their ability to control their symptoms. These feelings cause them to be more on guard or vigilant for the symptoms, which, ironically, makes them more vulnerable to noticing and experiencing the very symptoms they fear. This ultimately reinforces their beliefs about being helpless, creating a vicious cycle between anxious apprehension and cognitive arousal.

It is with this idea in mind that techniques to lower physical arousal were incorporated into treatment protocols. These strategies include progressive and passive muscle relaxation, diaphragmatic breathing, and guided imagery. They may also include general suggestions for increasing exercise and daily activity as well as encouragement to attend classes on yoga, mindfulness, meditation, Tai Chi, and so on. What all these strategies have in common is that they provide a way for the patient to gain some degree of control over his or her physical arousal.

In *progressive and passive muscle relaxation* the goal is to help patients gain a greater sense of control over their bodies. These strategies typically are practiced on a daily basis. As patients begin to master the exercise, they are better able to identify and decrease tension that might otherwise escalate into a full-blown panic attack. As patients become more confident in their ability to use relaxation strategies, they also enhance the perception of their ability to cope with anxiety and increase their threshold for activation of false alarms.

Diaphragmatic breathing (breathing retraining) also helps patients regain a sense of control over the somatic features of panic and anxiety by teaching them a method of breathing that increases relaxation and prevents hyperventilation. Recall that when a person is experiencing stress and anxiety, respiration rate often increases, which is characterized by the use of chest muscles and short, shallow breaths. This hyperventilation creates a cascade of somatic symptoms that can be interpreted by patients to mean that their body is out of control. To combat this tendency, patients are taught diaphragmatic breathing (i.e., breathing that involves in-and-out movement of the abdomen, not chest) at a regular rate (i.e., approximately 12 breaths per minute). This exercise is then practiced outside of therapy in many different situations. Patients quickly learn to regulate their breathing and come to recognize that this is an effective strategy on which they can rely in panic-provoking situations.

Cognitive Restructuring

Cognitive restructuring can be traced back to the seminal work of Aaron T. Beck, who was the first to propose a comprehensive theory that faulty information processing, characterized by an increased sense of vulnerability, may underlie the anxiety disorders (Beck et al., 1985). As is evident by its name, cognitive restructuring is aimed at correcting faulty information processing in patients with anxiety disorders. The process of cognitive restructuring involves the identification of maladaptive cognitions followed by a detailed analysis to identify potential biases or errors in logic (i.e., cognitive distortions). This process may be done in a formal manner, such as by using a dry board and "three-column record" (consisting of thoughts, feelings, and behaviors) in session to help patients identify and examine the thoughts, beliefs, and assumptions elicited during an episode of anxiety, worry, or panic, as well as their subsequent behaviors. Alternately, cognitive restructuring may be done in a less explicit manner, such as by presenting individuals with a series of questions (i.e., the Socratic method) during the session to determine their idiosyncratic maladaptive beliefs and then helping them to challenge the validity of these cognitions by guiding them to alternate possibilities.

Exposure

As detailed earlier, avoidance behaviors maintain anxiety disorders in that they strengthen the individual's fear through the process of negative reinforcement. *Exposure* is a powerful strategy used to extinguish the association between a trigger (stimulus) and anxiety response. Exposure therapy involves systematically having the individual confront a range of anxiety-provoking stimuli. Indeed, according to Teasdale (1993), one of the most effective ways of changing maladaptive emotions involves directly altering emotionally driven behaviors (e.g., the avoidance responses). This is in accordance with emotional processing theory (Foa et al., 2006; Foa & Kozak, 1986), which states that emotion networks representing fear- and anxiety-related behavior incorporate a defined mutual circuit and must be accessed for therapeutic change to occur.

The goal of exposure is to have the individual confront personally relevant and context-specific anxiety-provoking stimuli (which can be internal or external) in order to access his or her particular fear network, and then to prevent (behavioral and/or cognitive) avoidance so that the fear diminishes in the presence of the stimulus and thus results in extinction of his or her maladaptive response. According to Otto, Smits, and Reese (2004), repeated confrontations of the feared stimuli under controlled conditions are required in order to unlearn fears and avoidance behaviors, with the goal being to extinguish (i.e., dissipate) fear as patients increase their sense of safety in the presence of these stimuli. Otto et al. also pointed out that successful exposure requires clear and unambiguous tests of the fearful assumptions, such as paying direct attention to objective occurrences during exposure and decreasing both safety behaviors (in terms of use and availability) as well as distraction (cognitive avoidance). This fits with modern definitions of extinction that account for active learning of new meanings in relation to original fear cues and emphasize that the learning must be context dependent.

By eliminating avoidance responses, individuals learn to tolerate their symptoms (i.e., habituate to them) as well as disconfirm (i.e., restructure) negative beliefs. This leads to the extinction of an association between the anxiety-provoking stimuli and the maladaptive avoidance response. In a course of typical exposure therapy, the individual will first complete an exposure exercise in session with the guidance of the therapist, with subsequent practice done with less assistance and in between sessions.

Note that most exposure-based treatments involve the creation of a hierarchy of least anxiety-provoking to most anxiety-provoking stimuli. On the basis of this individualized hierarchy, patients are exposed to each of these stimuli in a progressive, systematic fashion. This allows them to learn to tolerate anxiety in less stressful situations first, making it easier to alter the urge to escape. This lesson is then generalized from mildly anxiety-provoking situations to more difficult situations. Therapy progresses and builds on successful past accomplishments, ultimately eroding the connections between the stimulus and the fear response.

CASE EXAMPLE

The following case example demonstrates the use of CBT to target the psychopathological mechanisms involved in the maintenance PD with agoraphobia. Specifically, the three mechanisms targeted were (a) interpretative bias (the individual overestimates the danger of experiencing a panic attack, believing he will die or "go crazy" during a panic attack), (b) avoidance behavior (the individual avoids situations that are associated with a panic attack), and (c) fear of a panic attack (the individual misinterprets benign bodily symptoms as signs of imminent danger).

Presenting Problem

Jason is a 43-year-old man who sought treatment for panic attacks and phobic avoidance (i.e., agoraphobia). He experienced his first panic attack 3 years ago while on vacation in another state. Since that time, he has experienced several panic attacks each week. When he experienced the first attack, he believed he was "going crazy" and since then has feared that during a panic attack he would "go crazy and end up locked in a psychiatric hospital." He did everything he could to avoid experiencing panic attacks, and he tried to limit his activities because he feared if he had a panic attack in public it would increase the likelihood that he would end up being committed to a psychiatric hospital. By the time Jason started treatment, he was avoiding riding in trains and elevators, entering crowded places (e.g., movie theaters), traveling outside of a 20-mile radius around his home, and a number of social situations. As a result of the agoraphobia, Jason had difficulty getting to work on a regular basis and was in danger of losing his job. He was diagnosed according to *DSM–IV–TR* with PD with agoraphobia.

Psychological Interventions

The therapist began CBT by educating Jason about the nature of anxiety, panic, and agoraphobia. The goal was to give Jason the message that PD is a relatively common and well-researched condition that is treatable and not a precursor to "going crazy." Jason found this information useful because "going crazy" was his primary fear during panic attacks. To bolster the psychoeducation phase, Jason was advised to read information about PD on the Internet provided by the Anxiety Disorders Association of America (http://www.adaa.org). This reinforced the information provided during the session and greatly reduced his belief that panic attacks could end in the catastrophic event he feared. The primary mechanisms targeted with this intervention were interpretative bias ("Panic attacks are harmful") and fear of panic attacks ("If I feel a sense of depersonalization, it means I am going crazy").

The treatment then focused on cognitive restructuring. With the assistance of his therapist, Jason was able to identify his catastrophic thoughts. Most of these involved ideas and images that he would "go crazy" and end up in a psychiatric hospital. He also feared that he would have a heart attack during a panic attack. As a result, Jason often avoided situations in which escape was difficult because he believed that if he was stuck in a situation and experienced a panic attack, one of these consequences would occur. The therapist began challenging Jason's catastrophic thoughts in session and generated more realistic thoughts to replace the anxiety-provoking ones. In addition, Jason began to use the information he had received about PD to challenge his catastrophic thoughts. In fact, Jason was able to recall several situations during which he felt anxious but was unable to escape (e.g., a time he was stuck on a subway train) and realized that the anxiety always passed without any of the catastrophes he feared occurring. The primary mechanism targeted with this intervention was Jason's fear of symptoms of a panic attack ("I will go crazy during a panic attack"; "I will have a heart attack during a panic attack").

The final intervention was exposure therapy. The primary mechanism targeted was avoidance. The remaining sessions involved systematic exposure to feared agoraphobic situations (e.g., using subway trains and buses; going into elevators; going into social situations; and going on trips of increasing distance from his home, with the ultimate goal of traveling to Miami, Florida). As is typical in exposure therapy, the therapist started with items low on Jason's fear hierarchy (e.g., items that Jason reported avoiding when possible but was able to do if necessary) to strengthen his coping skills for situations in which the anxiety would be more overwhelming as well as to demonstrate the effectiveness that repeatedly facing a situation within a short period of time has on reducing anxiety and disconfirming negative predictions. Jason was then instructed to practice each assigned item three times during the week in between sessions. For example, the first week he rode the subway train for one stop, the next week three stops, the next week six stops, and so on. This strategy was effective, and repeated exposure to low- and then high-level anxiety-provoking situations resulted in a rapid decrease in his anxiety (habituation). As a result, Jason experienced a significant decrease in his phobic behavior.

CONCLUSION

Anxiety disorders, as defined by the *DSM*, are believed to be distinct diagnostic categories. Although there is quite a bit of symptom divergence among individuals with different anxiety disorders (e.g., a person with an SP vs. a person with OCD), in fact, as we have presented throughout this chapter, the core symptoms and underlying behavioral psychopathological mechanisms are quite similar. Anticipatory anxiety, panic (fear), and avoidance are central components that exist within each of the anxiety disorders. Anxiety disorder categories represent distinct presentations of these central components that have their roots in evolutionary significant threats. Ultimately, understanding the core psychopathological mechanisms has implications for the etiology and treatment of anxiety disorders.

REFERENCES

American Psychiatric Association. (1952). *Diagnostic and statistical manual of mental disorders*. Washington, DC: Author.

American Psychiatric Association. (1980). *Diagnostic and statistical manual of mental disorders* (3rd ed.). Washington, DC: Author.

American Psychiatric Association. (2000). *Diagnostic and statistical manual of mental disorders* (4th ed., text revision). Washington, DC: Author.

Anderson, K. C., & Insel, T. R. (2006). The promise of extinction research for the prevention and treatment of anxiety disorders. *Biological Psychiatry, 60,* 319–321.

Barlow, D. H. (2002). *Anxiety and its disorders: The nature and treatment of anxiety and panic* (2nd ed.). New York: Guilford Press.

Barlow, D. H., Allen, L. B., & Choate, M. L. (2004). Towards a unified treatment for emotional disorders. *Behavior Therapy, 35,* 205–230.

Beck, A. T., & Clark, D. A. (1988). Anxiety and depression: An information processing perspective. *Anxiety Research, 1,* 23–26.

Beck, A. T., & Clark, D. A. (1997). An information processing model of anxiety: Automatic and strategic processes. *Behaviour Research and Therapy, 35,* 49–58.

Beck, A. T., Emery, G., & Greenberg, R. L. (1985). *Anxiety disorders and phobias: A cognitive perspective.* New York: Basic Books.

Borkovec, T. D. (1994). The nature, functions, and origins of worry. In G. C. L. Davey & F. Tallis (Eds.), *Worrying: Perspectives on theory, assessment, and treatment* (pp. 5–33). New York: Wiley.

Borkovec, T. D., Hazlett-Stevens, H., & Diaz, M. L. (1999). The role of positive beliefs about worry in generalized anxiety disorder and its treatment. *Clinical Psychology and Psychotherapy, 6,* 126–138.

Broadhurst, P. L. (1957). Emotionality and the Yerkes–Dodson law. *Journal of Experimental Psychology, 54,* 345–352.

Brown, T. A., & Barlow, D. H. (2005). Dimensional versus categorical classification of mental disorders in the fifth edition of the *Diagnostic and Statistical Manual of Mental Disorders* and beyond: Comment on the special section. *Journal of Abnormal Psychology, 114,* 551–556.

Bryant, R. A. (2003). Early predictors of posttraumatic stress disorder. *Biological Psychiatry, 53,* 789–795.

Butler, G., & Mathews, A. (1983). Cognitive processes in anxiety. *Advances in Behaviour Research and Therapy, 5,* 51–62.

Clark, D. M. (1986). A cognitive approach to panic. *Behaviour Research and Therapy, 24,* 461–470.

Clark, D. M. (1999). Anxiety disorders: Why they persist and how to treat them. *Behaviour Research and Therapy, 37,* S5–S27.

Clark, D. M., & McManus, F. (2002). Information processing in social phobia. *Biological Psychiatry, 51,* 92–100.

Clark, D. M., & Wells, A. (1995). A cognitive model of social phobia. In R. G. Heimberg, M. Liebowitz, D. Hope, & F. Scheier (Eds.), *Social phobia: Diagnosis, assessment and treatment* (pp. 69–93). New York: Guilford Press.

Cox, B. J., Clara, I. P., & Enns, M. W. (2002). Posttraumatic stress disorder and the structure of common mental disorders. *Depression and Anxiety, 15,* 168–171.

Craske, M. G. (1999). *Anxiety disorders: Psychological approaches to theory and treatment.* Denver, CO: Westview Press/Basic Books.

Craske, M. G., & Pontillo, D. C. (2001). Cognitive biases in anxiety disorders and their effect on cognitive behavioral treatment. *Bulletin of the Menninger Clinic, 65*(Suppl.), 58–77.

Eich, E. (1995). Searching for mood dependent memory. *Psychological Science, 6,* 67–75.

Foa, E. B., Huppert, J. D., & Cahill, S. P. (2006). Emotional processing theory: An update. In B. O. Rothbaum (Ed.), *The nature and treatment of pathological anxiety* (pp. 3–24). New York: Guilford Press.

Foa, E. B., & Kozak, M. J. (1986). Emotional processing of fear: Exposure to corrective information. *Psychological Bulletin, 99,* 20–35.

Gauthier, J. (1999). Bridging the gap between biological and psychological perspectives in the treatment of anxiety disorders. *Canadian Psychology, 40,* 1–11.

Hirsch, C. R., Clark, D. M., & Mathews, A. (2006). Imagery and interpretations in social phobia: Support for the combined cognitive biases hypothesis. *Behavior Therapy, 37,* 223–236.

Kelly, M. M., & Forsyth, J. P. (2007). Observational fear conditioning in the acquisition and extinction of attentional bias for threat: An experimental evaluation. *Emotion, 7,* 324–335.

Kessler, R. C., Berglund, P., Demler, O., Jin, R., & Walters, E. E. (2005). Lifetime prevalence and age-of-onset distributions of *DSM–IV* disorders in the National Comorbidity Survey Replication. *Archives of General Psychiatry, 62,* 593–602.

Kessler, R. C., Chiu, W. T., Demler, O., & Walters, E. E. (2005). Prevalence, severity, and comorbidity of the 12-month *DSM–IV* disorders in the National Comorbidity Survey Replication. *Archives of General Psychiatry, 62,* 615–627.

Klein, D. F. (1993). False suffocation alarms, spontaneous panics, and related conditions: An integrative hypothesis. *Archives of General Psychiatry, 50,* 306–317.

Krueger, R. F., Watson, D., & Barlow, D. H. (2005). Toward a dimensionally based taxonomy of psychopathology. *Journal of Abnormal Psychology, 114,* 491–493.

LeDoux, J. E. (1996). *The emotional brain.* New York: Simon & Schuster.

Mathews, A. (1990). Why worry? The cognitive function of anxiety. *Behaviour Research and Therapy, 28,* 455–468.

McNally, R. J. (1994). Cognitive bias in panic disorder. *Current Directions in Psychological Science, 3,* 129–132.

Michael, T., Blechert, J., & Vriends, N. (2007). Fear conditioning in panic disorder: Enhanced resistance to extinction. *Journal of Abnormal Psychology, 116,* 612–617.

Nathan, P. E., & Gorman, J. M. (2007). *A guide to treatments that work* (3rd ed.). New York: Oxford University Press.

Otto, M. W., Smits, J. A. J., & Reese, H. E. (2004). Cognitive–behavioral therapy for the treatment of anxiety disorders. *Journal of Clinical Psychiatry, 65*(Suppl. 5), 34–41.

Rachman, S. (1993). Obsessions, responsibility, and guilt. *Behaviour Research and Therapy, 31,* 149–154.

Rachman, S. (1997). A cognitive theory of obsessions. *Behaviour Research and Therapy, 35,* 793–802.

Rachman, S. (1998). A cognitive theory of obsessions: Elaborations. *Behaviour Research and Therapy, 36,* 385–401.

Rachman, S., & de Silva, P. (1978). Abnormal and normal obsessions. *Behaviour Research and Therapy, 16,* 233–238.

Rapee, R. M., & Heimberg, R. (1997). A cognitive–behavioral model of anxiety in social phobia. *Behaviour Research and Therapy, 35,* 741–756.

Roemer, L., & Orsillo, S. M. (2002). Expanding our conceptualization of and treatment for generalized anxiety disorder: Integrating mindfulness/acceptance-based approaches with existing cognitive–behavioral models. *Clinical Psychology: Science and Practice, 9,* 54–68.

Salkovskis, P. M. (1985). Obsessional–compulsive problems: A cognitive–behavioral analysis. *Behaviour Research and Therapy, 11,* 271–277.

Smith, K., & Bryant, R. A. (2000). The generality of cognitive bias in acute stress disorder. *Behaviour Research and Therapy, 38,* 709–715.

Smits, J. A. J., Powers, M. B., Cho, Y. C., & Telch, M. J. (2004). Mechanism of change in cognitive–behavioral treatment of panic disorder: Evidence for the fear of fear mediational hypothesis. *Journal of Consulting and Clinical Psychology, 72,* 646–652.

Smits, J. A. J., Rosenfield, D., McDonald, R., & Telch, M. J. (2006). Cognitive mechanisms of social anxiety reduction: An examination of specificity and temporality. *Journal of Consulting Clinical Psychology, 74,* 1203–1212.

Soares, J. F., & Ohman, A. (1993). Preattentive processing, preparedness, and phobias. *Behaviour Research and Therapy, 31,* 87–96.

Stein, D. J. (2006). Advances in understanding the anxiety disorders: The cognitive–affective neuroscience of "false alarms." *Annals of Clinical Psychiatry, 18,* 173–182.

Taylor, S., & Rachman, S. (1994). Stimulus estimation and the overprediction of fear. *British Journal of Clinical Psychology, 33,* 173–181.

Teasdale, J. D. (1993). Emotion and two kinds of meaning: Cognitive therapy and applied cognitive science. *Behaviour Research and Therapy, 31,* 339–354.

Warda, G., & Bryant, R. A. (1998). Cognitive bias in acute stress disorder. *Behaviour Research and Therapy, 36,* 1177–1183.

Wegner, D. M., Schneider, D. J., Carter, S. III, & White, L. (1987). Paradoxical effects of thought suppression. *Journal of Personality and Social Psychology, 53,* 636–647.

Wells, A. (1999). A metacognitive model and therapy for generalized anxiety disorder. *Clinical Psychology and Psychotherapy, 6,* 86–95.

Widiger, T. A., & Coker, L. A. (2003). Mental disorders as discrete clinical conditions: Dimensional versus categorical classification. In M. Hersen & S. M. Turner (Eds.), *Adult psychopathology and diagnosis* (4th ed., pp. 3–35). New York: Wiley.

Yerkes, R. M., & Dodson, J. D. (1908). The relation of strength of stimulus to rapidity of habit-formation. *Journal of Comparative Neurology and Psychology, 18,* 459–482.

Zajonc, R. B. (1984). On the primacy of affect. *American Psychologist, 39,* 117–123.

6

DISTINGUISHING RISK FACTORS FROM SYMPTOMS: ARE EATING DISORDERS SIMPLY DISORDERED EATING?

JANET POLIVY AND C. PETER HERMAN

According to Fairburn and Walsh (2002), an *eating disorder* (ED) is "a persistent disturbance of eating behavior or behavior intended to control weight, which significantly impairs physical health or psychosocial functioning" (p. 171). As we discuss in this chapter, various diagnostic criteria have been used to define the precise elements that constitute an ED, but the two main features are clearly (a) disturbed eating or weight control and (b) interference with physical and/or psychological health. The EDs have existed for a long time, and they manifest today in the same manner as they have in the past: Self-starvation and episodes of binge eating and purging have been reported for centuries, and the clinical presentation of anorexia nervosa (AN) has not changed in more than 150 years, when cases described in the medical literature were clearly AN as we know it today (Bemporad, 1997). Finally, EDs are relatively rare. Although many women engage in some form of dieting, relatively few develop an ED (Wilson, 2002). The 12-month prevalence is less than 0.1% for AN and around 1% for bulimia nervosa (BN; Hoek, 2006). Although there have been reports of increases in incidence of the disorders from 1900 to 1970 (e.g., Hoek & van Hoeken, 2003), the recent estimate of 8 cases of AN and 12 cases of BN per 100,000 still make them infrequent, to say the least.

In this chapter, we attempt to distinguish between, on the one hand, risk factors that may cause or contribute to the development of EDs and on the other hand, the actual symptoms that comprise the EDs, their side effects, and their consequences. We do not review the empirical research on risk factors for EDs because several very good and complete reviews already exist (see e.g., Jacobi, 2005; Jacobi, Hayward, de Zwaan, Kraemer, & Agras, 2004). For simplicity's sake, we also limit our discussion to the two eating disorders most clearly defined and most intensively studied: AN and BN. We begin by discussing early theoretical approaches to understanding EDs, and then we present the diagnostic criteria and consider means of identifying those with EDs (assessment/measurement), so that we can define the symptoms of the disorders and understand the relation of these symptoms to risk factors that predict the development of EDs. Finally, we discuss some of the clinical implications of conflating risk factors and symptoms.

THEORIES OF EATING DISORDERS

Theories about the development of EDs appeared in some number in the 1960s and 1970s. Hilde Bruch had been studying AN (as well as obesity, which was then itself regarded as an ED) for decades and published a seminal volume in 1973 detailing her theorizing about AN and obesity. (BN had not yet been identified as a separate disorder.) She discussed the influences of society and of family interactions on the development of vulnerable adolescents and integrated these social factors with individual factors (e.g., genetics and biology) into a comprehensive model. She also provided rich clinical descriptions of the disorders. She pointed out the importance of body image distortions in AN and identified the struggle for control over one's body and one's self that marks the disorder. She also described the deficits in self-awareness and emotional awareness, hunger awareness, and maturity/individuation that were later incorporated into the Eating Disorder Inventory (EDI; Garner, Olmsted, & Polivy, 1983a). According to Bruch, these cognitive distortions and psychological struggles represent parts of the disorder and underlie the abnormal behaviors that are more specifically associated with food and weight. She drew a distinction between societal pressure to make one's body shape conform to a socially acceptable image and the disturbance of body image and distorted attitudes that can result from such pressure and that characterize the EDs and separate them from normal dieting. She classified sociocultural and family factors as contributors or risk factors for the development of an ED but saw the results of these pressures—that is, the body image distortions and negative feelings about the self—as aspects of the disorder itself. Clinical theorists such as Bruch thus made a distinction between symptoms of EDs and risk factors (e.g., contributing factors or triggering factors) that produce or elicit the symptoms. For Bruch, the symptoms of ED went beyond disturbances in eating per se to include disturbances in cognition, perception, and emotion.

Theorizing about EDs since Bruch's time has focused on the contributions to the development of EDs (e.g., Polivy & Herman, 2002; Striegel-Moore, 1997) of the three broad, general areas on which she focused (i.e., the social/cultural environment, the family, and the individual). However, since the late 1980s there has been a change in the way that the disorders are viewed and conceptualized. The distinction between characteristics of the person that reflect the existence or effects of the disorder and characteristics that contribute to the development of the disorder are less clear cut today than they were previously. The so-called risk factors (i.e., contributors to or predictors of the disorder) in much contemporary research seem to include many characteristics that earlier theorists saw as symptoms of the disorder itself. For example, qualities such as body image dissatisfaction/distortion; negative feelings about the self, including low self-esteem or feelings of ineffectiveness; and unrealistic performance expectations or perfectionism were all seen by early theorists as aspects of ED pathology (Bruch, 1973, 1978; Crisp, 1980; Garfinkel & Garner, 1982; Selvini-Palazzoli, 1978; Strober, 1980). Nowadays, these same traits are among the most widely studied risk factors for EDs (for reviews, see Jacobi et al., 2004, and Polivy & Herman, 2002). This shift in the construal of the role played by characteristics such as body dissatisfaction raises the question of what constitutes a *symptom* of a disorder and what constitutes a *risk factor* for that same disorder. In this chapter, we explore this distinction and attempt to determine what effect (if any) the labeling of certain characteristics as risk factors as opposed to symptoms has on theory and research aimed at understanding and treating EDs.

DIAGNOSTIC CRITERIA FOR ANOREXIA NERVOSA AND BULIMIA NERVOSA

The criteria for diagnosing AN and BN ought to help to answer the question of what constitutes a risk factor and what constitutes a symptom. After all, if something is a diagnostic criterion for the disorder (i.e., part of the disorder itself), then it should be regarded as a symptom, not a risk factor (i.e., something that precedes and increases the probability of developing the disorder). Diagnosis of EDs has generally been based on observable behavioral symptoms. In the 1970s, diagnosis of AN was based on the six Feighner criteria (Feighner et al., 1972), which specified (a) age of onset of 10 to 25 years; (b) suppression of food intake resulting in weight loss of 10% to 25% of premorbid weight; (c) distortion of attitudes concerning eating, food, or weight to the point of denial of illness and failure to recognize nutritional needs in the pursuit of extreme thinness, but also sometimes including hoarding of food or other unusual responses toward food; (d) no medical illness or biological condition that might be responsible for the loss of appetite and weight; (e) no other diagnosed psychiatric disorder; and (f) at least two of the following symptoms: amenorrhea, lanugo hair, bradycardia (resting pulse of 60 beats per minute or less), periods of hyperactivity, episodes of binge eating, or vomiting. The third item on this list (distortion of attitudes) is a psychological (and possibly less objective) symptom, but the definition rested primarily on physical and behavioral symptoms specific to eating and weight. It is worth noting here that several features of EDs that Bruch and other contemporary theorists considered inherent to the disorders (e.g., body image distortion, lack of awareness, maturity fears) were not included among the standard psychiatric research and clinical criteria for ED.

When the American Psychiatric Association's *Diagnostic and Statistical Manual of Mental Disorders* was brought up to date and ultimately emerged as the fourth edition, *DSM–IV* (American Psychiatric Association, 1994), AN and BN both included primarily behavioral/physical symptoms. For AN, these symptoms consisted of maintaining a body weight at 85% or less of normal (for height and age), reflecting the behavior of eating minimally and eliminating altogether the intake of many "fattening" foods; placing excessive value on weight for evaluating self-worth, experiencing the body as fat despite emaciation, or fearing fatness; plus, in postmenarcheal females, amenorrhea for at least 3 menstrual cycles (although this criterion seems likely to be dropped in the upcoming *DSM–V*; Mitchell, Cook-Myers, & Wonderlich, 2005). Two types of AN are specified: a restricting type, consisting exclusively of self-starvation, and a binge eating/purging type, wherein the self-starvation is punctuated by repeated episodes of binge eating and/or purging behavior. For BN, the *DSM–IV* diagnostic criteria are recurrent episodes of binge eating, compensatory behaviors to reduce the impact of taking in these excess calories (both bingeing and compensation occurring at least two times a week), and one cognitive/psychological symptom (namely, excessive dependence on weight and shape for self-evaluation). Two subtypes of BN are likewise identified on the basis of whether purging behavior is present (i.e., purging vs. nonpurging types). The defining characteristics of these disorders for diagnostic purposes thus include both physical/behavioral symptoms and at least one psychological/cognitive symptom; both types of ED are thus described as consisting of physical and cognitive eating and body-related symptoms.

In addition to extreme thinness, AN patients manifest other physical symptoms, such as endocrine (e.g., estrogen) disturbances as well as a variety of serologic, cardiac, electroencephalograph, and physical symptoms of starvation (American Psychiatric Association, 1994), but these symptoms appear to be merely side effects of starvation. Other psychological aspects are present in AN, such as depressed mood, obsessive–compulsive behaviors, insomnia, social withdrawal, and decreased sex drive, which also may all be secondary effects of malnutrition. Similarly, BN patients display physical manifestations of their disorder, such as metabolic or dental problems, electrolyte imbalances, enlarged parotid glands, and cardiac disorders (American Psychiatric Association, 1994), all of which may be secondary to bingeing and purging. Depression and anxiety are often present in BN but may represent secondary reactions to the disorder rather than symptoms per se (Beumont, 2002; Polivy & Herman, 2002). *DSM–IV* lists these features of the disorder but because they are not criteria for diagnosing the disorders their actual status is not clear, and this is not clarified in *DSM–IV*.

The major ED diagnostic criteria thus appear to be pathological eating behaviors (starving, bingeing, purging, compensating) and their effects (losing a lot of weight and maintaining low weight), plus the psychological distortion of body image (seeing oneself as fat), overconcern with weight and shape, and use of weight and shape for self-evaluation. In our view, this focus on eating-related features misses important aspects of the disorders.

Some psychological features of AN have been noted that are not part of the diagnostic criteria and that do not seem to be sequelae of starvation. Perfectionism, feelings of ineffectiveness, and a need for control over one's body and environment characterize AN patients (American Psychiatric Association, 1994; Jacobi et al., 2004), and these may be present both before significant weight loss has occurred and/or after weight restoration (e.g., Kaye et al., 1998). Patients with the binge/purge subtype of AN also display various impulsive behaviors in addition to bingeing, such as drug or alcohol abuse, sexual acting out, stealing, self-mutilation, and unstable moods (e.g., Garfinkel, 2002). Binge/purge AN patients tend to exhibit premorbid characteristics such as higher childhood weight and increased incidence of familial obesity, as well as borderline, narcissistic, or antisocial personality traits (Garfinkel, 2002). These patients appear to have a worse prognosis (Beumont, 2002).

Similarly, in BN, purging patients exhibit more psychopathology than do nonpurgers. They often exhibit self-injury, comorbidity with other disorders, and anxiety about eating/gaining weight (Garfinkel, 2002). BN patients tend to be impulsive, which may manifest as sexual acting out, stealing, or intentional self-harm (Polivy & Herman, 2002). BN patients tend to be secretive about their disorder; they attempt to hide evidence of their binges, are ashamed of their behavior, and in general engage in the binge eating when alone (Polivy & Herman, 1993).

One other symptom not explicitly specified in the *DSM–IV* diagnostic description but widely recognized as characteristic of ED patients is a relentless pursuit of thinness (Bruch, 1973). Given current idealization of thinness in Western society, this desire for thinness is not easy to discriminate from the motivation driving normal dieting as seen in many young women (Polivy & Herman, 1987). Compared with the normal dieters, ED patients manifest not only a fear of fatness that may resemble a phobia but also tend to base their self-worth almost entirely on their body shape and weight (McFarlane, McCabe, Jarry, Olmsted, & Polivy, 2001). But is overconcern with weight and shape exclusive to EDs? There is evidence to suggest that normal, chronic dieters share this characteristic. For example, although not as extreme as ED patients in their reliance on weight and shape for determining their self-worth, restrained eaters (chronic dieters) also place a greater than normal emphasis on weight and shape in their self-evaluations (Trottier, McFarlane, Olmsted, & Polivy, 2005). How then do we discriminate having an ED from so-called normal dieting?

The diagnostic criteria for EDs are focused on behaviors and attitudes related to eating, weight, and body shape, but separating these behaviors and attitudes from those present in nonpathological, normal dieters may be difficult because the difference, if any, may be no more than a matter of degree. Both *DSM–IV* and clinical descriptions of the EDs do, however, include psychological features that although not diagnostic or defining criteria are nevertheless acknowledged to be present alongside the eating pathology. These references to "associated features" that are not necessarily central to the disorder raise the question of what exactly these associated features represent. Are they part of the disorder itself, or consequences of the disorder, or contributing (risk) factors that play some role in causing the disorder to develop, or something else? Would an exclusively eating-related disorder that did not include any of these associated psychological features be debilitating enough to qualify as a true disorder, or would an exclusively eating-related disorder be merely "severe dieting" (see, e.g., Polivy & Herman, 1987)?

IDENTIFYING PEOPLE WITH EATING DISORDERS

Do the assessment techniques for diagnosing EDs help discriminate individuals with true EDs from avid dieters? Early screening instruments developed to measure the EDs (e.g., the Eating Attitudes Test [Garner, Olmsted, Bohr, & Garfinkel, 1982]; the Bulimia Test [Hawkins & Clement, 1980]) focused solely on eating attitudes and behaviors. Conceptualizations that emphasized the importance of cognitive and personality symptoms of the disorders (e.g., Bruch, 1973, 1978; Crisp, 1980; Garfinkel & Garner, 1982; Selvini-Palazzoli, 1978; Strober, 1980) led to the development of a widely used inventory, the EDI, to measure ED pathology as it was defined at the time (before the advent of *DSM–IV*, so the symptoms measured were not the diagnostic criteria later specified in *DSM–IV*).

In 1983, a chapter describing the newly published and validated EDI began: "This chapter describes a new psychometric instrument designed to assess a broad range of behavioral and attitudinal characteristics of anorexia nervosa and bulimia" (Garner, Olmsted, & Polivy, 1983b, p. 173). Similarly, the journal article reporting the development of this measure stated that the shortcoming of the other measures then available to assess symptoms of AN and BN was that none of them tapped "psychological dimensions which have been postulated to be more fundamentally related to anorexia nervosa and bulimia" (Garner, Olmsted, & Polivy, 1983a, p. 16). Thus, the EDI was developed as a multifaceted measure not only of actual disordered eating behaviors but also of associated psychological characteristics. The psychological problems measured by this scale were included specifically to differentiate nonclinical eating disturbances in groups such as normal dieters from true EDs (Garner et al., 1983a, 1983b; Garner, Olmsted, Polivy, & Garfinkel, 1984), on the grounds that the latter included certain psychopathological elements (not necessarily eating related) that combined with the eating problems displayed by some normal dieters to produce true EDs.

Garner et al. (1983a, 1983b) derived the eight subscales of the EDI conceptually and/or deductively from the theories about the underlying psychological features of EDs offered by clinicians such as Bruch (1973, 1978), Selvini-Palazzoli (1978), Crisp (1980), and Strober (1980), as well as from clinical descriptions of the behavioral aspects of the disorder (e.g., Beumont & Smart, 1976; Bruch, 1973, 1978; Russell, 1979). The subscales of the original EDI include two mainly behaviorally focused symptom scales: (a) Drive for Thinness (i.e., excessive dieting and avoidance of weight gain amounting to a fear of fatness) and (b) Bulimia (i.e., episodes of uncontrolled binge eating, often followed by self-induced vomiting or other compensatory behaviors). Cognitively oriented subscales include Body Dissatisfaction (i.e., the belief that parts of the body are too large or unattractive), Interpersonal Distrust (i.e., feelings of alienation and an inability to form close relationships or express one's feelings to another person), Interoceptive Awareness (measuring the lack of ability to recognize and label bodily feelings of hunger or emotion), and Maturity Fears (i.e., the wish to retreat to a prepubertal stage of life to avoid the demands of adulthood). The remaining two subscales combine cognitive characteristics with what might be deemed personality attributes: (a) Perfectionism, or excessive expectations for superior personal achievement, and (b) Ineffectiveness, or feelings of general inadequacy, insecurity, worthlessness, and loss of control over one's life, all of which sounds very similar to the personality trait of low self-esteem or neuroticism. The EDI includes both eating and psychological subscales in order to provide a measure that could "meaningfully differentiate subgroups of patients or . . . distinguish those with serious psychopathology from 'normal' dieters" (Garner et al., 1983b, p. 174). The assumption was that although normal dieters might share certain behavioral patterns with individuals with EDs, only those with true EDs would show the cognitive, emotional, and personality aberrations captured in the nonbehavioral EDI subscales. These aberrations, although no doubt characteristic of those with true EDs, are nevertheless problematic from the standpoint of diagnosis and etiology.

Although the EDI has been widely used to identify individuals with EDs, the status of the different types of subscales remains problematic. It remains unclear whether the sorts of non-eating-related characteristics measured by the EDI reflect specific symptoms of an ED, general symptoms of psychopathology (present in many disorders, not specific to ED or to any other specific diagnostic category), or something else (risk factors, perhaps). What exactly is the connection between, say, the Interpersonal Distrust scale and EDs? Is interpersonal distrust uniquely associated with EDs and not other disorders? Is interpersonal distrust a symptom of EDs as well as other disorders? Or might interpersonal distrust be a risk factor for ED (i.e., a cause or predictor of ED, but not in itself a symptom of ED)?

The EDI was used specifically to examine the difference between nonclinical, weight-preoccupied dieters and individuals displaying true AN. These two groups were differentiated by the Ineffectiveness, Interpersonal Distrust, and Interoceptive Awareness subscales of the EDI more than by their eating behaviors and attitudes (Garner et al., 1984; Polivy & Herman, 1987). (As expected, the "differentiating" scales indicated more pathology among the individuals with AN than among dieters.) The nonclinical dieters could be further divided into two subgroups (by cluster analysis). One group had somewhat elevated scores only on Drive for Thinness, Body Dissatisfaction, Bulimia, and Perfectionism and seemed to be reasonably normal dieters, but the other (much smaller) group had elevated scores on all of the EDI subscales and appeared to be more pathologic, possibly exhibiting a subclinical variant of an ED (what today might be even be diagnosed as "eating disorder not otherwise specified").

Many studies (e.g., Joiner, Heatherton, & Keel, 1997; Nudelman, 1988; G. J. Taylor, Parker, Bagby, & Bourke, 1996) have assessed the symptoms of EDs as defined and measured by the EDI. Evidence has accumulated that such qualities as ineffectiveness (e.g., White & Litovitz, 1998) and perfectionism (e.g., Halmi et al., 2000; Joiner, Heatherton, & Keel, 1997) are present in those with the disorder and are associated strongly with degree of ED severity and negative prognosis for outcome. Some researchers (e.g., Kaye et al., 1998; Srinivasagam et al., 1995) have noted, however, that some of these characteristics, such as perfectionism, persist after recovery from the ED. The role of perfectionism is further clouded by the fact that perfectionism is construed and measured in different ways in the literature. Perfectionism as measured by the EDI does seem to be related to the degree of ED pathology, remitting with other ED symptoms, whereas trait perfectionism is what persists after the disorder remits (Sutandar-Pinnock, Woodside, Carter, Olmsted, & Kaplan, 2003). It has therefore been suggested that trait perfectionism might be a predisposing contributor to the disorder—in other words, a risk factor rather than an actual symptom of the disorder (Srinivasagam et al., 1995). We will return to this issue shortly.

The EDI is still fairly widely used to diagnose ED pathology, but it is no longer the most frequently used ED assessment tool. The Eating Disorder Examination (EDE), a semistructured interview, is currently the most widely used assessment instrument for EDs (Fairburn & Cooper, 1993). It consists of questions comprising four subscales that measure (a) restrained eating; (b) concerns about eating; (c) shape and weight; and (d) severity and frequency of particular eating-disorder behaviors, such as binge eating or purging. This instrument is focused specifically on eating-related behaviors and attitudes, with no attempt to assess what is labeled in *DSM–IV* "associated psychological features." The self-report version of the EDE (the EDE–Q) assesses the frequency of overeating episodes (both *objective* binge episodes, defined as consumption of a large amount of food in a brief period of time during which one feels a loss of control over eating, and *subjective* binge episodes, in which there is a subjective feeling of being out of control even though the amount of food eaten need not be large). This questionnaire is considered to be a reasonable substitute for the EDE interview for assessing most ED symptoms, except for binge eating, which appears to be frequently overestimated by the questionnaire (Rieger, Wilfley, Tein, Marino, & Crow, 2005). Other current assessment measures that are used less frequently focus on specific eating- or weight/shape-related behaviors or attitudes (for discussion of such measures see e.g., Garner, 2002; Touyz, Polivy, & Hay, 2008). The one relatively recent measure that does include assessment of more general psychopathology along with specific ED issues is the Structured Interview for Anorexic and Bulimic Disorders (Fichter, Herpertz, Quadflieg, & Herpertz-Dahlman, 1998). This interview is not widely used, however. The assessment of EDs thus seems to have moved away from broader psychological pathology to focus on the particular behaviors and attitudes of the disorder that are specifically eating related.

This refocusing of the identification of EDs almost exclusively onto the eating-related symptoms has altered the discussion of the disorders. Because the assessment and diagnostic procedure is now so closely tied to the eating aspects of the disorder, other features of the disorders formerly viewed as symptoms are being treated differently. Many of these features are now being viewed not as symptoms but as contributors to or causes of the disorder; they have become risk factors.

SEARCHING FOR RISK FACTORS

For almost 2 decades now, researchers have been trying to identify etiological contributors to EDs. Risk factor research began in earnest in the 1980s, when hundreds of studies began to examine cognitive and personality attributes that might cause or at least contribute to the development of the disorders. (The terms *cause* and *contributor* are used liberally throughout the literature, with *cause* generally appearing to reflect a more powerful force than *contributor*. The distinction between these terms is not well defined, however. The term *contributor* would seem to imply that it operates in concert with other contributors; a cause, however, could (but need not) operate on its own.) The sorts of psychological associated features discussed even in *DSM–IV* as somehow being part of the disorders (even if they are not explicit diagnostic criteria) have been increasingly investigated as causal agents rather than as aspects of the pathology itself. Thus, attention has shifted from defining and understanding EDs themselves to identifying risk factors that predict them. The same characteristics that earlier might have been seen as part of the disorder are now seen as producing the disorder.

It is not entirely clear what the purpose is of all of this activity investigating risk factors. Why is it useful or important to identify risk factors? We acknowledge that there are "obvious" answers to these questions, but we intend to challenge these answers. In the remainder of this chapter, we explore several questions raised by the advent of the risk factor approach to understanding EDs. For instance, does knowing that *in utero* complications are associated with a greater risk of developing an ED in adolescence suggest strategies to prevent the disorder in at-risk individuals? Does this statistical association mean that all persons whose mothers experienced complications during their pregnancy should be (somehow) "treated"? Are we prepared to intervene for all those who do not have the disorder but have the risk factor? Should they all at least be tracked, if not treated? Moreover, are risk factors anything more than statistical associations; that is, does identifying risk factors contribute to understanding and preventing the disorder? How much better do we understand EDs if we know that they are predicted by *in utero* complications? Also, most important, does identifying risk factors help us to treat people who already have the disorder (with or without that particular risk factor)? What sort of specific treatment might be suitable for someone who experienced *in utero* complications? These questions need to be addressed.

WHAT IS A RISK FACTOR?

What exactly is a risk factor? We need to understand the answer to this question in order to determine how important it is to identify risk factors for EDs. A *risk factor* is presumably an antecedent condition that is related in some way to the development of a disorder. Thus, a risk factor must precede the disorder in question; otherwise it is merely a correlate (Kazdin, Kraemer, Kessler, Kupfer, & Offord, 1997; Kraemer et al., 1997; Schmidt, 2002). Kazdin et al. (1997) stated that "A risk factor is defined as a characteristic, experience, or event that, if present, is associated with an increase in the probability (risk) of a particular outcome" (p. 377). Therefore, the presence of a risk factor should be associated with an increased incidence of the disorder. Schmidt (2002) also pointed out that a risk factor should appear repeatedly in multiple studies. Insofar as studies of possible risk factors cast a wide empirical net, the chances that a particular factor will be statistically associated with EDs in a single study simply by chance becomes a true threat. If a particular factor is associated with a disorder only sometimes, then it is unlikely to be predictive, let alone causal. Kazdin et al. warned that the relation between a particular risk factor and the pathological outcome to which it is related is conditional, depending on various features of the risk factor, such as its duration, intensity, and when in the person's development exposure occurs. Thus, risk factors are not necessarily static properties but have more complex relations to outcomes. Finally, the outcomes in question are probabilistic, not inevitable. "Risk factors influence the likelihood of an outcome rather than determine the outcome" (Kazdin et al., 1997, p. 379.)

Kazdin et al. (1997) further distinguished between risk factors, which are associated with increases in the occurrence of adverse or undesirable outcomes, and *protective factors*, which are "antecedent conditions associated with a decrease in the likelihood of undesirable outcomes or with an increase in the likelihood of positive outcomes" (p. 377). Protective factors have as many explanatory and treatment implications as do risk factors. The proper study of risk factors, then, requires an examination of both the adverse influences (the risk factors) and the desirable, protective factors. Aside from their respective negative and positive valence, however, risk factors and protective factors are identical.

Schmidt (2002) stated that the most important aspect of a risk factor is that its elimination also eliminates the disorder. This formulation is probably too extreme insofar as a given risk factor is unlikely to be the only risk factor, so eliminating it does not eliminate all risk. As C. B. Taylor (2005) more temperately noted, "The ultimate test of a risk factor is to demonstrate that its reduction leads to a reduced incidence of the disorder" (p. 2). Taylor continued, "No risk factor for eating disorders has yet passed this test" (p. 2). According to Taylor, no protective factors or screening variables for dividing individuals into low/no-risk versus high-risk categories have been identified. We may thus legitimately proceed to the question of whether a risk factor can be changed, either by therapy, development, or some other process. A risk factor that changes is known as a *variable risk factor*, whereas one that is immutable (gender, date of birth, etc.) is called a *fixed marker*. If a variable risk factor fulfills Schmidt's and Taylor's criterion and changes the probability of developing the disorder when the risk factor itself is changed, then it is a *causal risk factor*, but if it does not affect the risk of developing the disorder, then it is merely a *variable marker* (Kazdin et al., 1997; Kraemer et al., 1997).

Most of the characteristics studied as risk factors for EDs are presumed to be variable risk factors, but that presumption may or may not be warranted.

Jacobi et al.'s (2004) comprehensive analysis of the research investigating risk factors for EDs indicates that many of the so-called risk factors actually appear to be correlates rather than causes. As they put it, "Few of the putative risk factors were reported to precede the onset of the disorder" (p. 19). In other words, the main criterion of precedence is not always established for these supposed risk factors. For example, Jacobi et al. concluded that whereas the lack of interoceptive awareness appears to be a variable risk factor for EDs (i.e., it can be changed, and changes in it are associated with changes in the incidence of EDs), perfectionism and self-concept deficits are actually correlates, not predictors, of EDs (i.e., they do consistently precede the onset of the disorder, but they do not occur reliably in patients exhibiting the disorder); all of these characteristics, however, have been described as risk factors. This is an example of correlates that may actually be symptoms of the disorder being seen as risk factors.

Proposing something as a potential risk factor also implies an understanding of causality of the disorder; that is, it helps to have some idea about what causes the disorder in order to propose that a particular factor contributes to it. In reality, however, the sort of research ordinarily used to explore risk factors does not allow one to conclude anything more than that risk factors reflect only statistical associations, allowing for more accurate prediction but not necessarily contributing to explanation or causal analysis. Fairburn and Harrison (2003) concluded that "virtually nothing is known about the individual causal processes involved, or about how they interact and vary across the development and maintenance of the disorders" (p. 408).

Our lack of understanding of the causal behavioral mechanisms underlying EDs leaves us with little conceptual framework for investigating EDs. The list of variables that have been studied as potential risk factors for EDs indicates the variety and breadth of characteristics that have been implicated (for a list of putative risk factors that have been studied in the ED literature, see Table 6.1). No single study can look at all of them, but there is no strong theoretical basis for choosing which ones should or will be explored in any given study. Indeed, the exploration of risk factors does not require much in the way of theoretical analysis. A more popular way to select risk factors for investigation is more empirical, casting a wide net to find characteristics that may turn out to be significant predictors of the disorder. The plethora of such studies with minimal conceptual assistance to direct attention in particular directions has resulted in the sort of list of potential risk factors listed in Table 6.1. Moreover, a strongly empirical approach limits the sorts of conclusions that can be drawn from the data. Replication becomes essential because of the enhanced possibility that the findings, not having been predicted by theory, are simply chance outcomes; if we are to make sense of them rather than treat

TABLE 6.1

Risk Factors Identified in the Literature as Possible Contributors to the Development of Eating Disorders

Type of Factor	Factor
Sociocultural	Female gender (femininity in males)
	Adolescence
	Western culture
	Race (Asian and Black may be protective)
	Ethnicity
	Social class (upper and upper middle class)
	Peer and media idealization of thinness
	Urban location
Family	Either parent dieting, obese, or diagnosed with an eating disorder
	Family history of affective disorders, anxiety disorders, substance use/abuse, personality disorders
	Enmeshed or hypercritical family
Developmental/environmental	Early childhood eating problems
	Activities emphasizing the body (e.g., ballet, gymnastics)
	Being teased in childhood/adolescence
	Sexual or physical abuse (bulimia nervosa)
Genetic	Chromosome 1 (anorexia nervosa) or 10 (bulimia nervosa)
	First-degree relative with an eating disorder
Physiological	Premature birth or complications at birth
	Birth between April and June
	Early puberty
	High body mass index
Personality/psychological	Low self-esteem
	Body dissatisfaction
	Body shame
	Dieter/restrained eater
	Perfectionism
	Obsessiveness
	Rigidity
	Fearfulness/anxiety
	Identity diffusion/confusion
	Overcompliance
	Social inhibition
	Depression/negative affect

Note. From *Eating disorders* (p. 20), by S. Touyz, J. Polivy, and P. Hay, 2008, Cambridge, MA: Hogrefe & Huber. Copyright 2008 by Hogrefe & Huber. Adapted with permission.

them as purely descriptive, the findings need to be integrated into a new theory. The current, mainly empirical literature is thus largely a hodgepodge of studies on patients, students, or more general populations, using cross-sectional, prospective, retrospective, and case analysis methods, with seemingly random sets of measures and with findings that are themselves seemingly random when not mutually contradictory.

An additional problem plaguing the risk factor literature reflects confusion about the appropriate level of specificity of risk factors for EDs. Should a risk factor be specific to a particular disorder, or can it be more general and predict an increased incidence for a wider set of disorders? Schmidt (2002) suggested that a risk factor should be associated with only one disorder, yet many of the factors identified as risk factors for EDs (e.g., low self-esteem) may not be specific threats for EDs per se but may instead predispose an individual to any of a variety of disorders. Does this disqualify them as risk factors for EDs?

It is not clear why a risk factor must be specific to a particular disorder. In fact, longitudinal studies suggest the presence of characteristics such as negative self-concept, low self-esteem, or higher ineffectiveness prior to the onset of an ED (e.g., Bardone, Vohs, Abramson, Heatherton, & Joiner, 2000; Joiner, 1999; Joiner, Heatherton, Rudd, & Schmidt, 1997; Patton, Selzer, Coffey, Carlin, & Wolfe, 1999; Stice, 2001; Stice, Hayward, Cameron, Killen, & Taylor, 2000; Stice & Shaw, 2003). However, as Jacobi et al. (2004) pointed out, most reports of negative self-concept in patients with EDs are retrospective or not predictive of actual ED diagnosis. Even when negative affectivity (which encompasses negative emotionality; depression; ineffectiveness; and even, in some studies, body dissatisfaction) did have some predictive power in longitudinal studies, these characteristics do not appear to be specific for EDs, inasmuch as they also precede conditions such as affective disorders and substance abuse (e.g., Crocker & Wolfe, 2001; Jacobi et al., 2004). Jacobi et al. concluded that psychiatric morbidity and negative affectivity were nonspecific, variable risk factors of unknown potency. In addition, the psychological pathology seen by theorists such as Bruch (1973) as related to the behavioral manifestations of EDs includes extremely low self-esteem and negative feelings about the self as well as perfectionism, impulsivity, and deficits in identity formation and feelings of control (Polivy & Herman, 2002), all of which may be present in other psychological pathologies. Thus, the specificity–generality question applies not only to risk factors but also to symptoms (as might be predicted once we acknowledge the prevailing confusion over whether a particular characteristic is best thought of as a risk factor or a symptom). This question—whether these broad psychological characteristics represent variable risk factors that predispose an individual to develop an ED or whether they are correlates, symptoms, or early manifestations of the disorder itself—has not yet been specifically addressed, but we discuss it shortly. For the last decade or more, however, such characteristics have been assumed to be (and described and studied as) risk factors for EDs (see, e.g., Jacobi et al., 2004). Because most (if not all) of these broad psychological defects are often present in other psychiatric disorders as well as in EDs, they cannot be said to be specific risk factors for EDs.

These psychological deficits, however, although they may be nonspecific, may nevertheless be crucial to the disorder. In the absence of these psychological deficits, does one truly have an ED, or is one merely a weight-preoccupied dieter? Are extreme weight concern and eating abnormalities alone enough to render one as truly having an ED? We may here be the victims of terminology: The term *eating disorder* suggests that it is eating alone that is disordered. Most clinical accounts of EDs, however, note that the disorder resides not only in the domain of eating per se but also in more central and far-reaching aspects of personality. This discussion brings us back to the issue of what the disorder is, and when it actually begins. Are these psychological deficiencies risk factors that are present premorbidly, and contribute to the development of an ED, or are they an indication that a disorder is present, or at least imminent and may manifest itself, perhaps as an ED but perhaps as a different disorder entirely?

RISK FACTORS OR SYMPTOMS?

As Jacobi et al. (2004) pointed out, "Drawing the line between the exposure to a risk factor and the beginning of a disorder can be . . . difficult" (p. 34). Schmidt (2002) similarly cautioned that disentangling which came first, the putative risk factor or the disorder, is a difficult task. She noted that clinical syndromes may be preceded by months of subclinical symptoms, and separating subclinical symptoms from contributory risk factors with any degree of certainty may not be possible. Wonderlich (2002) questioned the nature of the relationship between personality and EDs: Do certain personality traits increase the risk of developing an ED, is a particular personality profile the result of the ED, or are EDs and personality unrelated except insofar as both are influenced by some third variable (e.g., biological predisposition)? Wonderlich observed further that empirical studies, which tend to produce straightforward and fairly simple-minded correlational findings, rarely test any of these models. What all of these commentators appear to be reacting to is the blurred distinction between risk factors and actual manifestations or symptoms of a disorder.

In the rush to discover causal contributors to EDs, researchers tend to find risk factors among the attributes that have been identified as being associated with EDs, and even among the attributes that have been identified as discriminating factors (i.e., factors that separate patients from nonpatients). Personality factors (e.g., perfectionism, impulsivity, ineffectiveness/low self-esteem, need for control, and ego/identity deficits that may contribute to the focus on body shape as a source of self-esteem) that were formerly seen as a manifestation of the disorder (and thus whose own causes would normally be sought in attempts to understand EDs) have been relabeled as risk factors for ED rather than part of the disorder. Such characteristics, which we might have been inclined to regard as "effects" for which "causes" might be sought, are now themselves seen as potential causes or risk factors. Thus, for instance, many prospective risk factor studies (e.g., Bardone et al., 2000; Bardone-Cone, Abramson, Vohs, Heatherton, & Joiner, 2006; Joiner, 1999; Joiner, Heatherton, Rudd, & Schmidt, 1997; Patton et al., 1999; Stice, 2001; Stice et al., 2000; Stice & Shaw, 2003; Stice & Whitenton, 2002; Vohs et al., 2001) have indicated that perfectionism and low self-esteem or ineffectiveness, often in interaction with such variables as dieting and/or body dissatisfaction, predict increases in eating-related ED symptomatology. Similarly, high levels of psychiatric morbidity, along with severe dieting, prospectively predict the development of actual EDs; adolescent girls who were both severe dieters and in the group characterized as most psychologically disordered had a 1 in 4 chance of developing an ED within 1 year (Patton et al., 1999). These psychological deficits, formerly seen as symptoms of the disorder, have thus begun to be reconstrued as risk factors for the development of EDs. In what is perhaps a reflection of this shift, newer measures designed to assess the symptoms of EDs (e.g., the EDE and EDE–Q; Fairburn & Beglin, 1994) have returned to an emphasis on measuring strictly eating- and weight-related physical, behavioral, and cognitive symptoms of AN and BN.

What difference does it make if certain characteristics migrate from symptoms to risk factors? Theoretically speaking, if prevention efforts were directed at these factors, it might not matter whether they were called *risk factors* or *symptoms*. Unfortunately, though, prevention efforts (e.g., Baranowski & Hetherington, 2001; Huon, 1994; Posavac, Posavac, & Weigel, 2001; Rocco, Ciano, & Balestrieri, 2001; Smolak, Levine, & Schermer, 1998; Stice, Chase, Stormer, & Appel, 2001) have tended to target the eating- and body-related attitudes and behaviors, perhaps because they are seen as easier to treat but perhaps also because it seems to make more sense to treat symptoms than to treat risk factors. Thus, prevention programs focus on combating idealization of thinness and dieting but do not address the personal deficiencies. It might thus be more useful to regard these personal deficiencies as symptoms of the disorder, deserving of therapeutic attention when patients are in treatment (e.g., Fairburn, Cooper, & Shafran, 2003).

Removing a symptom is taken as evidence that the disorder is improving or remitting; if a risk factor is removed, the disorder should be prevented (or at least become less likely). However, attacking risk factors does not inspire the same confidence that one is making progress against the disorder that comes with removing a symptom per se. Is any given risk factor necessary or sufficient in and of itself to produce or prevent an ED? Dieting and/or the idealization of thinness, for example, is considered a risk factor for EDs, but AN was equally prevalent in previous times when women did not diet or value thinness (Bemporad, 1997). This stark fact suggests that dieting is not necessary for the development of an ED, and the equally stark fact that millions of women diet without ever developing an ED means that dieting is also not sufficient for the development of an ED. How much of a risk factor is something that is neither necessary nor sufficient to the development of a disorder? Correspondingly, how worthwhile is it to "treat" a risk factor whose removal is no guarantee that the disorder will be in any way attenuated? Many recent researchers (e.g., Bardone et al., 2000; Joiner, Heatherton, & Keel, 1997; Patton et al., 1999; Stice, 2001; Stice et al., 2000; Stice & Shaw, 2003; Stice & Whitenton, 2002; Vohs et al., 2001) have posited that factors such as dieting, low self-esteem, perfectionism, and body dissatisfaction operate in an interactive fashion (possibly along with additional factors) to increase the risk of developing an ED. However, with the nature of the interaction unspecified, how confident can we be that removing any single one of these factors will suffice to prevent the disorder? Perhaps several of them may have to be targeted to achieve a detectible reduction in the prevalence of EDs. Is such an effort even feasible? By relegating certain characteristics from the category of symptom to the category of risk factor, then, we reduce the likelihood that they will be treated directly. We also change our view of the nature of the disorder, downgrading certain features so that they are no longer seen as central aspects. The personality deficits, in our view, are not secondary; they are what convert intense dieting into an ED.

The most widespread treatment for EDs—cognitive–behavioral treatment (Fairburn et al., 2003)—currently addresses itself to disordered eating behaviors such as binge eating; dietary restraint; and the reliance on eating, weight, and shape for self-evaluation. If the disorder does include associated psychological features such as self-esteem deficits, perfectionism, and emotional problems, then therapy should address these, too, which is what Fairburn et al. (2003) suggested. In effect, Fairburn et al. demanded that low self-esteem be regarded as pathological in and of itself (or at least in conjunction with eating pathology) rather than being merely a predictor of the development of eating pathology.

What makes one person a strict dieter and the other an ED patient? Is it merely a question of how little is eaten, how much weight is lost, how often one binges, or how fat one feels? These symptoms, we submit, do not adequately differentiate the strict dieter and the ED patient. There are profound implications for treatment: If EDs are more than pathological eating behaviors and related attitudes, then it is not appropriate for treatment to focus exclusively on normalizing eating and body image.

CLINICAL IMPLICATIONS OF CONFLATING RISK FACTORS AND SYMPTOMS

Separating risk factors from symptoms is clearly a difficult task. The difference between the two is more than merely semantic, however. It matters what one calls these characteristics—*risk factors, symptoms, sequelae,* or something else. How we deal with risk factors and symptoms in practical terms makes a difference, and if we treat these two categories of characteristics differently, then it is important to identify them properly so that the appropriate action can be taken. Symptoms presumably should get treatment attention, but what should be done about risk factors? Those that are fixed obviously cannot be treated, and if they are fixed and general (i.e., widespread and pertinent to many disorders) it is not clear that they even provide useful preventative information. Does it help to know that females are more likely than males to develop an ED and that EDs are most likely to happen during adolescence? What can we do with this knowledge? If we are able to add that some of these adolescent females are invested in the thin ideal and are restricting their eating to lose weight, is this enough of a combined risk to justify intervening? To date, prevention programs have been targeting adolescent dieting and idealization of thinness. The programs involve psychoeducation or group discussions among adolescent girls about problems associated with dieting (e.g., Baranowski & Hetherington, 2001; Huon, 1994; Posavac et al., 2001; Rocco et al., 2001; Smolak et al., 1998; Stice et al., 2001). These programs generally report decreases in pathological eating and attitudes, as assessed on self-report questionnaires, although Franko (2001) found that getting at-risk adolescent girls to participate in prevention programs can be difficult. The small sample sizes in these studies, the absence of control groups, and the short duration of study and follow-up make it difficult to determine whether any actual ED cases were prevented or whether the obtained improvements involved changes beyond the boundaries of normal dieting, body image, and self-esteem. After all, because these at-risk young women do not yet have EDs, there is a problem of measurement: How do we determine whether they have improved as a result of the preventive intervention? In principle, we should be looking at long-term data on the actual incidence of EDs. Do the interventions actually make EDs less probable? Because of the short time-lines of these studies, however, and because the actual incidence of EDs is very low in any case, ED incidence is not a practical outcome measure. Instead, researchers tend to use what might be termed "analogue" measures—paper-and-pencil measures of eating-related pathology—and scores on these measures are rarely, if ever, in the truly pathological range. The success of these prevention programs is typically assessed in terms of a reduction in scores on these analogue measures, but such a reduction by no means represents clear evidence of treatment success if by *treatment success* we mean a demonstrable prevention of the onset of an ED. These intervention efforts at least try to use risk factor information in a practical, preventive manner, but it is important to note that aside from the measurement issue, there remains the problem of avoiding the central personality deficits. Just as the symptoms of EDs have been "purified" to exclude the personality deficits, so too have the risk factors that tend to serve as the targets of interventions.

The core psychopathology of overvaluing a thin physique and using it to determine one's self-worth (obviously closely related to the "risk factors" of dieting, thinness idealization, and body dissatisfaction) has been identified as a principal ED-maintaining process that should be the main target of cognitive–behavioral treatment of EDs (e.g., Fairburn et al., 2003). How is this principal ED-maintaining process any different, though, from the risk factor of believing that thinness is desirable and that one should diet—beliefs that characterize as many as half of adolescents and young women? Is it simply a matter of degree? Is the key term here *overvaluing* thinness (as opposed to merely valuing it)? Where is the line between normal body image concern and overvaluing thinness? Should we treat normal dieting? Who and what should actually be treated?

The failure to distinguish between risk factors for a disorder and symptoms of the disorder itself has implications for treatment and prevention of disorders. There is a good chance that we may both overtreat certain features and undertreat others. First, with regard to overtreatment, if we misidentify something (e.g., dieting, valuing thinness) as a risk factor and use broadscale prevention programs to treat it, then we may needlessly (and at great expense) treat many individuals who are not really at risk and at the same time fail to target treatments properly for those who are actually evincing the disorder. Second, with regard to undertreatment, if we misidentify something (e.g., a damaged self) as a risk factor rather than as a core element of the pathology itself, then we may be inclined to ignore it in our treatment efforts, especially if there is no easy treatment suggesting itself. We may rationalize our failure to treat it by convincing ourselves that even though it is a risk factor, it is not necessarily a crucial one; after all, given the huge array of risk factors that have been empirically identified, they cannot all be crucial, can they? In addition, there is correspondingly little reason to be confident that diminishing or eliminating one risk factor will necessarily have much impact on the disorder. If we are to avoid the twin perils of overtreatment and undertreatment, we thus need to be more careful in defining risk factors to be sure that they are not merely normal behavior (e.g., dieting), actual contributory agents for an ED, or not real symptoms (e.g., a damaged self) indicating that the disorder is already present.

CONCLUSIONS

It is not clear that all of the characteristics nominated as risk factors for EDs fulfill the criteria of preceding the onset of the disorder and of demonstrably changing the likelihood of developing the disorder. When the risk factor remains after the disorder is supposedly remitted, further questions arise. Moreover, psychological deficits that were formerly seen as part of the disorder have often been relegated to the status of risk factors rather than symptoms, meaning that they do not get treated. Ben-Tovim (2003) pointed out that after 3 decades of intensive research, EDs remain difficult to treat or prevent. One reason for this disappointing situation may be that we are confusing risk factors, correlates, and symptoms of EDs.

REFERENCES

American Psychiatric Association. (1994). *Diagnostic and statistical manual of mental disorders* (4th ed.). Washington, DC: Author.

Baranowski, M. J., & Hetherington, M. M. (2001). Testing the efficacy of an eating disorder prevention program. *International Journal of Eating Disorders, 29,* 119–124.

Bardone, A. M., Vohs, K. D., Abramson, L., Heatherton, T. F., & Joiner, T. E. (2000). The confluence of perfectionism, body dissatisfaction, and low self-esteem predicts bulimic symptoms: Clinical implications. *Behavior Therapy, 31,* 265–280.

Bardone-Cone, A. M., Abramson, L. Y., Vohs, K. D., Heatherton, T. F., & Joiner, T. F., Jr. (2006). Predicting bulimic symptoms: An interactive model of self-efficacy, perfectionism, and perceived weight status. *Behaviour Research and Therapy, 44,* 27–42

Bemporad, J. R. (1997). Cultural and historical aspects of eating disorders. *Theoretical Medicine, 18,* 401–420.

Ben-Tovim, D. I. (2003). Eating disorders: Outcome, prevention and treatment of eating disorders. *Current Opinion in Psychiatry, 16,* 65–69.

Beumont, P. J. V. (2002). Clinical presentation of anorexia nervosa and bulimia nervosa. In C. G. Fairburn & K. D. Brownell (Eds.), *Eating disorders and obesity: A comprehensive handbook* (pp. 162–170). New York: Guilford Press.

Beumont, P. J. V., & George, G. C. W. (1976). Some personality characteristics of patients with anorexia nervosa. *British Journal of Psychiatry, 11,* 223–226.

Bruch, H. (1973). *Eating disorders: Obesity, anorexia and the person within.* New York: Basic Books.

Bruch, H. (1978). *The golden cage: The enigma of anorexia nervosa.* Cambridge, MA: Harvard University Press.

Crisp, A. H. (1980). *Anorexia nervosa: Let me be.* New York: Grune & Stratton.

Crocker, J., & Wolfe, C. T. (2001). Contingencies of self-worth. *Psychological Review, 108,* 593–623.

Fairburn, C. G., & Beglin, S. J. (1994). Assessment of eating disorders: Interview or self-report questionnaire? *International Journal of Eating Disorders, 16,* 363–370.

Fairburn, C. G., & Cooper, Z. (1993). The eating disorder examination (12th ed.). In C. G. Fairburn & G. T. Wilson (Eds.), *Binge eating: Nature, assessment, and treatment* (pp. 317–360). New York: Guilford Press.

Fairburn, C. G., Cooper, Z., & Shafran, J. (2003). Cognitive behaviour therapy for eating disorders: A "transdiagnostic" theory and treatment. *Behaviour Research and Therapy, 41,* 509–528.

Fairburn, C. G., & Harrison, P. J. (2003). Eating disorders. *The Lancet, 361*, 407–416.

Fairburn, C. G., & Walsh, B. T. (2002). Atypical eating disorders (eating disorder not otherwise specified). In C. G. Fairburn & K. D. Brownell (Eds.), *Eating disorders and obesity: A comprehensive handbook* (2nd ed., pp. 171–177). New York: Guilford Press.

Feighner, J. P., Woodruff, R. A., Winokur, G., Munoz, R., Robins, E., & Guze, S. B. (1972). Diagnostic criteria for use in psychiatric research. *Archives of General Psychiatry, 26*, 57–63.

Fichter, M. M., Herpertz, S., Quadflieg, N., & Herpertz-Dahlman, B. (1998). Structured interview for anorexic and bulimic disorders for *DSM–IV* and *ICD–10*: Updated (third) revision. *International Journal of Eating Disorders, 24*, 227–249.

Franko, D. L. (2001). Rethinking prevention efforts in eating disorders. *Cognitive and Behavioral Practice, 8*(3), 265–270.

Garfinkel, P. E. (2002). Classification and diagnosis of eating disorders. In C. G. Fairburn & K. Brownell (Eds.), *Eating disorders and obesity: A comprehensive handbook* (pp. 155–161). New York: Guilford Press.

Garfinkel, P. E., & Garner, D. M. (1982). *Anorexia nervosa: A multidimensional perspective*. New York: Brunner/Mazel.

Garner, D. M. (2002). Measurement of eating disorder psychopathology. In C. G. Fairburn & K. D. Brownell (Eds.), *Eating disorders and obesity: A comprehensive handbook* (2nd ed., pp. 141–146). New York: Guilford Press.

Garner, D. M., Olmsted, M. P., Bohr, Y., & Garfinkel, P. E. (1982). The eating attitudes test: Psychometric features and clinical correlates. *Psychological Medicine, 12*, 871–878.

Garner, D. M., Olmsted, M. P., & Polivy, J. (1983a). Development and validation of a multidimensional eating disorder inventory for anorexia nervosa and bulimia. *International Journal of Eating Disorders, 2*, 15–34.

Garner, D. M., Olmsted, M. P., & Polivy, J. (1983b). The Eating Disorder Inventory: A measure of cognitive–behavioral dimensions of anorexia nervosa and bulimia. In P. L. Darby, P. E. Garfinkel, & D. M. Garner (Eds.), *Anorexia nervosa: Recent developments* (pp. 173–184). New York: Liss.

Garner, D. M., Olmsted, M. P., Polivy, J., & Garfinkel, P. E. (1984). Comparison between weight-preoccupied women and anorexia nervosa. *Psychosomatic Medicine, 46*, 255–266.

Halmi, K. A., Sunday, S. R., Strober, M., Kaplan, A., Woodside, D. B., Fichter, M., et al. (2000). Perfectionism in anorexia nervosa: Variation by clinical subtype, obsessionality, and pathological eating behavior. *American Journal of Psychiatry, 157*, 1799–1805.

Hawkins, R. C., & Clement, P. F. (1980). Development and construct validation of a self-report measure of binge-eating tendencies. *Addictive Behaviors, 5*, 219–226.

Hoek, H. W. (2006). Incidence, prevalence and mortality of anorexia nervosa and other eating disorders. *Current Opinion in Psychiatry, 19*, 389–394.

Hoek, H. W., & van Hoeken, D. (2003). Review of the prevalence and incidence of eating disorders. *International Journal of Eating Disorders, 34,* 383–396.

Huon, G. F. (1994). Towards the prevention of dieting-induced disorders: Modifying negative food- and body-related attitudes. *International Journal of Eating Disorders, 16,* 395–399.

Jacobi, C. (2005). Psychological risk factors for eating disorders. In S. Wonderlich, J. E. Mitchell, M. de Zwaan, & H. Steiger (Eds.), *Eating disorders review: Part 1* (pp. 59–85). Oxford, England: Radcliffe Publishing.

Jacobi, C., Hayward, C., de Zwaan, M., Kraemer, H. C., & Agras, W. S. (2004). Coming to terms with risk factors for eating disorders: Application of risk terminology and suggestions for a general taxonomy. *Psychological Bulletin, 130,* 19–65.

Joiner, T. E. (1999). Self-verification and bulimic symptoms: Do bulimic women play a role in perpetuating their own dissatisfaction and symptoms? *International Journal of Eating Disorders, 26,* 145–151.

Joiner, T. E., Heatherton, T. F., & Keel, P. K. (1997). Ten-year stability and predictive validity of five bulimia-related indicators. *American Journal of Psychiatry, 154,* 1133–1138.

Joiner, T. E., Heatherton, T. F., Rudd, M. D., & Schmidt, N. B. (1997). Perfectionism, perceived weight status, and bulimic symptoms: Two studies testing a diathesis–stress model. *Journal of Abnormal Psychology, 106,* 145–153.

Kaye, W. H., Greeno, C. G., Moss, H., Fernstrom, J., Fernstrom, M., Lilenfeld, L. R., et al. (1998). Alterations in serotonin activity and psychiatric symptoms after recovery from bulimia nervosa. *Archives of General Psychiatry, 55,* 927–935.

Kazdin, A. E., Kraemer, H. C., Kessler, R. C., Kupfer, D. J., & Offord, D. R. (1997). Contributions of risk factor research to developmental psychopathology. *Clinical Psychology Review, 17,* 375–406.

Kraemer, H. C., Kazdin, A. E., Offord, D. R., Kessler, R. C., Jensen, P. S., & Kupfer, D. J. (1997). Coming to terms with the terms of risk. *Archives of General Psychiatry, 54,* 337–343.

McFarlane, T., McCabe, R., Jarry, J., Olmsted, M. P., & Polivy, J. (2001). Weight- and shape-related self-evaluation in women with eating disorders, dieters, and non-dieters. *International Journal of Eating Disorders, 29,* 328–335.

Mitchell, J., Cook-Myers, T., & Wonderlich, S. (2005). Diagnostic criteria for anorexia nervosa: Looking ahead to *DSM–V*. *International Journal of Eating Disorders, 37,* S95–S97.

Nudelman, S. (1988). Dissimilarities in eating attitudes, body image distortion, depression, and self-esteem between high-intensity male runners and women with bulimia nervosa. *International Journal of Eating Disorders, 7,* 625–634.

Patton, G. C., Selzer, R., Coffey, C., Carlin, J. B., & Wolfe, R. (1999). Onset of adolescent eating disorders: Population based cohort study over 3 years. *British Medical Journal, 318,* 765–768.

Polivy, J., & Herman, C. P. (1987). The diagnosis and treatment of normal eating. *Journal of Consulting and Clinical Psychology, 55,* 635–644.

Polivy, J., & Herman, C. P. (1993). Etiology of binge eating: Psychological mechanisms. In C. Fairburn (Ed.), *Binge eating* (pp. 173–205). London: Guilford Press.

Polivy, J., & Herman, C. P. (2002). Causes of eating disorders. *Annual Review of Psychology, 53,* 187–213.

Posavac, H. D., Posavac, S. S., & Weigel, R. G. (2001). Reducing the impact of media images on women at risk for body image disturbance: Three targeted interventions. *Journal of Social and Clinical Psychology, 20,* 324–340.

Rieger, E., Wilfley, D., Stein, R. I., Marino, V., & Crow, S. J. (2005). A comparison of quality of life in obese individuals with and without binge eating disorder. *International Journal of Eating Disorders, 37,* 234–240.

Rocco, P. L., Ciano, R. P., & Balestrieri, M. (2001). Psychoeducation in the prevention of eating disorders: An experimental approach in adolescent schoolgirls. *British Journal of Medical Psychology, 74,* 351–358.

Russell, G. F. M. (1979). Bulimia nervosa: An ominous variant of anorexia nervosa. *Psychological Medicine, 9,* 429–448.

Schmidt, U. (2002). Risk factors for eating disorders. In C. G. Fairburn & K. D. Brownell (Eds.), *Eating disorders and obesity: A comprehensive handbook* (2nd ed., pp. 247–250). New York: Guilford Press.

Selvini-Palazzoli, M. P. (1978). *Self-starvation: From individual to family therapy in the treatment of anorexia nervosa* (2nd ed.). New York: Jason Aronson.

Smolak, L., Levine, M. P., & Schermer, F. (1998). A controlled evaluation of an elementary school primary prevention program for eating problems. *Journal of Psychosomatic Research, 44,* 339–353.

Srinivasagam, N. M., Kaye, W. H., Plotnicov, K. H., Greeno, C., Weltzin, T. E., & Rao, R. (1995). Persistent perfectionism, symmetry, and exactness after long-term recovery from anorexia nervosa. *American Journal of Psychiatry, 152,* 1630–1634.

Stice, E. (2001). A prospective test of the dual-pathway model of bulimic pathology: Mediating effects of dieting and negative affect. *Journal of Abnormal Psychology, 110,* 1–12.

Stice, E., Chase, A., Stormer, S., & Appel, A. (2001). A randomized trial of a dissonance-based eating disorder prevention program. *International Journal of Eating Disorders, 29,* 247–262.

Stice, E., Hayward, C., Cameron, R. P., Killen, J. D., & Taylor, C. B. (2000). Body-image and eating disturbances predict onset of depression among female adolescents: A longitudinal study. *Journal of Abnormal Psychology, 109,* 438–444.

Stice, E., & Shaw, H. (2003). Prospective relations of body image, eating, and affective disturbances to smoking onset in adolescent girls. *Journal of Consulting and Clinical Psychology, 71,* 129–135.

Stice, E., & Whitenton, K. (2002). Risk factors for body dissatisfaction in adolescent girls: A longitudinal investigation. *Developmental Psychology, 38,* 669–678.

Striegel-Moore, R. (1997). Risk factors for eating disorders. In M. S. Jacobson, J. Rees, N. H. Golden, & C. E. Irwin (Eds.), *Annals of the New York Academy of Sciences:*

Vol. 817. Adolescent nutritional disorders: Prevention and treatment (pp. 98–109). New York: New York Academy of Sciences

Strober, M. (1980). Personality and symptomatological features in young, nonchronic anorexia nervosa patients. *Journal of Psychosomatic Research, 24*, 353–359.

Sutandar-Pinnock, K., Woodside, D. B., Carter, J. C., Olmsted, M. P., & Kaplan, A. S. (2003). Perfectionism in anorexia nervosa: A 6–24-month follow-up study. *International Journal of Eating Disorders, 33*, 225–229.

Taylor, C. B. (2005). Update on the prevention of eating disorders. In S. Wonderlich, J. E. Mitchell, M. de Zwaan, & H. Steiger (Eds.), *Eating disorders review: Part 1* (pp. 1–14). Oxford, England: Radcliffe.

Taylor, G. J., Parker, J. D. A., Bagby, R. M., & Bourke, M. P. (1996). Relationships between alexithymia and psychological characteristics associated with eating disorders. *Journal of Psychosomatic Research, 41*, 561–568.

Touyz, S., Polivy, J., & Hay, P. (2008). *Eating disorders.* Cambridge, MA: Hogrefe & Huber.

Trottier, K., McFarlane, T., Olmsted, M., & Polivy, J. (2005). Weight-related other evaluation in eating disorders. *Eating and Weight Disorders, 10*, 258–263.

Vohs, K. D., Voelz, Z. R., Pettit, J. W., Bardone, A. M., Katz, J., Abramson, L. Y., et al. (2001). Perfectionism, body dissatisfaction, and self-esteem: An interactive model of bulimic symptom development. *Journal of Social and Clinical Psychology, 20*, 476–497.

White, J. H., & Litovitz, G. (1998). A comparison of inpatient and outpatient women with eating disorders. *Archives of Psychiatric Nursing, 12*, 181–194.

Wilson, G. T. (2002). The controversy over dieting. In C. G. Fairburn & K. D. Brownell (Eds.), *Eating disorders and obesity: A comprehensive handbook* (2nd ed., pp. 93–97). New York: Guilford Press.

Wonderlich, S. (2002). Personality and eating disorders. In C. G. Fairburn & K. D. Brownell (Eds.), *Eating disorders and obesity: A comprehensive handbook* (2nd ed., pp. 204–209). New York: Guilford Press.

7

ALCOHOL AND DRUG USE DISORDERS

CLARA M. BRADIZZA AND PAUL R. STASIEWICZ

The purpose of this chapter is to examine the learning processes and behavioral mechanisms involved in the development and maintenance of alcohol and drug use disorders. Substance use disorders are characterized by repeated substance use despite significant physical, social, or occupational problems. Problematic substance use can lead to substance dependence, which includes difficulty cutting down use, tolerance, and withdrawal (American Psychiatric Association, 1994). Alcohol and drug tolerance occurs when there is a need for increased amounts of the substance in order to maintain the same effect. Withdrawal symptoms can begin during initial uses of the substance and can intensify following heavy or prolonged use. Most classes of drugs (e.g., alcohol, cocaine, amphetamines) have characteristic withdrawal syndromes. For example, alcohol withdrawal symptoms include hand tremor, nausea, transient hallucinations, psychomotor agitation, anxiety, and grand mal seizures, whereas cocaine withdrawal includes dysphoric mood, vivid dreams, insomnia or hypersomnia, increased appetite, and psychomotor retardation or agitation (American Psychiatric Association, 1994).

Not all individuals who use alcohol or drugs develop significant problems. The 2002 National Survey on Drug Use and Health (Substance Abuse and Mental Health Services Administration, 2003) found that 51% of Americans

199

age 12 and older regularly (at least once a month) drank alcohol, and 8.3% regularly used an illicit drug. In contrast to these rates of regular substance use, the survey found that 9.4% of the sample met *Diagnostic and Statistical Manual of Mental Disorders* (4th ed. rev.; American Psychiatric Association, 1994) criteria for any substance abuse or dependence diagnosis during the past year. Of this 9.4%, 68% (6.4% of the total sample) were diagnosed with only an alcohol use disorder, and the remaining 32% (3.0% of the total sample) were diagnosed with only a drug use disorder or with both an alcohol and drug use disorder. These statistics indicate that approximately 19% of regular alcohol users and 36% of regular drug users meet diagnostic criteria for substance abuse or dependence. It is clear that substance abuse presents a significant health problem among adults and adolescents in the United States; however, not all individuals who use alcohol or drugs incur substantial physical, psychological, or social problems. A number of social and psychological factors have been demonstrated to increase risk for developing a substance abuse problem, including deviance proneness (e.g., Jessor & Jessor, 1977; Windle & Davies, 1999), family and peer influences (e.g., Barnes, Farrell, & Dintcheff, 1997; Zucker & Fitzgerald, 1991), positive outcome expectancies for substance use (e.g., Cooper, Russell, Skinner, & Windle, 1992; Goldman, Darkes, & Del Boca, 1999), personality traits (e.g., Barnes, Murray, Patton, Bentler, & Anderson, 2000; Sher, Trull, Bartholow, & Vieth, 1999), and negative affect or tension reduction (e.g., Cappell & Herman, 1972; Greeley & Oei, 1999).

Learning theory provides a foundation for understanding the processes that underlie the acquisition and maintenance of substance use disorders (Vogel-Sprott & Fillmore, 1999). We have chosen to focus on two readily observable learning processes that enjoy the greatest empirical support in explaining the process of addiction in humans: (a) operant conditioning and (b) classical conditioning. These learning processes affect the behavioral mechanisms of action that are thought to influence the development and maintenance of substance abuse disorders, including positive and negative reinforcement. After we review these basic learning processes and mechanisms, we review and evaluate influential models of substance use that utilize classical and operant conditioning processes and the resulting behavioral mechanisms to explain the onset and maintenance of addiction. Models that focus more heavily on conditioning processes (i.e., conditioned withdrawal [Wikler, 1965], conditioned compensatory response [Siegel, 1983], conditioned appetitive models [Stewart, de Witt, & Eikelboom, 1984], and operant conditioning models [Bigelow & Silverman, 1999; Higgins, 1997]) are discussed first, followed by those that rely to a proportionately greater extent on affective–cognitive processing to explain addiction (affective processing model of negative reinforcement [Baker, Piper, McCarthy, Majeskie, & Fiore, 2004] and the two-factor model of negative reinforcement [Stasiewicz & Maisto, 1993]).

It is important to define major terms at the outset. For ease of reading, and to present information more succinctly, we use the term *drug* to refer both to alcohol and to other substance use, unless otherwise noted. We also use the terms *substance use disorders* and *addiction* interchangeably to refer to the problematic use of drugs and alcohol. We view these two terms as involving both physiological processes, such as tolerance and withdrawal, and psychological changes, such as craving, positive and negative affect, and outcome expectancies that set apart addicted individuals from those who engage in nonproblematic use. We refer to classical and operant conditioning as *processes*, even though they are more accurately defined by a strict set of procedures. The motivational products of these learning procedures are purported to drive behavior; that is, positive and negative reinforcement provide the impetus for drug seeking and, as such, are proposed to be the behavioral mechanisms underlying drug use.

CLASSICAL CONDITIONING

Classical conditioning, also know as *Pavlovian* and *respondent conditioning*, forms the basis of many theories of the etiology and maintenance of alcohol and drug use disorders. In its simplest form, classical conditioning involves the pairing of a neutral stimulus (conditioned stimulus [CS]; e.g., buzzer) with a stimulus (unconditioned stimulus [UCS]; e.g., bright light) that naturally evokes a response (unconditioned response [UCR]; e.g., eyeblink) in the absence of any learning. After multiple pairings of the CS with the UCS and the resultant UCR, the CS itself comes to evoke a conditioned response (CR; Pavlov, 1927). Alcohol and drugs can serve as powerful UCSs in both humans and nonhuman animals. CSs can include a variety of environmental and contextual stimuli, such as drug paraphernalia (e.g., injection works), the sight and taste of an alcoholic beverage (e.g., gin and tonic), or features of the context in which a substance is regularly consumed (e.g., living room; Bouton & Nelson, 1998). When paired with a drug UCS, the previously neutral CS can elicit a range of CRs, including physiological, behavioral, affective, and/or cognitive changes. These CRs may simulate the effects of the drug or they may be opposite in direction to the effects of the drug UCR (Grabowski & O'Brien, 1981; O'Brien, Testa, O'Brien, Brady, & Wells, 1977; Siegel, 1983). These drug CRs have been implicated as a factor in contributing to drug withdrawal (Wikler, 1965), tolerance (Siegel, 1983), and relapse (Baker et al., 2004).

OPERANT CONDITIONING

Operant conditioning, also frequently termed *instrumental learning*, occurs when a behavioral response produces a consequence that is significant to the organism. Reinforcement and punishment are defined by their effect on specific behavioral responses. Manipulations that increase a behavior are termed *reinforcers*, whereas a *punishment* decreases a behavior. *Reinforcers* are defined as events that increase the appearance of a targeted behavior, and they fall into two main categories: positive and negative. *Positive reinforcers* are those whose presentation increases the frequency of a target behavior. For example, a hungry rat is placed in a cage in which bar pressing is followed by the provision of food pellets. Bar pressing increases in frequency because it is being positively reinforced by the food pellet. In contrast, the removal of a *negative reinforcer* will also increase a behavior. For example, a rat receives mild electric footshock on being placed in a cage, and it can stop the footshock by pressing a bar. Bar pressing behavior increases because of its consequences (i.e., allowing the rat to escape the footshock). Note that negative reinforcement is distinct from punishment: A negative reinforcer increases a behavior, whereas a punishment decreases a behavior. For example, the frequency of bar pressing can be decreased when each bar press is followed by a mild footshock.

CLASSICAL AND OPERANT CONDITIONING: HOW ARE THEY SIMILAR?

Classical and operant conditioning are procedural in nature; that is, they are defined by a specific set of procedures that vary depending on whether the investigator is attempting to conduct a classical or operant conditioning paradigm. However, despite differences in protocol for the two conditioning processes, there are significant similarities. Classical and operant conditioning are termed *associative learning processes* in that they both involve the acquisition of knowledge about reliable environmental relationships. Most learning theorists agree that the value of conditioning processes to the organism is in the acquisition of information regarding the reliable prediction of relationships between important environmental or contextual events (e.g., Bouton, 1991; Rescorla, 1988, 1990). This knowledge regarding the predictable association between one event and another is posited to assist the human or nonhuman animal in adapting to its environment; this resulting adaptation is likely to increase its chances of survival (Domjan, 2005; Skinner, 1981). Both laboratory studies and naturalistic environments in which learning factors operate will most often involve both operant and classical conditioning components (Grabowski & O'Brien, 1981). This can be illustrated by a situation in which an individual repeatedly consumes alcohol in the same context. For example, an individual who regularly drinks in the same bar may develop classically conditioned responses to the sight of the bar, which functions as a CS. Following the consumption of an alcoholic beverage by the individual, the presence of alcohol in the body functions as a UCS. This UCS results in UCRs, such as the pleasant physiological effects of alcohol (i.e., relaxation, warmth). Following repeated associations of the bar context (CS) with the presence of the alcohol in the body (UCS) and the physiological effects of the alcohol (UCR), the bar context (CS) can come to elicit the physiological CRs in response to entering the bar, factors that contribute to processes such as alcohol craving, tolerance, and conditioned withdrawal. In addition to the action of classical conditioning factors in this situation, operant factors are at work. The bar context can serve as a discriminative stimulus (S^D) for drinking, signaling the onset of the rewarding effects of the drug. As a result, the bar context becomes associated with the immediate positive effects of alcohol, a reinforcer that helps maintain continued bar drinking. In this example, classical and operant conditioning processes work concurrently to maintain alcohol use.

BEHAVIORAL MECHANISMS IN ADDICTION

Classical and operant conditioning processes result in behavioral mechanisms of action that influence the occurrence of specific behaviors. Classical conditioning processes assist in identifying potentially appetitive or aversive situations. Operant conditioning procedures produce motivational states that increase or decrease a targeted behavior. Procedures that increase the frequency of a specific behavior are termed *reward procedures,* and those that decrease the occurrence of a behavior are termed *punishment.* The most relevant behavioral mechanisms for explaining drug use involve processes that increase a behavior—in this case, alcohol or drug use. Reward processes are operant in nature and consist primarily of positive and negative reinforcement. Both positive and negative reinforcement strengthen the occurrence of a behavior, which is reflected in the term *reinforcement. Positive* and *negative* refer to the perceived pleasantness or aversiveness of the outcome, respectively. When a behavior produces a biologically important pleasant outcome (e.g., food or sex), it is designated as *positive reinforcement.* Alternatively, a behavior that allows an organism to escape (terminate) or avoid a biologically important unpleasant event (e.g., physical pain, hunger) is termed *negative reinforcement.* It is the perceived effect of the stimulus on the organism (pleasant or unpleasant) that motivates behavior. Pleasant consequences (e.g., a cocaine high) increase motivation to repeatedly seek out the stimulus whereas aversive consequences (e.g., headache, vomiting) result in avoidance of contact with the stimulus.

BEHAVIORAL MECHANISMS IN ADDICTION:
DEVELOPMENT AND MAINTENANCE OF DRUG ABUSE

We now review six models that attempt to explain the acquisition and persistence of drug abuse (see Table 7.1). All of these models attempt to

TABLE 7.1

Comparison of Learning Models and Hypothesized Behavioral Mechanisms

Model	Reference(s)	Learning	Mechanism	Motivation
Conditioned withdrawal	Wikler (1965)	Classical conditioning	Negative reinforcement	Withdrawal relief
Conditioned compensatory	Siegel (1983)	Classical conditioning	Negative reinforcement	Withdrawal relief
Conditioned appetitive	Stewart et al. (1984)	Classical conditioning	Positive reinforcement	Pleasure
Operant conditioning	Higgins (1997); Bigelow (2001)	Operant conditioning	Positive reinforcement	Pleasure
Negative reinforcement	Baker et al. (2004)	Classical and operant conditioning	Negative reinforcement	Withdrawal relief, negative affect reduction
Two-factor reformulation	Stasiewicz and Maisto (1993)	Classical and operant conditioning	Negative reinforcement	Negative affect reduction

explain continued consumption of drugs, despite the often wide-ranging negative effects that are a result of frequent and excessive drug use. Drug use has been characterized as progressing from impulsive to compulsive use (Koob et al., 2004). At first, drug use is viewed as motivated by impulsivity and the effects of positive reinforcement. *Impulsive* disorders are experienced as "an increasing sense of tension or arousal . . . pleasure, gratification or relief at the time of committing the act, and possibly regret, self-reproach or guilt following the act (Koob et al., 2004, p. 739). Alternatively, *compulsive* use is seen as driven primarily by negative reinforcement and is characterized by "anxiety and stress before committing the compulsive repetitive behavior, and relief from the stress by performing the compulsive behavior" (Koob et al., 2004, p. 739). Compulsive drug use can be viewed as consisting of verbal, physiological, and behavioral responses that result in a "drug-acquisitive motivational state" (Baker, Morse, & Sherman, 1987, p. 258). It is this motivation or drive to engage in addictive drug use that these models attempt to explain. The models we present in this chapter involve negative and positive reinforcement to explain the underlying motivational state that fuels problematic drug use. Some models focus more on behaviorally or physiologically observable processes (e.g., classical and operant conditioning), whereas others maintain that these types of more objectively verifiable processes result in cognitive and affective conditions (i.e., negative affect) that motivate behavior. All of the models involve both classical conditioning and operant conditioning process; what differs is the relative emphasis these models place on classical versus operant processes. However, all of the models posit that the motivation to continue drug use in the face of significant negative consequences is driven by negative and positive reinforcement.

Models that primarily focus on the role of associative learning processes include the *conditioned withdrawal model* (Wikler, 1965), the *conditioned compensatory response model* (Siegel, 1983), *operant conditioning models* (Bigelow & Silverman, 1999; Higgins, 1997), and the *conditioned appetitive model* (Stewart et al., 1984). Models that incorporate cognitive elements include the *affective processing model of negative reinforcement* (Baker et al., 2004) and the *two-factor model of negative affect* (Stasiewicz & Maisto, 1993).

Conditioned Withdrawal Model

Put forth by Abraham Wikler and his colleagues, the conditioned withdrawal model proposes that escape from drug withdrawal symptoms, both conditioned and unconditioned, can function as a primary motivator of compulsive alcohol and drug use (Ludwig & Wikler, 1974; Wikler, 1965). Through a process of classical conditioning, drug cues (CSs) become associated with signs of drug withdrawal (UCS). Each administration of a drug involves both drug effects and unconditioned drug withdrawal. Whereas initial administrations of a drug result primarily in unconditioned drug withdrawal responses (UCRs), repeated drug use results in conditioned withdrawal symptoms that are triggered by internal and environmental cues (CSs) that have been repeatedly associated with unconditioned withdrawal. An operant conditioning process ensues in which individuals can effectively escape aversive withdrawal symptoms through continued drug use. In this case, drug withdrawal symptoms become an S^D that signals relief from the drug withdrawal syndrome through continued drug use. A number of studies have supported this model by demonstrating that withdrawal symptoms can be conditioned in humans (e.g., O'Brien et al., 1977; O'Brien, O'Brien, Mintz, & Brady, 1975) and nonhuman animals (e.g., Goldberg & Schuster, 1967; Wikler & Pescor, 1967). This model has also been used to explain the association between cognitive constructs such as craving and repeated substance use. Ludwig and Stark (1974) found that craving seemed most highly correlated with degree and extent of prior withdrawal experiences, which supports their contention that individuals experience cravings during episodes of conditioned or unconditioned withdrawal.

Conditioned Compensatory Response Model

The conditioned compensatory response model proposes that a significant contributor to drug tolerance and craving in humans and nonhuman animals is the result of CRs that are opposite in direction to the unconditioned effects of the drug (Siegel, 1979, 1983). These CRs develop as a result of a classical conditioning process in which the presence of a drug in the body functions as a US and the associated drug administration procedure that precedes the drug effect (e.g., drug injection, preparation and consumption of alcohol beverage) functions as a CS. Initially, the administration of the drug results only in the unconditioned drug effects (UCRs). With repeated administrations of the drug, environmental (i.e., drug context) and sensory (e.g., taste of the alcoholic beverage) cues produce CRs that are opposite in direction to the unconditioned effects of the drug. In this way, the CRs compensate for the drug effects that are contributing to increased tolerance, particularly when the drug is repeatedly administered in the same context. This increased tolerance fuels escalating drug use because increasing amounts of the drug are necessary to obtain the same effect. Siegel (1983) also argued that conditioned compensatory responses contribute to the development of withdrawal symptoms, which are often opposite to the pharmacological effect of the drug. Across a number of different drugs, conditioning effects tend to be context specific (e.g., Hinson & Siegel, 1986; Siegel, 1975, 1977), thereby accounting for the observation that drug tolerance is greater (Siegel, Hinson, Krank, & McCully, 1982) and is acquired more rapidly (Le, Poulos, & Cappell, 1979) when the drug is administered in the same context. Siegel also suggested that these compensatory responses may underlie drug craving. As tolerance to the appetitive unconditioned effects of the drug increases, there is a decrease in the pleasurable direct effects of the drug. At the same time, conditioned compensatory responses increase, which are perceived by the organism as aversive and may underlie the experience of drug craving.

The conditioned compensatory model has features similar to Wikler's (1965) conditioned withdrawal model. Most (although not all) drug withdrawal symptoms are in the direction opposite of the drug effect (Grabowski & O'Brien, 1981). As a result, the CRs for both the withdrawal and compensatory conditioning models are opposite in direction to the drug effects, resulting in similar predictions for both models.

Appetitive Operant Conditioning Model

In contrast to the negative reinforcement models (e.g., conditioned withdrawal model, conditioned compensatory model), an operant conditioning conceptualization focuses on the function of drugs as unconditioned positive reinforcers. Drug-seeking behavior conforms to the same operant conditioning principles as other unconditioned positive reinforcers (e.g., sex, water, food; Higgins & Heil, 2004). Reinforcement through drug consumption is viewed as a biologically normal event. Drug self-administration behavior is viewed as central to substance use disorders and is controlled by its consequences (Cohen, Liebson, & Faillace, 1971, 1972, 1973). Drugs of abuse function as positive reinforcers that strengthen and maintain drug self-administration behavior.

Both human and infrahuman research has shown that drug administration can be viewed as an operant behavior that is maintained and modified by its consequences (Bigelow, 2001).

An operant model posits that drug abuse disorders stem from deficiencies in the environmental contingencies of reinforcement rather than from defects within the individual. That is, the individual's environment does not contain adequate sources of positive reinforcement, and drug use, which results in immediate and powerful rewards, becomes a frequent source of reinforcement. The strength of drug use as a reinforcer increases, particularly as other forms of positive reinforcement in the environment decrease (e.g., fewer friends, loss of job). Much of the operant research has focused on discerning the impact of various schedules of reinforcement on drug use behaviors (Bigelow, 2001). Laboratory research has demonstrated that human drug self-administration can be decreased by arranging reinforcement of alternative responses that are incompatible with drug use (Carroll, 1993; Higgins, 1997). This expanded operant view examines how the availability of a concurrent array of environmental reinforcers can influence drug use behavior in problem drug users from a behavioral economic perspective (Carroll & Campbell, 2000; Vuchinich & Tucker, 1983, 1988). This research has highlighted the impact of magnitude and delay of reinforcement on drug use behavior (Madden, Petry, Badger, & Bickel, 1997; Vuchinich & Simpson, 1998). In general, longer delays discount or reduce the impact of alternative reinforcers to drug use, with drug abusers demonstrating greater discounting effects over similar periods of time compared with nonproblem users or nonusers.

Conditioned Appetitive Model

The conditioned appetitive motivational model (Stewart et al., 1984) proposes that the presence of the drug in the body activates appetitive motivational mechanisms that are involved in the initiation and reinitiation (i.e., relapse) of drug-seeking behavior. Through a process of classical conditioning, initially neutral stimuli associated with a drug come to elicit a positive motivational state similar to that elicited by the drug itself. Subsequent exposure to these conditioned incentive stimuli activates an appetitive (or positive) motivational state that primes the individual to reinitiate drug taking. Because these stimuli maintain the behavior on which they are contingent, they are said to act as reinforcers, and they are called *conditioned reinforcers*. According to Stewart et al. (1984), "a conditioned reinforcing stimulus acts to maintain behavior not by virtue of satisfying some drive or need but rather by acting as a persistent goad to response generation" (p. 263). This model helps explain relapse to substance use after long periods of abstinence by suggesting that conditioned cues in the environment act as CSs to increase the incentive value of the drug. Similar to the operant conditioning model, this appetitive motivational model suggests that it is primarily a positive rein-forcement process that drives drug use. The appetitive motivational model proposes that cravings result from the desire for a drug's pleasant effects. This positive-incentive account of appetitive behaviors stands in contrast to the drive-reduction (i.e., negative reinforcement) views that attribute appetitive actions to the need or drive-reducing properties of goal objects or incentives. For example, the conditioned withdrawal and conditioned compensatory models are two such negative reinforcement models that suggest that it is neg-ative reinforcement factors (e.g., relief of withdrawal and other aversive drug effects) that underlie both craving and drug use.

Affective Processing Model of Negative Reinforcement

Baker et al. (2004) proposed a negative reinforcement model of drug abuse in which escape or avoidance of negative affect is the primary underly-ing cause of drug addiction. All substances of addiction produce withdrawal symptoms, and pleasurable drug use effects often co-occur with unpleasant or aversive withdrawal symptoms. Withdrawal symptoms increase during an acute episode of drug use as drug effects dissipate. In addition to the impact of acute withdrawal during an episode of drug use, withdrawal symptoms may intensify over multiple drug use episodes as drug quantity and frequency increase over time. Baker et al. pointed out that different drugs of abuse typ-ically have varying physiological withdrawal syndromes; however, all drugs of abuse share negative affect as a common withdrawal symptom. In addition to withdrawal-based negative affect, drug users also contend with chronic situ-ationally induced (e.g., family arguments, work stress) and intrapersonal (e.g., sadness, anger, hopelessness) negative affect, particularly as drug use escalates.

The experience of negative affect produces unique interoceptive cues; over time, these internal sensations come to reliably signal affective changes through a process of classical conditioning. Baker et al. (2004) proposed that over time, drug users come to discriminate these internal sensations from others and learn to respond to lower levels of these internal cues. This is sup-ported by evidence indicating that humans (e.g., Murphy & Zajonc, 1993) and nonhuman animals (e.g., Kim, Siegel, & Patenall, 1999) can effectively process interoceptive cues, particularly those that are affectively laden, even when they are outside of conscious awareness. The experience of negative affect, whether it is part of a drug withdrawal syndrome or precipitated by situational or cognitive triggers, increases the incentive value of drug use. Like any aversive state, negative affect provides the motivation to escape through continued drug use and/or relapse following a period of abstinence. Studies have supported the idea that drug use is an effective, predictable, and efficient means of relieving negative affect (Marlatt & Gordon, 1985; Wetter et al., 1994).

Whereas other models such as the conditioned compensatory response model (Siegel, 1983), the conditioned withdrawal model (Wikler, 1965), and the operant conditioning model (e.g., Bigelow, 2001) emphasize the role of external or environmental cues in precipitating relapse, the affective processing model of negative reinforcement emphasizes the role of internal, negative affect as the primary cue for drug use. Baker et al. (2004) proposed that most individuals are usually unaware of their motivations for substance use; the addicted individual becomes proficient at detecting very low levels of negative affect before these levels are even consciously perceptible. As a result, over time, the escape responses to negative affect become conditioned to increasingly lower levels of negative affect. The process by which escape responses become conditioned to lower levels of negative affect was first demonstrated by Solomon and Wynne (1954). In their research with dogs on avoidance responding, they observed that avoidance latencies shortened considerably with training. They also noted that overt signs of anxiety disappeared with training and appeared not to exist during short-latency responses. Finally, they reported that the reappearance of fear during long-latency responses was followed by a return to short-latency responses for the next several trials. This set of observations led them to introduce a new principle, called *anxiety conservation*. The *conservation of anxiety hypothesis* was later extended by Stampfl and Levis (Levis, 1985; Stampfl & Levis, 1967, 1969, 1973), who used a serial CS paradigm. This principle of anxiety conservation has subsequently been further extended to explain the role of negative emotional states in substance use and substance use disorder (Stasiewicz & Maisto, 1993).

Two-Factor Model of Negative Affect

Negative affect is a common determinant of relapse to addictive use of alcohol and other drugs (Marlatt & Gordon, 1985). Several of the drug conditioning models reviewed earlier (e.g., Siegel, 1983; Wikler, 1965) propose that negative emotional states may act as CSs capable of eliciting conditioned drug responses because the individual has a history of using the drug in the presence of specific emotional states. Although the nature of the CR may differ, the drug conditioning models suggest that the CR develops from an association between internal and external stimuli (CS) and the drug effects (UCS). This view acknowledges the role of conditioned drug responses as mediating variables in drug consumption. An alternative view, based on Mowrer's (1947) two-factor avoidance theory, emphasizes aversive emotional learning and includes conditioned aversive emotional responses (CERs) as mediating variables in drug consumption (Stasiewicz & Maisto, 1993). In an effort to provide a theoretical framework for understanding the role of negative affect in the maintenance of substance use and substance use disorder,

Stasiewicz and Maisto (1993) used Mowrer's two-factor theory to extend existing drug-conditioning frameworks.

Among the set of drug-conditioning models, the role of negative affect in the maintenance of substance use disorder has been conceptualized in several ways. For example, the conditioned withdrawal model (Wikler, 1965), the conditioned compensatory response model (Siegel, 1983), and the conditioned appetitive model (Stewart et al., 1984) view negative affective states as CSs; both Siegel (1983) and Stewart et al. (1984) state that negative affect may increase the incentive value of the drug. Finally, from an operant conditioning perspective, negative affective states have been viewed as S^Ds (Pomerleau, 1981). These models tend to view negative emotional states as an originating event (CS or S^D) or a sequence of conditioned events that lead to drug consumption. However, Stasiewicz and Maisto (1993) remarked that this view does not give full consideration to the origin of the negative emotional response. They argued that a more complete explanation of the role of negative affect in the maintenance of substance use would incorporate learning principles that describe how the emotional response is acquired and maintained.

Mowrer (1947) proposed that two processes were involved in avoidance conditioning, providing two responses: (a) a CER and (b) a conditioned avoidance response. The CER results from the pairing of a "neutral" stimulus with a painful event, which is, in essence, a classical conditioning process. When associated with painful events, these "neutral" stimuli (e.g., a particular room, a person's voice) acquire the capacity to produce aversive emotional reactions (e.g., fear, anxiety) in the absence of the original painful stimulation. The conditioned avoidance response is an instrumental response. That is, the response is instrumental in changing the environment of the organism insofar as it reduces or eliminates the aversive stimulation. In this way, learning of an aversive emotional response occurs through classical conditioning, whereas learning of the avoidance response occurs through operant conditioning. In addition, the CER motivates behavior, whereas any response by the individual that reduces or eliminates this state is assumed to serve as a reinforcer of behavior. From this perspective, substance use is conceptualized as a behavioral avoidance response. For example, drug use will be rewarding to the extent that it results in a reduction or elimination of the CER.

Stasiewicz and Maisto (1993) also noted that the instrumental response of drug use (and the drug's effects) may function as one component of a more complex behavioral avoidance response that may require the addition of one or more associated behaviors (e.g., drinking and engaging in some other activity) before the response is effective in terminating the aversive CS. This view acknowledges that the drug effects alone may not always be sufficient for reducing or eliminating the aversive cues but that they may do so in combination with an activity that directs attention away from the aversive CS. The attention-allocation model of drinking (Steele & Josephs, 1988, 1990; Steele,

Southwick, & Pagano, 1986) provides an explanation of how the combined response of drinking and engaging in a distracting activity may result in a greater reduction in negative affect than either response alone.

COMMON THEMES

In this review, we have emphasized that the transition from substance use to substance abuse involves principles of learning. Although the particular emphasis on classical versus operant conditioning processes may vary among models, all of the models presented in this chapter propose that these learning processes are involved in the development and maintenance of substance abuse and dependence. All of the models emphasize either positive and/or negative reinforcement as the mechanism underlying the development of behavioral patterns of substance use. Finally, several models reviewed posit that drug use behavior becomes more efficient over time or, stated another way that the individual learns to respond more quickly to lower levels of interoceptive states thought to provide the motivation to engage in drug use (e.g., aversive withdrawal states, negative emotional states). Learning processes such as the anxiety conservation hypothesis (Solomon & Wynne, 1954) and, by extension, serial CS conditioning (e.g., Stampfl, 1988) are ideally suited to explain this observation.

To varying degrees, all of the models reviewed here focus on urges or cravings as mediators of the relationship between exteroceptive or interoceptive cues and substance use. With the exception of the conditioned appetitive model, urges or cravings are most often associated with the aversive or unpleasant effects of drug use. For example, urges or cravings are thought to be part of a complex withdrawal process (conditioned withdrawal model, negative reinforcement model), the development of tolerance and the need for increasing amounts of the drug (conditioned compensatory model), and negative emotional states (two-factor theory). Although urges and cravings may not take center stage in an operant conditioning model, they are most likely to emerge under conditions where the occurrence of a previously rewarded response (i.e., drug consumption) is blocked. In this regard, Amsel (1958) demonstrated that nonreward of a previously rewarded response produced an emotional response, which he called *frustration*. Support for the notion that urges and cravings are primarily associated with aversive states comes from a growing number of laboratory-based studies demonstrating that cue-elicited negative emotion (e.g., depressed mood, anger) elicits craving for drugs of abuse (e.g., Childress, Ehrman, McLellan, MacRae, & O'Brien, 1994; Coffey, Stasiewicz, Hughes, & Brimo, 2006; Cooney, Litt, Morse, Bauer, & Gaupp, 1997; Stasiewicz et al., 1997).

Although positive reinforcement may play a particularly important role during initial exposures to drug effects, the role of negative reinforcement assumes increasing importance as the individual learns that the drug allevi-ates unpleasant affective states, including aversive states associated with drug deprivation (i.e., withdrawal). Thus, the transition from initial substance use to substance abuse involves a shift from positive to negative reinforcement. As discussed earlier, a behavior will be negatively reinforced (rewarded, and as a result, strengthened) when it allows an organism to escape (terminate) or avoid a biologically-important unpleasant event (e.g., physical pain, drug withdrawal, anxiety). All of the models described address the role of aversive physical and/or emotional states as important antecedents to drug use among drug-dependent persons. For example, the conditioned withdrawal model, the conditioned compensatory response model, and the conditioned appetitive model view the aversive states as CSs; both the conditioned compensatory response model and the conditioned appetitive model claim that aversive states may increase the incentive value of the drug. An operant conditioning model would describe aversive physical or emotional states as S^Ds that set the occasion for drug use. Finally, both the negative reinforcement model and the two-factor model view the negative emotional state itself as a CR that provides the motivation for the individual to seek out and engage in substance use to allevi-ate the unpleasant affective state. With the exception of the two-factor model, these models state that aversive states that motivate continued drug use are the result of repeated exposures to the drug. The two-factor model, with its empha-sis on CERs, suggests that the aversive emotional state occurs independently of drug use and that drug use and related behaviors function to reduce these unpleasant states. Thus, with the possible exception of the conditioned appet-itive model, escape or avoidance learning is a central feature of these models.

CLINICAL IMPLICATIONS

We have reviewed here several learning-based models of drug depen-dence with regard to their role in the development and maintenance of drug dependence. Whether a particular model adopts an operant or classical con-ditioning framework (or both), all of the models would suggest that treatment must involve the learning of new relations between events. How each treat-ment approach differs is related to the relative importance each model assigns to the role of external (e.g., sight of preferred drinking context) versus inter-nal events (e.g., withdrawal states, emotional responses) and their relationship to substance use.

For example, models of drug dependence based on operant learning, such as the contingency management model, opt for reinforcing behaviors that are incompatible with substance use as well as drug abstinence itself (as verified by objective assessments). Indeed, treatment-outcome studies that have used a contingency management approach have been largely successful in reducing drug use among individuals diagnosed with a substance use disorder (Lussier, Heil, Mongeon, Badger, & Higgins, 2006). In contrast, models of drug dependence that feature classical conditioning processes rely more on exposure and response prevention treatments. For example, in a recent study by Coffey et al. (2006), exposure to trauma cues in a sample of patients with comorbid alcohol dependence and posttraumatic stress disorder resulted in a decrease in negative emotional responding and alcohol craving. The finding that alcohol craving elicited by negative emotional imagery decreases when imagery-elicited negative emotion is reduced may have important theoretical implications. Specifically, the data support Stasiewicz and Maisto's (1993) two-factor model of addiction and a recent reformulation of Baker et al.'s (2004) negative reinforcement model of drug addiction. These findings point to the importance of negative emotion in the maintenance of substance dependence. The data also suggest that for substance-dependent individuals who use substances in response to negative emotion, extended exposure to negative emotional cues without the negatively reinforcing effects of drugs may serve as extinction trials that weaken the relation between negative emotion and substance use. The results from Coffey et al.'s study are consistent with treatment strategies suggested by researchers who use exposure to interoceptive cues (e.g., negative emotion, racing heartbeat) to treat co-occurring substance use and panic disorder (Otto, Powers, & Fischmann, 2005; Otto, Safren, & Pollack, 2004). The physiological components of withdrawal are an important set of cues that have the capacity to motivate drug-taking behavior. Aversive emotional responses to these physiological cues may also need to be extinguished through exposure and response prevention techniques. This is the equivalent of providing exposure to autonomic cues of anxiety in patients with panic disorder. Finally, images, thoughts, and memories that function as CSs may constitute a large part of the stimulus complex that is maintaining substance use (Stasiewicz & Maisto, 1993). From a conditioning perspective, if cognitions possess either appetitive or aversive properties, then this effect is assumed to be the result of a conditioning process (Bradizza, Stasiewicz, & Maisto, 1994; Kirsch, Lynn, Vigorito, & Miller, 2004). Therefore, extended exposure to these cognitive stimuli is predicted to result in extinction of the conditioned appetitive or aversive emotional responses.

CASE EXAMPLE

We now provide a case example to illustrate how negative reinforcement may influence alcohol use in an alcohol-dependent individual.

The client is a 50-year-old retired man living with his two young children (ages 8 and 10). His presenting complaint was that his drinking was interfering with his ability to adequately parent his children. On the alcohol version of the Inventory of Drug Taking Situations (Annis, Turner, & Sklar, 1997), the client reported often drinking heavily in response to situations involving negative emotions and interpersonal conflict. According to the client, alcohol helped him to "calm down and relax" when he was angry. The Timeline FollowBack (Sobell, Maisto, Sobell, & Cooper, 1979) was administered to assess the extent of the client's alcohol use during the 180 days prior to the pretreatment assessment and during the 3-month treatment period at the posttreatment assessment. In addition, several measures of negative affect and mindfulness were administered to assess changes in these variables before and following a course of treatment. Pre- and posttreatment summary information for this client are presented in Table 7.2. At the pretreatment assessment, he reported consuming 13 drinks per drinking day. He reported abstaining on 38% of days during the pretreatment assessment period. Finally, he reported drinking heavily (≥ 5 drinks per day) on 52% of days during the pretreatment assessment period.

The client's pretreatment goal was to reduce his drinking to a level that did not interfere with his ability to parent. He planned to limit his drinking in social situations and when in the presence of his children. The treatment

TABLE 7.2
Pre- and Posttreatment Scores on Questionnaire Measures

Measure	Range	Pretreatment	Posttreatment
TLFB			
Drinks per drinking day		13	5
% days abstinent	0–180	38	91
% heavy drinking days	0–180	52	4
AAAQ			
Approach	0–80	61	5
Avoidance	0–80	36	77
PANAS			
Positive Affect	10–50	43	44
Negative Affect	10–50	26	13
MAI			
Anger–Arousal	8–40	19	17
Anger-Eliciting Situations	7–35	12	7
Hostile Outlook	4–20	15	9
Anger-In	5–25	11	11
Anger-Out	2–10	10	9
KIMS			
Observing	12–60	47	44
Describing	8–40	29	34
Act With Awareness	10–50	34	38
Accepting Without Judgment	9–45	28	39
AAQ	1–63	37	31

Note. TLFB = Timeline FollowBack; AAAQ = Approach and Avoidance of Alcohol Questionnaire; PANAS = Positive and Negative Affect Schedule; MAI = Multidimensional Anger Inventory; KIMS = Kentucky Inventory of Mindfulness Skills; AAQ = Acceptance and Action Questionnaire.

approach involved 12 sessions of cognitive–behavioral treatment for alcohol dependence plus an affect regulation training (ART) component designed specifically for individuals who report drinking heavily in response to negative emotional situations. The cognitive–behavioral treatment component included sessions that provided skills for coping with high-risk drinking situations as well as relapse prevention skills.

The ART component focused on the role of negative emotions in substance use and included sessions designed to increase a person's ability to identify and label emotions, prolonged direct experiencing of negative emotions, and mindfulness skills for managing negative emotions and cravings. The prolonged direct experiencing component comprised four sessions of imaginal exposure to the client's highest-rated negative emotional drinking triggers. The direct experiencing of negative emotion without experiencing the usual consequences (e.g., substance use, avoidance) is intended to increase the client's ability to tolerate (and accept) unpleasant emotions, reduce maladaptive emotional responses (through nonreinforcement), and increase self-efficacy for regulating negative affect.

Mindfulness has been described as the act of paying attention in a particular way. In the ART treatment, breath was used as an anchor for the client's attention. Mindfulness involves attending to one's breathing and bringing attention back to the present moment whenever the mind wanders. Thoughts, sensations, feelings, and urges are to be observed in a nonjudgmental way. The therapist began by teaching the client to pay attention to his breathing, to be in the moment. As he became more comfortable with the act of mindfulness, the therapist extended the mindfulness exercise to situations that involved negative emotions and urges to drink. When an urge or negative emotion was presented, the client was instructed to be mindful of the changing physical sensations in his body that were associated with urges and emotions. In this way, he was instructed to stay with the urge and/or emotion and to observe how it changed. During the prolonged-exposure sessions, mindfulness skills were applied after the emotion was elicited through the guided imagery technique. At the beginning of treatment, the client indicated that he was confident that this approach would help him reduce his alcohol consumption.

The client described his most frequent negative emotional drinking situation and the situation in which he found it most difficult to resist drinking as "drinking at home after I yell at the kids for doing something wrong." The therapist conducted a thorough assessment of this situation, including visual cues (e.g., seeing the messy living room, the children's faces), thoughts (e.g., "What are they doing!"), physiological sensations (e.g., heart pounding, face flushed), and response-produced cues (e.g., the stinging sensation in his hand after hitting the wall in anger). As the client reported these cues, the therapist began developing a negative affect imagery scene that would be used during the first prolonged-exposure session. Several other negative affect imagery scenes also were developed based on the client's self-report. During the prolonged-exposure sessions the therapist revised the imaginal scene content as additional cues emerged during the scene presentations.

At posttreatment, the client demonstrated improvement on several alcohol consumption variables. He had greatly decreased the number of drinks per drinking day, from 13 pretreatment to 5 posttreatment, and he had reduced his number of heavy drinking days from 52% of available drinking days to 4%. Percentage days abstinent from alcohol increased from 38% at pretreatment to 91% at posttreatment. Finally, on the Approach and Avoidance of Alcohol Questionnaire (McEvoy, Stritzke, French, Lang, & Ketterman, 2004) there was a substantial decrease in the client's approach inclinations (from 61 to 5) toward drinking alcohol and a corresponding increase in avoidance inclinations toward alcohol (from 36 to 77).

On measures of affect, the client reported a substantial decrease in negative affect as assessed by the Positive and Negative Affect Schedule (Watson, Clark, & Tellegen, 1988). There also was a pre- to posttreatment decrease on several subscales of the Multidimensional Anger Inventory (Siegel, 1986), in particular the Anger-Eliciting Situations scale, which assesses anger in response to a range of potentially anger-provoking situations, and the Hostile Outlook scale, which is an attitudinal parameter of anger. Further complementing these changes were increases in mindfulness on the Kentucky Inventory of Mindfulness Skills (Baer, Smith, & Allen, 2004). The client reported increases in posttreatment scores on the Observing, Describing, and Accepting with Awareness subscales of the Kentucky Inventory of Mindfulness Skills. On the Acceptance and Action Questionnaire (Hayes et al., 2004), a measure of experiential avoidance, the client's score decreased from 37 at pretreatment to 31 at posttreatment, indicating less avoidance.

At the posttreatment assessment, the client reported that he was continuing to use the affect-regulation skills he had learned in treatment. He also reported feeling less angry and more in control of his emotions and stated that these changes have resulted in him spending more time engaged in family activities with his children. In addition, because he was drinking less, he reported having much more energy. He took a part-time job while his kids were in school and reported losing 30 pounds because of his increased activity.

This case study illustrates the interconnectedness of negative affect and alcohol dependence (through negative reinforcement) and suggests that a reduction in negative affect may be one mechanism by which treatment for alcohol dependence works. Indeed, the use of an emotion-focused intervention demonstrates that emotional experiencing and subsequent reductions in negative affect are associated with positive alcohol treatment outcomes.

CONCLUSIONS

In this chapter, we have reviewed models that apply learning principles to enhance the understanding of common behavioral mechanisms of drug dependence. We also have discussed the implications of these models and their proposed behavioral mechanisms for the treatment of drug dependence. The view of behavioral mechanisms of drug dependence emerging from this review is that our assessments must be able to capture the many ways that learning principles combine to produce complex human behavior such as drug dependence. It is likely that a combination of learning principles will provide a much more clinically relevant description of the development and maintenance of drug dependence than do existing classical conditioning or operant models alone. Moreover, the application of learning principles to explain the role of cognitive or expectancy constructs in drug dependence (Bradizza et al., 1994; Kirsch et al., 2004) and the neurobiological adaptation to drug effects (Hyman, Malenka, & Nestler, 2006) paves the way for development of an integrative model of drug dependence capable of incorporating findings from diverse theoretical perspectives (e.g., Tryon, 2005). Finally, by elucidating the behavioral mechanisms, such as negative and positive reinforcement, that contribute to the development and maintenance of drug dependence, scientists can work to develop or enhance interventions that can modify the underlying learning processes that support drug dependence.

REFERENCES

American Psychiatric Association. (1994). *Diagnostic and statistical manual of mental disorders* (4th ed.). Washington, DC: Author.

Amsel, A. (1958). The role of frustrative nonreward in noncontinuous reward situations. *Psychological Bulletin, 55*, 102–119.

Annis, H. M., Turner, N. E., & Sklar, S. M. (1997). *Inventory of Drug-Taking Situations: User's guide*. Toronto, Ontario, Canada: Addiction Research Foundation of Ontario.

Baer, R. A., Smith, G. T., & Allen, K. B. (2004). Assessment of mindfulness by self-report: The Kentucky Inventory of Mindfulness Skills. *Assessment, 11*, 191–206.

Baker, T. B., Morse, E., & Sherman, J. E. (1987). The motivation to use drugs: A psychobiological analysis of urges. In P. C. Rivers (Ed.), *Nebraska Symposium on Motivation: Vol. 34. Alcohol use and abuse* (pp. 257–321). Lincoln: University of Nebraska Press.

Baker, T. B., Piper, M. E., McCarthy, D. E., Majeskie, M. R., & Fiore, M. C. (2004). Addiction motivation reformulated: An affective processing model of negative reinforcement. *Psychological Review, 111*, 33–51.

Barnes, G. M., Farrell, M. P., & Dintcheff, B. A. (1997). Family socialization effects on alcohol abuse and related problem behaviors among female and male adolescents. In R. W. Wilsnack & S. C. Wilsnack (Eds.), *Gender and alcohol: Individual and social perspectives* (pp. 156–175). New Brunswick, NJ: Rutgers Center of Alcohol Studies.

Barnes, G. E., Murray, R. P., Patton, D., Bentler, P. M., & Anderson, R. E. (2000). *The addiction-prone personality.* Dordrecht, The Netherlands: Kluwer Academic.

Bigelow, G. E. (2001). An operant behavioral perspective on alcohol abuse and dependence. In N. Heather, T. J. Peters, & T. Stockwell (Eds.), *International handbook of alcohol dependence and problems* (pp. 299–315). New York: Wiley.

Bigelow, G. E., & Silverman, K. (1999). Theoretical and empirical foundations on contingency management treatments for drug abuse. In S. T. Higgins & K. Silverman (Eds.), *Motivating behavior change among illicit-drug abusers: Research on contingency management interventions* (pp. 15–31). Washington, DC: American Psychological Association.

Bouton, M. E. (1991). Context and retrieval in extinction and in other examples of interference in simple associative learning. In L. Dachowski & C. F. Flaherty (Eds.), *Current topics in animal learning* (pp. 25–53). Hillsdale, NJ: Erlbaum.

Bouton, M. E., & Nelson, J. B. (1998). The role of context in classical conditioning: Some implications for cognitive behavior therapy. In W. O'Donohue (Ed.), *Learning and behavior therapy* (pp. 59–84). Needham Heights, MA: Allyn & Bacon.

Bradizza, C. M., Stasiewicz, P. R., & Maisto, S. A. (1994). A conditioning reinterpretation of cognitive events in alcohol and drug cue exposure. *Journal of Behavior Therapy and Experimental Psychiatry, 25,* 15–22.

Cappell, H., & Herman, C. P. (1972). Alcohol and tension reduction: A review. *Quarterly Journal of Studies on Alcohol, 33*(1-A), 33–64.

Carroll, M. E., (1993). The economic context of drug and non-drug reinforcers affects acquisition and maintenance of drug-reinforced behavior and withdrawal effects. *Drug and Alcohol Dependence, 33,* 201–210.

Carroll, M. E., & Campbell, U. C. (2000). A behavioral economic analysis of the reinforcing effects of drugs: Transition states of addiction. In W. K. Bickel & R. E. Vuchinich (Eds.), *Reframing health behavior change with behavioral economics* (pp. 63–87). Mahwah, NJ: Erlbaum.

Childress, A. R., Ehrman, R., McLellan, A. T., MacRae, J., & O'Brien, C. P. (1994). Can induced moods trigger drug-related responses in opiate abuse patients? *Journal of Substance Abuse Treatment, 11,* 17–23.

Coffey, S. F., Stasiewicz, P. R., Hughes, P. M., & Brimo, M. L. (2006). Trauma-focused imaginal exposure for individuals with co-morbid posttraumatic stress disorder and alcohol dependence: Revealing mechanisms of alcohol craving in a cue reactivity paradigm. *Psychology of Addictive Behaviors, 20,* 425–435.

Cohen, M., Liebson, I., & Faillace, L. (1971). Moderate drinking by chronic alcoholics: A schedule-dependent phenomenon. *Journal of Nervous and Mental Disease, 153,* 434–444.

Cohen, M., Liebson, I., & Faillace, L. (1972). A technique for establishing controlled drinking in chronic alcoholics. *Diseases of the Nervous System, 33,* 46–49.

Cohen, M., Liebson, I., & Faillace, L. (1973). Controlled drinking by chronic alcoholics over extended periods of free access. *Psychological Reports, 32,* 1107–1110.

Cooney, N. L., Litt, M. D., Morse, P. A., Bauer, L. O., & Gaupp, L. (1997). Alcohol cue reactivity, negative-mood reactivity, and relapse in treated alcoholic men. *Journal of Abnormal Behavior, 106,* 243–250.

Cooper, M. L., Russell, M., Skinner, J. B., & Windle, M. (1992). Development and validation of a three-dimensional measure of drinking motives. *Psychological Assessment, 4,* 123–132.

Domjan, M. (2005). Pavlovian conditioning: A functional perspective. *Annual Review of Psychology, 56,* 179–206.

Goldberg, S. R., & Schuster, C. R. (1967). Conditioned suppression by a stimulus associated with nalorphine in morphine dependent monkeys. *Journal of the Experimental Analysis of Behavior, 10,* 235–243.

Goldman, M. S., Darkes, J., & Del Boca, F. K. (1999). Expectancy mediation of biopsychosocial risk for alcohol use and alcoholism. In I. Kirsch (Ed.), *How expectancies shape experience* (pp. 233–263). Washington, DC: American Psychological Association.

Grabowski, J., & O'Brien, C. P. (1981). Conditioning factors in opiate use. *Advances in Substance Abuse, 2,* 69–121.

Greeley, J., & Oei, T. (1999). Alcohol and tension reduction. In K. E. Leonard & H. T. Blane (Eds.), *Psychological theories of drinking and alcoholism* (2nd ed., pp. 14–53). New York: Guilford Press.

Hayes, S. C., Strosahl, K., Wilson, K. G., Bissett, R. T., Pistorello, J., Toarmino, D., et al. (2004). Measuring experiential avoidance: A preliminary test of a working model. *Psychological Record, 54,* 553–578.

Higgins, S. T. (1997). Applying learning and conditioning theory to the treatment of alcohol and cocaine abuse. In B. A. Johnson & J. D. Roache (Eds.), *Drug addiction and its treatment: Nexus of neuroscience and behavior* (pp. 367–385). Philadelphia: Lippincott Williams & Wilkins.

Higgins, S. T., & Heil, S. H. (2004). Principles of learning in the study and treatment of substance abuse. In M. Galanter & H. D. Kleber (Eds.), *Textbook of substance abuse treatment* (3rd ed., pp. 81–87). Arlington, VA: American Psychiatric Press.

Hinson, R. E., & Siegel, S. (1986). Pavlovian inhibitory conditioning and tolerance to pentobarbital-induced hypothermia in rats. *Journal of Experimental Psychology: Animal Behavior Processes, 12,* 363–370.

Hyman, S. E., Malenka, R. C., & Nestler, E. J. (2006). Neural mechanisms of addiction: The role of reward-related learning and memory. *Annual Review of Neuroscience, 29,* 565–598.

Jessor, R., & Jessor, S. L. (1977). *Problem behavior and psychosocial development.* New York: Academic Press.

Kim, J. A., Siegel, S., & Patenall, V. R. (1999). Drug-onset cues as signals: Intra-administration associations and tolerance. *Journal of Experimental Psychology: Animal Behavior Processes, 25,* 491–504.

Kirsch, I., Lynn, S. J., Vigorito, M., & Miller, R. R. (2004). The role of cognition in classical and operant conditioning. *Journal of Clinical Psychology, 60,* 369–392.

Koob, G. F., Ahmed, S. H., Boutrel, B., Chen, S. A., Kenny, P. J., Markou, A., et al. (2004). Neurobiological mechanisms in the transition from drug use to drug dependence. *Neuroscience & Biobehavioral Reviews, 27,* 739–749.

Le, A. D., Poulos, C. X., & Cappell, H. (1979, November 30). Conditioned tolerance to the hypothermic effect of ethyl alcohol. *Science, 206,* 1109–1110.

Levis, D. J. (1985). Implosive theory: A comprehensive extension of conditioning theory of fear/anxiety to psychopathology. In S. Reiss & R. R. Bootzin (Eds.), *Theoretical issues in behavior therapy* (pp. 49–82). New York: Academic Press.

Ludwig, A. M., & Stark, L. H. (1974). Alcohol craving: Subjective and situational aspects. *Quarterly Journal of Studies on Alcohol, 35,* 899–905.

Ludwig, A. M., & Wikler, A. (1974). "Craving" and relapse to drink. *Quarterly Journal of Studies on Alcohol, 35,* 108–130.

Lussier, J. P., Heil, S. H., Mongeon, J. A., Badger, G. J., & Higgins, S. T. (2006). A meta-analysis of voucher-based reinforcement therapy for substance use disorders. *Addiction, 101,* 192–203.

Madden, G. J., Petry, N. M., Badger, G. J., & Bickel, W. K. (1997). Impulsive and self-control choices in opioid-dependent patients and non-drug-using patients: Drug and monetary rewards. *Experimental and Clinical Psychopharmacology, 5,* 256–262.

Marlatt, G. A., & Gordon, J. R. (1985). *Relapse prevention: Maintenance strategies in the treatment of addictive behaviors.* New York: Guilford Press.

McEvoy, P. M., Stritzke, W. G. K., French, D. J., Lang, A. R., & Ketterman, R. L. (2004). Comparison of three models of alcohol craving in young adults: A cross-validation. *Addiction, 99,* 482–497.

Mowrer, O. H. (1947). On the dual nature of learning—A re-interpretation of "conditioning" and "problem-solving." *Harvard Educational Review, 17,* 102–148.

Murphy, S. T., & Zajonc, R. B. (1993). Affect, cognition, and awareness: Affective priming with optimal and suboptimal stimulus exposures. *Journal of Personality and Social Psychology, 64,* 723–739.

O'Brien, C. P., O'Brien, T. J., Mintz, J., & Brady, J. P. (1975). Conditioning of narcotic abstinence symptoms in human subjects. *Drug and Alcohol Dependence, 1,* 115–123.

O'Brien, C. P., Testa, T., O'Brien, T. J., Brady, J. P., & Wells, B. (1977, March 11). Conditioned narcotic withdrawal in humans. *Science, 195,* 1000–1002

Otto, M. W., Powers, M. B., & Fischmann, D. (2005). Emotional exposure in the treatment of substance use disorders: Conceptual model, evidence, and future directions. *Clinical Psychology Review, 25,* 824–839.

Otto, M. W., Safren, S. A., & Pollack, M. H. (2004). Internal cue exposure and the treatment of substance use disorders: Lessons from the treatment of panic disorder. *Anxiety Disorders, 18*, 69–87.

Pomerleau, O. F. (1981). Underlying mechanisms in substance abuse: Examples from research on smoking. *Addictive Behaviors, 6*, 187–196.

Pavlov, I. P. (1927). *Conditioned reflexes* (G. V. Anrep, Trans.). London: Oxford University Press.

Rescorla, R. A. (1988). Pavlovian conditioning: It's not what you think it is. *American Psychologist, 43*, 151–160.

Rescorla, R. A. (1990). The role of information about the response–outcome relation in instrumental discrimination learning. *Journal of Experimental Psychology: Animal Behavior Processes, 15*, 262–270.

Sher, K. J., Trull, T. J., Bartholow, B. D., & Vieth, A. (1999). Personality and alcoholism: Issues, methods, and etiological processes. In K. E. Leonard & H. T. Blane (Eds.), *Psychological theories of drinking and alcoholism* (2nd ed., pp. 54–105). New York: Guilford Press.

Siegel, S. (1975). Evidence from rats that morphine tolerance is a learned response. *Journal of Comparative and Physiological Psychology, 89*, 90–95.

Siegel, S. (1977). Morphine tolerance acquisition as an associative process. *Journal of Experimental Psychology: Animal Behavior Processes, 3*, 1–13.

Siegel, S. (1979). The role of conditioning in drug tolerance and addiction. In J. D. Keehn (Ed.), *Psychopathology in animals: Research applications* (pp. 143–168). New York: Academic Press.

Siegel, S. (1983). Classical conditioning, drug tolerance, and drug dependence. In R. G. Smart, F. B. Glaser, Y. Israel, H. Kalant, R. E. Popham, & W. Schmidt (Eds.), *Research advances in alcohol and drug problems* (Vol. 7, pp. 207–246). New York: Plenum Press.

Siegel, S. (1986). The Multidimensional Anger Inventory. *Journal of Personality and Social Psychology, 51*, 191–200.

Siegel, S., Hinson, R. E., Krank, M. D., & McCully, J. (1982, April 23). Heroin "overdose" death: The contribution of drug-associated environmental cues. *Science, 216*, 426.

Skinner, B. F. (1981, July 31). Selection by consequences. *Science, 213*, 501–504.

Sobell, L. C., Maisto, S. A., Sobell, M. B., & Cooper, A. M. (1979). Reliability of alcoholics' self-reports of drinking and related behaviors one year prior to treatment in an outpatient treatment program. *Behaviour Research and Therapy, 17*, 157–160.

Solomon, R. L, & Wynne, L. C. (1954). Traumatic avoidance learning: The principles of anxiety conservation and partial irreversibility. *Psychological Review, 61*, 353–385.

Stampfl, T. G. (1988). The relevance of laboratory animal research to theory and practice: One-trial learning and the neurotic paradox. *The Behavior Therapist, 11*, 75–79.

Stampfl, T. G., & Levis, D. J. (1967). Essentials of implosive therapy: A learning-theory-based psychodynamic behavioral therapy. *Journal of Abnormal Psychology*, 72, 496–503.

Stampfl, T. G., & Levis, D. J. (1969). Learning theory: An aid to dynamic therapeutic practice. In L. D. Eron & R. Callahan (Eds.), *The relationship of theory to practice in psychotherapy* (pp. 85–114). Chicago: Aldine.

Stampfl, T. G., & Levis, D. J. (1973). *Implosive therapy: Therapy and technique*. Morristown, NJ: General Learning Press.

Stasiewicz, P. R., Gulliver, S. B., Bradizza, C. M., Rohsenow, D. J., Torris, R., & Monti, P. M. (1997). Exposure to negative emotional cues and alcohol cue reactivity with alcoholics: A preliminary investigation. *Behaviour Research and Therapy*, 35, 1143–1149.

Stasiewicz, P. R., & Maisto, S. A. (1993). Two-factor avoidance theory: The role of negative affect in the maintenance of substance use and substance use disorder. *Behavior Therapy*, 24, 337–356.

Steele, C. M., & Josephs, R. A. (1988). Drinking your troubles away: I. An attention-allocation model of alcohol's effect on psychological stress. *Journal of Abnormal Psychology*, 97, 196–205.

Steele, C. M., & Josephs, R. A. (1990). Alcohol myopia: Its prized and dangerous effects. *American Psychologist*, 45, 921–933

Steele, C. M., Southwick, L., & Pagano, R. (1986). Drinking your troubles away: The role of activity in mediating alcohol's reduction of psychological stress. *Journal of Abnormal Psychology*, 95, 173–180.

Stewart, J., de Wit, H., & Eikelboom, R. (1984). Role of unconditioned and conditioned drug effects in the self-administration of opiates and stimulants. *Psychological Review*, 91, 251–268.

Substance Abuse and Mental Health Services Administration. (2003). *Results from the 2002 National Survey on Drug Use and Health: National Findings* (DHHS Publication No. SMA 03-3836). Rockville, MD: Author.

Tryon, W. W. (2005). Possible mechanisms for why desensitization and exposure therapy work. *Clinical Psychology Review*, 25, 67–95.

Vogel-Sprott, M., & Fillmore, M. T. (1999). Learning theory and research. In K. E. Leonard & H. T. Blane (Eds.), *Psychological theories of drinking and alcoholism* (2nd ed., pp. 292–327). New York: Guilford Press.

Vuchinich, R. E., & Simpson, C. A. (1998). Hyperbolic temporal discounting in social drinkers and problem drinkers. *Experimental Clinical Psychopharmacology*, 6, 292–305.

Vuchinich, R. E., & Tucker, J. A. (1983). Behavioral theories of choice as a framework for studying drinking behavior. *Journal of Abnormal Psychology*, 92, 408–416.

Vuchinich, R. E., & Tucker, J. A. (1988). Contributions from behavioral theories of choice to an analysis of alcohol abuse. *Journal of Abnormal Psychology*, 97, 181–195.

Watson, D., Clark, L. A., & Tellegen, A. (1988). Development and validation of brief measures of positive and negative affect: The PANAS Scales. *Journal of Personality and Social Psychology, 54,* 1063–1070.

Wetter, D. W., Smith, S. S., Kenford, S. L., Jorenby, D. E., Fiore, M. C., Hurt, R. D., et al. (1994). Smoking outcome expectancies: Factor structure, predictive validity, and discriminant validity. *Journal of Abnormal Psychology, 103,* 801–811.

Wikler, A. (1965). Conditioning factors in opiate addictions and relapse. In D. M. Wilner & G. G. Kassebaum (Eds.), *Narcotics* (pp. 85–100). New York: McGraw-Hill.

Wikler, A., & Pescor, F. T. (1967). Classical conditioning of a morphine abstinence phenomenon, reinforcement of opioid drinking behavioral and "relapse" in morphine addicted rats. *Psychopharmacologia, 10,* 103–117.

Windle, M., & Davies, P. T. (1999). Depression and heavy alcohol use among adolescents: Concurrent and prospective relations. *Development and Psychopathology, 11,* 823–844.

Zucker, R. A., & Fitzgerald, H. E. (1991). Early development factors and risk for alcohol problems. *Alcohol Health & Research World, 15,* 18–24.

INDEX

Coping mechanisms, avoidance behavior as, 154
Corpus Callosum morphology, 26
Cost biases, 160
Craving
    for alcohol, 213
    and appetitive motivational model, 208
    and conditioned withdrawal model of drug abuse, 204, 205
    as mediator, 211
CVD (Cognitive Vulnerability to Depression) Project, Temple–Wisconsin, 8
    design of, 111–113
    diagnostic criteria for hopelessness depression in, 109
    findings from, 114
        Axis II personality functioning, 123
        cognitive and stress generation, 121–122
        cognitive vulnerability and course of depression, 119–120
        cognitive vulnerability–stress interaction and prospective development of depression, 120–121
        hopelessness as mediator, 118
        and modification of cognitive style, 131
        negative cognitive style as specific to hopelessness depression, 117
        negative cognitive style and suicidality, 120
        negative cognitive style and vulnerability to depression, 114–117
        protective role of social support, 123–124, 132
        rumination as mediator and moderator, 118–119
        self-referent information processing, 122–123
    and potential protective factors, 132
    theoretical issues to be addressed with, 132–133

DA. *See* Dopamine
DAS (Dysfunctional Attitudes Scale), 112
Deconstruction, of schizophrenia, 32–35
"Deficit syndrome," in schizophrenia, 18
Dementia, and schizophrenia as composite entity, 18
Dementia praecox, Kraepelin's definition of, 19, 31
Depression (bipolar), 89
    and context-processing deficits, 51
    See also Bipolar disorders
Depression (unipolar), 107–111
    Beck's cognitive theory of, 108, 108–109
    and clinical practice, 129–132
    and CVD Project, 8, 111, 132–133
        design of, 111–114
        diagnostic criteria for hopelessness depression in, 109
        findings from, 114–24
        and potential protective factors, 132
        theoretical issues to be addressed with, 132–133
    hopelessness depression (HD) subtype of, 108, 110, 115, 116, 117
    and mania, 79
    hopelessness as mediator in, 118
    individual differences in vulnerability to, 107–108
    response styles theory of, 118
Depression, major (MD), 109, 111, 115, 116, 117
    and childhood maltreatment, 127, 128
    in CVD Project, 115
    and rumination, 118, 119
Depressogenic cognitive style, 108
Developmental antecedents, of cognitive vulnerability to depression, 124–129
Diagnostic category, as phenotype for biological research (schizophrenia), 16–17, 18
Diagnostic and Statistical Manual of Mental Disorders (DSM–I)

Mindfulness, 215
   Kentucky Inventory of, 216
Mismatch negativity (MMN), 24,
   27–28
Modeling, by parents, 125–126
Moods
   vs. emotions, 88
   and vulnerability to bipolar disorder,
    95
Motor skills (bilateral), and schizo-
   phrenia, 20
Multidimensional Anger Inventory
   (MAI), 214, 216
Muscle relaxation, for anxiety disorders,
   166

National Institute of Mental Health,
   and psychosocial treatments for
   mania, 96
National Survey on Drug Use and
   Health (2002), 199–200
Negative affect, two-factor model of,
   204, 209–211, 212, 213
Negative affect imagery scenes, in case
   example, 215–216
Negative attributional style
   and CBT, 130
   of children, 127, 129
   and parental depression, 125
Negative cognitive style(s)
   and childhood maltreatment, 127–129
   and hopelessness depression, 110, 117
   of parents and children, 125–126
   reduction of, 131
   and rumination, 119
   and self-referent information pro-
    cessing, 122
   and suicidality, 120
   and vulnerability to depression,
    114–117
Negative emotional reactivity, and
   bipolar disorder, 78, 88–94,
   96, 98
   studies on, 89–94
Negative reinforcement, affective processing model of (drug abuse),
   204, 208–209, 212, 213

Negative reinforcers or reinforcement,
   202, 203, 211–212, 213
Neural network framework, 43
Neurobiology, of context processing,
   59–62
Neuroimaging endophenotypes, 28–29
Neurophysiological/psychophysiological
   endophenotypes, 21, 27–29
N400 component of event-related
   potential, 54–56
NMDA (N-methyhl-D-aspartate),
   63–64
Nucleus accumbens, 62–63, 80

Obesity, as eating disorder, 176
Obsessive–compulsive disorder (OCD),
   156–158
   and *DSM–III*, 142
   false alarms in, 157–158
   triggers in, 145
Operant conditioning, 201–202
   in appetitive operant conditioning
    model, 206–207
   and classical conditioning, 202–203
   in conditional avoidance response,
    210
   treatment implications of, 212–213

Panic, 146, 152
Panic attack, 145, 149, 152–153
   fear of (case example), 168
Panic disorder (PD), 152–154
   and *DSM–III*, 142
   and false alarm, 150
   fear of fear in, 153
   and panic attack, 152–153
   and somatic events, 158
   vicious cycle in, 155
Parallel distributed processing, 43
Parenting, and antecedents of cognitive
   vulnerability to depression,
   124–127, 131
   childhood maltreatment, 127–129
Parkinson's disease, 21
Pathological anxiety, 144, 146
Pavlovian conditioning, 201. *See also*
   Classical conditioning

ABOUT THE EDITORS

Kurt Salzinger, PhD, is senior scholar in residence at Hofstra University's Department of Psychology in Hempstead, New York, and is current president of the Eastern Psychological Association. Dr. Salzinger was executive director for science at the American Psychological Association (APA), professor of psychology at Hofstra University and Polytechnic University of New York, principal research scientist at the New York State Psychiatric Institute, program officer at the National Science Foundation, and president of the New York Academy of Sciences. He was a member of the APA Council and Board of Directors, president of APA's Divisions 1 (General Psychology) and 25 (Behavior Analysis), and president of the American Association of Applied and Preventive Psychology. He is chair of the board of the Cambridge Center for Behavioral Studies and a member of the Association of Behavior Analysis Council. Dr. Salzinger was the recipient of the National Science Foundation's Sustained Superior Performance Award and the American Psychopathological Association's Stratton Award; he is also a recipient of the "Most Meritorious Article" Award from the *Journal of Behavior Therapy and Experimental Psychiatry*. Dr. Salzinger was also Presidential Scholar for the Association for Behavior Analysis and is listed in *Who's Who in America*. He is a fellow in the American Association for the Advancement of Science, the New York Academy of Sciences, and the Association for Behavior Analysis. He is author or editor of 12 books, more than 140 articles and book chapters, and 24 columns. He has conducted research on the behavior of human beings, dogs, rats, and goldfish; schizophrenia; the verbal behavior of children and adults; and the history of psychology.

Mark R. Serper, PhD, is a professor in the clinical psychology program at Hofstra University in Hempstead, New York, and a supervisor in the Hofstra Psychology Evaluation and Research Center, where he oversees graduate clinical psychology students. He received his doctorate in clinical psychology from the State University of New York at Binghamton and completed a clinical internship and fellowship in neuropsychology at the Mount Sinai Medical School in New York City. Previously, he worked in the New York University/Bellevue Hospital Psychiatric Emergency Service. Currently, Dr. Serper and his students are examining the clinical and neurocognitive effects of cocaine on schizophrenia patients presenting for emergency treatment. He is specifically interested in attention and memory dysfunctions in schizophrenia patients who abuse cocaine. Dr. Serper is also interested in the neuropsychopharmacology of schizophrenia and in examining the attentional and cognitive deficits that underlie some types of schizophrenic clinical symptoms. He has examined the effects of classical and atypical antipsychotic medication on schizophrenia patients' clinical symptoms and neurocognition. Dr. Serper's clinical practice interests center on the neuropsychological assessment and cognitive–behavioral treatment in patients with traumatic brain injury and dementia.